Rivington

Rivington

The Story of a Village

PHOEBE HESKETH

COUNTRY BOOK CLUB
Newton Abbot 1974

To Aubrey
and the Children

Contents

List of Illustrations

Foreword

Here, upon this little toft and quillit of land shall be built a chapell. . .

From a document relating to the origins of the fifteenth century Rivington church.

Since we came to Rivington in 1931 all the people who lived here then have either disappeared or died. We have had four vicars, three schoolmasters, two postmistresses, and all new neighbours: I have not portrayed any one of them, or their relatives, or anyone living now. With the exception of ourselves, the Dapples and the Thatchers, all the Rivington characters are fictitious, though some of the incidents are true. And if I have occasionally coloured and twisted the threads of this story, it is because imagination grows fertile with time and memory.

For historical reference I have drawn upon W. F. Irvine's *A Short History of the Township of Rivington*, and George Birtill's *The Enchanted Hills*. My thanks are due also to Dorothy Owen whose very interesting researches into the origin of the Headless Cross Boggart I have included in this story with her kind permission, and to the Arts Council for help and encouragement.

Soul of the Village
Vanishing Feature of English Life

There are few villages within easy travelling distance of an industrial or administrative centre where the population type has not radically changed during the past forty years, and particularly since the last war.

The essence of village life lies in the fact that roadman and rector, shepherd and squire, live cheek by jowl, each knowing something of the other's way of life, thus breeding mutual respect one for the other.

Few villages exist within fifty miles of London where the former cottagers have not been driven into council housing estates, while the villages themselves have become cliques of middle-class commuters living segregated lives and entirely destroying the ideal of communal life of the village as it has existed for perhaps 400 years.

This I feel is possibly the greater tragedy as no legislation can stop it, and once the village spirit has gone the bricks and mortar are merely a museum piece, as interesting as Stephenson's 'Rocket' and of as little practical use today. Thomas Hardy knew that the heart of England lay in her countrymen and in her villages. Within a few years these will have ceased to exist.

(From P. Carmichael in the *Daily Telegraph*).

We Come to Live at Fisher House

South of the village green in Rivington, Lancashire, is a white Georgian house with a sloping lawn and garden surrounded by trees. Here, forty odd years ago we came to live, meaning to stay for a year only because it seemed too unmanagable for a newly-married couple. But the place has personality as well as character, and claimed us like an old friend. This is Fisher House with a fanlight above its jasmine-coloured door, and a sundial standing among a tangle of old-fashioned flowers. For more than two centuries marguerites, poppies, cornflowers and roses have blazed out their colours, faded, and died.

At that time Aubrey and I, in our early twenties and engaged to be married, were looking for a house. The last one we had seen was not far from the cotton mills which were to provide our bread and butter. Smoke drifted over gritstone cottages and blackened fields fenced with wire and rusty bedsteads. I remember saying to Aubrey: 'It's no good. I can't live here.' So then he thought of Rivington. We reached it by a climbing moorland road north of Bolton, which at the top gave us a glimpse of the sea. After coasting downhill we arrived at Rivington with its chapel, stone cottages, and prim School House to the left of the green, while on our right the church weathercock rose above high trees. Set back beyond the green and, like the church, half-hidden by trees, was a house to let.

The scarlet of a letter-box gleamed in a cottage wall identifying the post-office, so we went inside and asked about the house. They gave us a large, old-fashioned key to the back door, and a few minutes later we were letting ourselves into a huge stone-flagged kitchen where an antique stove was rusting away. Hooks in the ceiling spoke of hams and hard winters, while five black-tongued bells hanging stiff above the door were silent witnesses to days of servants. An even larger laundry had a similar, though rustier, stove, a wash-boiler, and two stone sinks.

Leading from the door with the bells was a narrow hallway darkened by brown paint; here a wallpaper's tortuous pattern was speckled with damp. But when we stood in the spacious drawing-room whose enlarged window looked out into encroaching trees, I felt the powerful atmosphere of the place. Though empty, the house was alive with echoes and footfalls. As for the bedrooms, three of them were more like dormitories—not to mention three replicas in the attic. Outside, apart from a garage, there were two loose-boxes and a saddle-room to cheer us, for we both rode, and I already kept a horse.

When we returned the key we asked questions, and learned from the postmistress that the house got its name from the Reverend John Fisher, a Cambridge scholar, who lived here all the time he was vicar of Rivington for a record run of fifty years —from 1763 to 1813. I remarked on the size of the bedrooms, and she told us that the vicar had also used the house as a school for boys, more than twelve of them boarders.

In spite of its size, dampness and dark paint, I fell in love with Fisher House. At the same time my grudging self realized that we couldn't afford its needs for re-decorating and central heating. More urgent needs, too, for new bath, sink, and kitchen-range. 'And think of the out-houses,' I groaned, 'and those smothering trees.'

Indeed, in half an acre of garden were crowded thirteen great forest trees. Mostly sycamores. But an immense beech leaned over the wall at the bottom of the garden—happily too far away to enclose us in its shade. Less happily a whitebeam and a rowan blocked out the sky from the drawing-room and bedroom above.

Electricity had not yet reached Rivington, and, looking back, it seems unbelievable that I was not in the least deterred by the prospect of trimming fifteen oil lamps, and cleaning two stoves and a cooker. The truth is, with the black world of industry wheeling and smouldering outside, we were bewitched by this house in a green oasis. Fortunately for us, Rivington lies on a watershed for Liverpool, and even today the village and surrounding moorland remain unchanged since 1847 when the valley with its farms, houses, and a chapel were flooded to form a chain of reservoirs.

On our second visit we fell even more under the spell of the place. From the back-yard you step right into the bracken that fringes the moors; and looking up eastwards is Rivington Pike with its square beacon tower. Two hundred yards above us to the left a chestnut tree (on that day) burned pink candles over the garden of the manse. In the distance a curlew's prolonged, stone-rolling cry awoke the moorland to the late northern spring. It was too much; we decided to take the house for a year's trial.

From then on every time we came over to strip walls, to distemper and paint, we felt ourselves under village inspection. Our first caller was Miss Whittle who lived behind the post-office. I descended a ladder to answer her knock. 'Just coom ter see 'ow yer getting on an' t'offer any 'elp,' she announced. 'An' so you've cum ter live 'ere,' she went on as she stepped inside. 'Well, I daresay as you'll not stay long.' This, after I'd told her we were managing on our own. She shook her head knowingly. 'Full o'dry-rot an' death-watch beetle—so they say. An' t'damp's summat terrible—but you'll 'ave found that out by now.' With her narrow face and pointed features Miss Whittle reminded me of a weasel. Her busy eyes made you feel she could see through the merest crack. After an active pause for inspection she went on to inform us that Fisher House is built on a marsh and infested with rats. 'They cum inside in th' autumn—you'll 'ear 'em scratting round t' skirtings on winter nights' She would have enlightened us still further had I not at this point told her that our move was only temporary. Whereupon, disappointed, she departed.

Next day she was back, surprising me as I walked the plank between two pairs of step-ladders to distemper the drawing-room ceiling. 'Oh!' she exclaimed gleefully, *'won't* yer 'ave a stiff neck in t'morning!'

Though I could have wrung her neck I was determined to finish the ceiling before nightfall. Miss Whittle seemed equally determined to stand her ground so that I learned a bookful about our neighbours and unguessed divisions across the village green. 'You'll be "church" people, I daresay?' she began hopefully. 'T'Colonel up at Moorside is "church", so's'is friend Mr March-banks. But Marchbanks's gardener's chapel sexton—that's Johnny Thatcher from t'manse. A queer lot, Thatchers. Don't 'old wi' sanitation.' In the challenging silence between us I re-called Johnny's apple-fresh appearance, and discounted this information.

'Then there's schoolmaster next door,' she persisted through the splosh splosh of my brush, 'e'es "church" but she's "chapel" ter t'bone an' won't own it. She an' t'vicar's wife is oil an' vinegar. . . .'

'And which are you, Miss Whittle?' I showered her with white drops, big as seagulls, but she was unquenchable. 'Me?' she replied like a knife, 'I treads in t'middle. Keeps in wi' all. Now yer left 'and neighbour, Mrs Dapple, as yer might expect, is "chapel".' Squawking at her joke she continued in higher key: 'But Mrs Marchbanks, 'er from Primrose Cottage beyond t' green, she's neither. No religion in 'er. Paints pictures an' starves 'er 'usband. Only a young couple too—trouble brewin' there. Queerest of all are Morels up at Sweetloves. Queer an' clever, fit in nowhere. Just you wait.'

'I can't wait to hear any more; it's getting dark.' Bucket in hand I rattled down the ladder and rattled her out of the house. When Aubrey appeared half an hour later I was lighting the one oil lamp, burning my fingers in irritation. 'I've discovered the first nettle.' Grimly I described Miss Whittle's invasion. 'She must be firmly grasped, or else. . . .'

She kept away for days—no doubt telling everyone else about us—and we were too occupied to think of her. Four layers of paper had to be scraped off hall and bedrooms, while the entire house needed decorating. We spent hours removing varnish, thick and black as tar, which disfigured the beautiful twelve-inch floorboards. This done, we despaired over the glazed chocolate paint which coated everything, including the carved Georgian surround to the drawing-room door. 'We must get help,' I decided looking from my blistered hands to the gloom of leaves outside. 'And it's so dark, even at midsummer. Can't we have some trees down?'

'One thing at a time,' Aubrey replied practically. 'How about a cup of tea?' I remembered there was no sugar, and ran round to the post-office to see if I could buy some. 'I'm sorry,' Mrs Seed shook her head, 'we're not allowed to sell anything but stamps.'

It seems strange that in a village which has a post-office and chapel on one side of the green, a church and school on the other, you can't buy so much as a packet of tea. Nor is there a pub since the *Black Lad* was pulled down over fifty years ago. 'If you want a pint of beer,' I told Aubrey, 'you'll have to refresh yourself at the village club.'

News of our predicament must have got around because one evening, to our delight, Mr Dapple from the cottage on our left knocked on the back door and said he'd be glad to give us a hand. And what a hand it proved to be. Every day after work he came in to hang wallpapers, burn off paint, and re-tile fireplaces. This freed us to spend hours clearing out the stables of old books and musty straw, broken boxes, tools, saddlery—and even pictures. Under what seemed the dust and debris of centuries I discovered a framed photograph filmed over with grime. Wondering who it could be, I rubbed away the dirt to discover a prim-faced elderly lady whose dark eyes gazed sorrowfully back at me. She was swathed in widow's weeds; not a wisp of hair escaped from the treble band of crêpe across her forehead. Like a cocoon she was bound in black up to the chin. I cleaned up the picture with growing curiosity, and next day showed it to Mr Dapple. He looked at it thoughtfully, 'Must be Aunt Dorcas,' he decided. 'She lived 'ere after John Fisher died.' I pressed him further, and learned how this Dorcas, after a brief marriage, enlivened a long widowhood by filling the large bedrooms with relations and friends in need of a holiday. She[1] had remained a spinster until the age of fifty when, after a courtship of nineteen years, she married a Mr Fincham, distrusted by her strongly 'chapel' mother because he was a churchman. The despairing daughter was driven to meet her lover in the summer-house while her mother was singing hymns in chapel. To make amends for this deceit, Dorcas, after her mother's death, wore mourning for twelve years before consenting to a marriage that was to last for only two.

One wonders if the nineteen years of uncertainty were not the more enjoyable because Aunt Dorcas advised all the young girls she knew to remain single until the age of fifty. Her bridegroom was far from good-looking; indeed, he was described as[2] 'tall, thin and shambling, with only one eye, for he lost the other holding a branch aside which obstructed her path in one of their lover-like walks, and a small twig entering it destroyed the sight.' Happily Dorcas cherished his blind eye 'as a mark of gallantry

[1] *Lancashire Memories* by Louisa Potter.
[2] ibid.

and devotion'. Qualities he displayed towards her until the very end when he died whispering her name over and over again.

After this Dorcas went into mourning for life. Louisa Potter's description of the widow is worth quoting:

> Fancy a tallish spare figure, with a stern grave face marked with the small-pox, and piercing black eyes, in crêpe and bombazines up to the throat, without a scrap of white to relieve the widow's cap. And such a cap. Not the little gauzy fabric we see now, becomingly adjusted behind the braided hair; this was a real widow's cap, with as strict an attention to the unbecoming as the most exacting husband could require. First, there was no hair visible; then her cap was composed of several tiers of broad-hemmed muslin, with a smooth round stick run through each hem; and a piece of muslin in the same fashion, went under the chin, and was pinned to the cap on each side. . . .
>
> When seven years had expired, she went into her second mourning, which only differed from the first in adopting a false front of straggling black hair; but if any of her relations died, then she took off the front until the mourning for them was over.[1]

Not only herself, but the entire house was put into mourning. Dorcas had the garden gate painted white edged with black; a black knocker hung on the white front door; and black crêpe was twisted around the sundial—so that its finger could no longer tell the passing hours. Indoors, the black-bordered white muslin curtains were looped up with black roses; and the late husband's hat, swathed in crêpe, was hung in the lobby—not only as a constant reminder but as a warning to possible thieves that a ghost, if not a man, lurked around the corner.

After such nursing of grief, along with cold vigils on the beloved's gravestone in the chapel yard—she had her own way there—Dorcas took to nursing the poor and the sick. And though her income was small, she was for ever inviting friends in need, as I have said, for a holiday—though even these were expected to help her sew for the poor. She concocted invalid dishes and herb remedies until the house became almost a dispensary for herbal cures—a habit which was to continue in Rivington till our day.

For all her good works, Dorcas suffered many troubles, most

[1] *Lancashire Memories* by Louisa Potter.

of which came from her neighbour and sister-in-law, Mrs John Fincham, a pretentious woman whose scalding remarks were only equalled by the vexatiousness of her peacock. This bird was encouraged to visit Fisher House garden where it stuffed itself on Dorcas's carefully sown peas and other cherished seeds. Words ran hot and high, but the peacock raids continued. Eventually Dorcas resolved her anger into a dissenter's contempt for the low intellect of these relations who, too conventional to think for themselves, supported the church.

Dorcas's niece, Eveline, a poetess (and also a niece of the Lancashire poet, Robert Leighton) married John Crompton from Rivington Hall, and after her aunt's death came to live at Fisher House. 'Wot wi' peacocks an' poetesses in t'dust, you'll be in good company,' Mr Dapple assured me.

After hearing this story I wondered who had painted the front door black—as it was on our arrival—and how, in spite of all, the house had an atmosphere of peace and friendliness. By now I was infected with its secrets, and felt every floorboard and cupboard creaking with life.

The hot July days burned down into August. We were to be married in September, and if the house was unfinished, the garden was a wilderness. We scythed the one-time lawn, grubbed out reverted michaelmas daisies, tore up bindweed, bracken and briars, and wrestled with willow-herb, just now flaunting magenta flowers. Each day ended with bonfires, bleeding hands and broken nails till I complained that no wedding-ring would ever slide over my swollen knuckles. Worst of all were the midges, stinging battalions loosed by fallen ranks of weed. They got into our hair, crawled down our backs, and bit us all over till we fled indoors for the relief of the ammonia bottle. Rivington, low-lying among reservoirs and trees, is renowned for its virulent breed of midges whose swarms are fostered by the soft, damp air. To watch people waiting for the seven o'clock bus on a summer evening was as good as being at the zoo. After two minutes hats came off and handkerchiefs came out as the victims flapped and scratched in the hopeless combat.

One day, feeling too tired and dusty to work any longer, I walked out of the garden, past the post-office and alongside the wall of the chapel yard. A man smoking a pipe and reading a book was leaning against it under the shade of a chestnut tree. A good-looking man, blue-eyed, grey-haired; and though he must have been fifty his complexion was pink and white as a girl's. I recognized Johnny Thatcher, alleged opponent of hygiene. 'Good-afternoon,' I said, a question in my voice. He smiled back: ' 'aving a walk? It's a pleasant enough day in Lancashire's pleasantest place.' He slipped the book into his pocket. 'Tennyson this afternoon—"The Lotus Eaters"—it's 'ot enough ter make anyone feel idle. Would yer care ter take a look round "chapel",?'

He led the way and I followed wondering what sort of a man was this who read Tennyson in his tea-break and whose appearance so wholly triumphed over no sanitation. Inside it was cold and musty; bare white walls, high pulpit and box-pews of dark oak added to the atmosphere of severity. Yet the sun washed through the clear windows on to well-polished wood. 'Just as it wer' built in 1703,' Johnny told me proudly, 'a place o' free thinking. Sithee!' He pointed above the door to a slab of rough stone on which was carved: 'Ye Rev. S. Newtone driven out ye church Bartol Sunday 1662.' ' 'e refused King's orders ter read t'new Prayer Book,' Johnny explained, 'so 'e an' 'is followers flit.' I learned how this indomitable band held services up on Noon Hill near Rivington Pike until winter and rain and snow drove them to meet at Moses Cocker Farm—a mile up the hill behind our house.

By now I was fidgetting to be off across the green and down Forty-One Steps to the stream. But Johnny wouldn't let me go before telling me that a weaving mill had once stood in this valley where, a hundred years ago, every farmer had also been a weaver. 'But there's naught changed in Rivington this century,' he concluded, 'only t'trees and people cum an' go.'

Indeed, no one travelling between Mersey and Ribble, much of it a waste of slag-heaps, factories, and indeterminate towns, could imagine a 'green and pleasant land' such as this. So that when we moved in I gave no thought to the rats and beetles that were to harry us from time to time. All I knew on that day of October sunshine with the whitebeam outside the drawing-room window unclasping its leaves, and the rowan gleaming with berries, was that we had come home.

2

New Acquaintances

Keeping animals is a good way of getting to know people, and it was through riding Mingo, my black Australian whaler, a trained polo pony and superb hunter, that I met two neighbours who were to play a large part in our lives. Each day in those early days I rode out in a new direction. A favourite way was behind Top Barn, belonging to Rivington Hall, half a mile up-hill from our house, and from there up the glen where a stream rushed and stumbled downhill in greeting. The road, rough as a stream-bed, led to Sweetloves, a lonely stone house, sometimes golden and sometimes grey, sheltering under the Pike. With one tall gable-end for sentinel, it faced east and west: 'Up the airy mountain; down the rushy glen.' Peat smoke spiralled from two chimneys; and the windows were scantily curtained. No one ever seemed to pass through that always-shut iron gate. Until the day I surprised a young woman struggling to lift it back on to its stone pivot. 'Can I help you?' I asked, jumping down and flinging the reins over a post. 'How kind of you,' she smiled and stood upright. 'Father gets so upset if the gate isn't properly fastened. Though there's no one to keep out here—except ghosts.'

Together we tugged, dragging the gate back into position. She picked up two large tins. 'Just going down to the bus. We're out of paraffin,' she explained, adding, 'Aren't you lucky to have a horse?'

'Sorry I can't give you a lift. But may I walk down to the village with you?' She nodded without introducing herself. So this must be Anna Morel, I thought, teacher and writer. Of medium height, she was slim, supple, and moved like a dancer gently swinging the two tins. Strands of dark auburn hair escaped from her brown beret. Though her face was pale and serious, her almost green eyes lit up with tiny candle-flames when she smiled. She seemed reluctant to talk, thus perhaps justifying her name in the village for being 'a one to herself'. However, I dared to ask after her father, a retired professor. 'He hardly sees anyone,' she said briefly. 'His life is spent in study and writing.' After another silence I also discovered that she had an elder sister. This piece of information, conveyed in five words, returned her to her own thoughts, and Mingo's slow progress down the stony glen prevented me from asking any more questions.

Another day, while slithering down this same steep hill, a girl of about my own age riding a light grey pony trotted towards us. Her fair hair was tied back in a Dick Turpin bow, and she wore moss-green corduroys. Here was Bryony Marchbanks from Primrose Cottage, across Sheephouse Lane, north of the green from us. 'Hello!' she greeted me, 'I'm glad we've met this way at last.' Because she spent hours painting in the fields, as Miss Whittle had told me, she was looked upon as an eccentric. Today she seemed friendly enough, and turned her pony to ride back home with me. A most entertaining companion she proved to be. She told me how she hated social life and village activities. 'I hate cooking too,' she smiled, 'so poor Humphrey has to get many meals out.' Indeed, this was the only time on our rides that she referred to her seemingly neglected husband. She was far more interested in Pegasus, her pony, a grey with a dash of Arab blood that Sir Alfred Munnings would have painted. We were both lost to domestic life, and our ponies, catching something of our mood, fired one another to non-stop gallops, unpremeditated and exhilarating.

All the same, Bryony was not the sporting type. When her painting moods were on she would abandon Pegasus and retire from my world. After two months of her company I told her I was going to have a baby, whereupon she pulled a face and refused to ride with me. For some reason she was agin babies.

Happily I had by now made friends with a genuine horse-woman who lived a mile or so away, and often rode with me. Astride her smart bay mare she looked as though she had been born in the saddle, and was scornful of Bryony's unhorsemanlike get-up and undisciplined performance. When I explained to her that owing to my condition the doctor had consented to gentle trotting only, she saw to it that we controlled our ponies and rode in a proper manner.

Mingo, however, had no intention of keeping to the rules. One February day of frost and sun with every stone set hard as a diamond in the sandy roads on the Pike, she began bouncing and fidgetting to be off home downhill. To check her career I turned her sideways till she skittered and skated alarmingly over patches of ice. It was useless to pull and saw at her mouth. Head up, in full control, she flexed her muscles and got away. I might have been astride a bullet cracking through the whistling air. Or racing down a river-bed. But her easy action and nimble feet made nothing of it. Frozen stones were flung up, trees flashed by, and there was nothing to do but sit down and enjoy the ride. Excitement mounted as we thundered down the tarmac of Sheephouse Lane, hooves beating a tattoo as we sped reckless of corners and two astonished motor-cyclists driven against the bank. Somehow we skidded round the circle of the green, jumped the banking wall, streamed across and up the drive.

Fifteen minutes later my companion trotted in. '*Well!*' she exclaimed at the sight of Mingo's heaving belly, dilated nostrils, and lathered neck, 'I can't imagine a better way of getting rid of a baby.'

But the baby was there to stay.

One spring afternoon after this, walking past Sweetloves, I came upon Bryony absorbed in painting. For once I persuaded her to put down her brush and tell me something about the Morel family. 'The Professor and the elder daughter, Rebecca, are both odd,' she began thoughtfully. 'No one ever sees him—he shuts himself up and writes day and night. I believe he used to be a brilliant lecturer, though his books never seem to get published. Anna writes a little too, but she doesn't get much chance, poor thing, with the two of them to look after. Every so often she takes a job and then has to give it up. Rebecca is dominating: she gives the impression she runs the place, and she certainly makes it revolve around her. But every now and then she flies off the handle. . . .' As she spoke I recalled a tall, gaunt figure striding down the glen in a long mac. and faded felt hat. 'I don't know her any better than you do,' Bryony went on. 'I don't really *know* anyone here, but the Sweetloves set-up interests me a lot.'

When I inquired about the vicarage she shook her head: 'Not in my line. You'll have to find out for yourself.' Absorbed in painting and riding, Bryony was not in the least interested in Rivington's history. And as for church and chapel, she mocked at both and supported neither. But I was soon caught up in the unholy cross-currents of the place, and discovered things which were to make living here feel like the fulfilment of destiny.

One afternoon, walking over the green with the Lombardy poplar in the vicarage garden on my left, I crossed Sheephouse Lane, went through the wicket-gate opposite, and instead of running down Forty-One Steps to the stream, I turned left for the green knoll north of the churchyard. According to a fifteenth-century document the original church of daub-and-wattle had stood here upon this 'little toft and quillit' of land. Toft and quillit. The inspired phrase exactly describes the green hillock looking west over water and woods; north and east to the long, brown-shouldered moors.

These ruminations led me to climb the churchyard wall with the intention of finding the grave of John Fisher, who, so Johnny had told me, lay to the west alongside the rubbish-dump. (He had little use for Church of England parsons.) I soon discovered the place, and went down on my knees to scrape the moss from the inscription. Here, sure enough, lay the Reverend John, a Peterhouse scholar, born 1739, elected vicar 1763, died 1813. Beside him was his wife, Esther, niece of Lord de Willoughby of Parham (a pillar of the chapel), and his sister and three sons, all of whom had been born in Fisher House, a fact which very likely prompted him to start a school.

An obstructive holly bush had thrust itself through a crack in the gravestone so that even if the good man had been called to sit up facing east at the sound of the last trump, he would have been prevented from doing so. I was actually kneeling under the holly when a brisk footstep behind me made me start up with embarrassment to face Mrs Mooney, the vicar's wife. She was carrying an armful of dahlias whose brilliant colours clashed with her wiry red hair. Small and slight, she had creamy skin freckled like a robin's egg. 'Doing an inspection of graves?' she enquired lightly. When I told her I was thinking of cutting down the holly bush her brown-flecked hazel eyes brightened in alarm. 'Never.' You mustn't do that. The holly is the holy tree; it allows the evil to escape through its leaves. That's why they're prickled, with our sins.'

I had no answer to this, recalling that some people called her fey, partly because she was Irish. All the same, she had both feet

on the ground—an important asset in a country parson's wife.
Meanwhile she was asking me to help her arrange the flowers. In
the vestry she chattered away, telling me about the family whose
thread runs through this story. And a good deal else besides. While
we emptied dead flowers into the railed-off dump behind the
Fishers, and arranged fresh ones on the vestry floor, she swept me
back to Anglo-Saxon times. Even then Rivington or Rowanton
—after the rowan tree—existed as a manor and belonged to
Alexander Pilkington. 'The Pilkington's were the big nobs before
the Conquest,' she nodded with authority and selected a flower-
show specimen. 'And after that they held sway hereabouts for
hundreds of years. In fact, this church was built in 1541 by
Richard Pilkington. And *aren't* we proud to know that his son,
James, was the first Protestant Bishop of Durham, and helped to
compile the New English Prayer Book. But alas,' she sighed
thrusting a recalcitrant dahlia into a narrow-necked altar vase,
'the locals disliked it so much that they stuck to the old service
until they were forced out of church. Johnny Thatcher never
tires of telling *that* story!' As she spoke a shaft of sun from a south
window glinted on her fierce red hair.

We walked back to the vicarage and she went on almost talking
to herself: 'It must have been hard for the vicar who stayed on
in the church with a handful of people. You see, although he was
a Royalist he was also a Puritan. *How* he must have suffered
during those Sunday "lip-services"—because nobody liked the
new prayer-book.' By now we were at the gate, and she invited
me in for tea. The large Victorian vicarage, the only house across
the green from us, was cold and gloomy. Apologizing for the
gone-out fire, she called her husband who, after a few moments,
appeared from the study. Tall, dark, and pale, he moved and
spoke with a gentle Celtic melancholy (he was Anglo-Irish) and
had an air of belonging somewhere else. Yet some chance remark
might suddenly focus his attention so that his light blue-grey eyes
would direct their straight gaze right into you.

Mrs Mooney handed him a cup of tea, which he drank
abstractedly—it might have been peat-water or poteen—while
fondling the ears of a white cat he addressed as Mimi. The cat,
rubbing his legs, purring like an engine, jumped on to his knee.
'Fisher House has a strong atmosphere,' he said dreamily nursing
Mimi, his tea forgotten. 'These old houses seem to absorb their

owners' personalities. Perhaps they even have memories stored up
in the walls. . . .' His wife paused in the act of re-filling my cup
to nod agreement: 'Yes indeed, when I last called I swear I heard
footsteps upstairs.'

'Now, Moira,' he cautioned, 'remember, no ghosts.'

'Very well. But there are strange enough living characters
around here to make up for any dead ones. Have you met Mrs
Twigg yet?' she asked, handing me a plate of ginger-nuts. When
I shook my head she described the woman wearing a cloak who
had once danced past me on the narrow path beside the stream.
I say 'danced' because her lilting movements couldn't be
described as a walk. On this occasion she had flung up her arms
including me with the trees in her 'Lovely morning!'

'She belongs to a fairy story. Draws water from the Yarrow
waterfall,' Mrs Mooney went on, 'and would certainly refuse
electricity in her cottage—even if it were offered. Anyhow, she
adds colour to the place, living by candlelight and all that.'

'Talking of candlelight,' interposed the vicar who was very
much a non-gossip, 'I happened to bring up the burning subject
—candles on the altar—at the last church council meeting. The
two farmers were against, of course, and so was Mr Plodder.
Being schoolmaster, I suppose he feels responsible to the parents
of his pupils. Most of them would disapprove of candles.'

'I don't believe that for one minute!' retorted his wife. 'It's
Mrs P. She's Methodist to the marrow—he just wouldn't dare.
We live in a nest of Calvinism,' she went on, turning to me. And
then, back to her husband: 'Have you forgotten that Bolton used
to be called the Geneva of the North?'

'Oh come, it's not so bad as that,' he answered gently. 'Anyway,
Colonel Darley—he's from Moorside, the big house—' he added
for my benefit, 'and Mr Marchbanks. . . .'

'The hunting husband of Bryony, your artist friend,' Mrs
Mooney interrupted her husband, determined to have her say.
'*She's* an oddity if you like. Sits all day in a field in front of an
easel, but won't go near the church—except to paint it. And
loathes hunting—that's what splits them. Funny isn't it,' she went
on, 'how hunting and high church—candles and all that—seem
to go together? Some people need colour and ceremony. The
Colonel's Master of Hounds, by the way, as you probably know
by now.'

The vicar turned to me: 'I'd be interested to hear your views, and your husband's, on this subject.' Being a newcomer I was surprised by his question, and somewhat taken aback. 'I'll have to think about it. But as we both ride and my husband hunts, we'll probably be in favour.'

'You've only to mention candles here,' Mrs Mooney remarked, 'and everyone thinks we're on the march to Rome.'

We must tread warily,' replied her husband, 'and respect tradition. Maybe they'll come to it in time. Country minds turn round as slowly as the seasons.'

'At any rate, dear, you must make them allow you a pot of gold paint for the weathercock—we'll soon get him spruced up.'

Suddenly I felt incorporated in the village, its problems and people, and was fascinated to hear how the old religious rivalry had eventually resolved itself by everyone going to church one Sunday and to chapel the next. Which made you wonder what the division had been about. Like a field after the harrow the green once more sprouted its peaceful grass. An inscription out-side the chapel: 'Here Let No Man Be Stranger', newly-painted in gold, seemed to offer a permanent olive branch. 'In Rivington today,' Mrs Mooney told me, "church" people go to chapel funerals, and "chapel" people attend church weddings. After all, our service *is* more effective. I wouldn't feel married in chapel.'

'And would you feel buried there, I wonder?' Her husband teased.

'I must admit that when it comes to hymns, they have us beat —singing the roof off on Sunday afternoons.' She turned to me. 'Have you heard Miss Whittle complain? She says it's impossible to have her afternoon nap with that noise going on.'

As she spoke a different kind of noise—uninhibited yells from eighteen-month-old lungs—assailed us. 'Oh, I'd forgotten David!' Mrs Mooney jumped up. 'He's been fastened in his pram all afternoon, poor mite.'

She dashed out of the room to return with her aggrieved infant, slow reproachful tears sliding down his shining cheeks. 'You're as bad as I am, Moira,' the vicar said, 'forgetting your own baby.' He gazed proudly at this gasping bundle of wet lashes and damp wool. I got up as Mrs Mooney sat down jigging the child on her knee. 'Oh, don't go just yet,' she begged. 'See, he's smiling at you already. Wait till you have a baby—you won't be able to go running and riding about the countryside then.'

As though to stem further remarks Mr Mooney shook my outstretched hand. 'I hope you'll be very happy here. I've a strong feeling that after a year you won't want to leave. There's something about the place. . . .' he hesitated, 'I never thought I'd settle down in this very scattered parish with such a small congregation. But it gets a hold on you.'

'Too few souls to save,' laughed his wife. 'But I really believe it was the birds made him decide to stay on.'

'The *birds?*'

'Why, yes, Mr Mooney has become quite an ornithologist—never goes out without his field-glasses. Though I tell him it looks bad in a vicar. People may feel they're being spied on—especially in the summer time. Among the bracken, you know.'

This novel thought brought to mind the long, lean figure often to be seen on Yarrow reservoir embankment, gazing fixedly into the distance—as though sighting eternity through a pair of field-glasses.

3

Village Characters and Events

During those early months Aubrey and I were getting ourselves
dug in—not an insuperable task considering that apart from our
house, School House on our right, and the vicarage opposite, there
were only seven cottages in the village. Two of these were in a
row with School House facing west over the green to the
forbidding vicarage. Between the green and the vicarage ran
Rivington Lane, the narrow road linking Horwich and Adlington, our nearest shopping centres, one two miles to the south, the
other two miles north.

School House, obviously, housed the schoolmaster, Mr Plodder,
and his wife. Both pulled their weight in the village. Apart from
the school managers' committee, he also served on the parish,
and the parochial church councils where his solid common
sense often grounded the vicar's imaginative flights. Mrs Plodder,
with her sleek brown hair, was neat, plump, and compact as a
partridge. She was also pale from too much polishing and too
little time in the open air. One never saw her out for a walk; she
was too busy with the Women's Institute—of which she was
president and pillar.

In this kind of work she was rivalled by Mrs Mooney who
propped up the Mothers' Union across the road. At a deeper
level Mrs P. felt the challenge of Mrs Mooney's unconscious
attraction for everyone—that red hair, those freckles and lively
eyes were too near at hand for comfort, whereas Mrs Plodder,
diffident and reserved, saw the world through spectacles. Many
a time must School House sitting-room have served as glaring-
post for vicarage kitchen. Rivalry was reflected even in their pets
because Mrs Plodder's fox-terrier, Bonzo, was ever ready to take
a piece out of the white cat's tail.

Next door to the Plodders lived Mrs Birdwhistle, a mighty
widow who, being childless, served as willing buffer between Mrs
Seed, the postmistress, her right-hand neighbour, and Miss

Whittle whose thatched cottage crouched in the shade behind the post-office, and whose ferret nose and ears were ever alert for movement afoot or rumours in the air. Not that she could find much to report against the Seeds, straightforward, hard-working country-folk. Between the rare moments of selling stamps, Mrs Seed spent most of her time by wash-tub or oven. Ronnie, her husband, dark and silent and blind in one eye, combined the tasks of sexton, verger, organist, and grave-digger for the church. (Johnny Thatcher was his 'chapel' rival.) Though the graves Ronnie dug were few, and his solo bell-ringing not arduous, the business of caring for church and churchyard required more than the strength of one. Certainly he was no Sir Launcelot, and the vicar declared that too often Ronnie turned his blind eye to these requirements.

Rivington post-office was far and happily removed from the efficiency of metal grilles and men with stampers and people hurrying in, looking at the clock, and hurrying out. Here was room for all the time in the world. Indeed, you had often to wait for who knows how long if Mrs Seed, in summertime, happened to be in the croft feeding the hens, or locking the church door in an early winter dusk. On one such occasion I whiled away many minutes watching their pony through the window stuffing himself with grass before the annual mowing of the green, eating a methodical circle around his tethering pole. On the window-ledge lacy-leaved plants curled and twisted, translucent against the glass; and from the ceiling a canary in a cage pulsed and hammered with song as though to burst open the bars. Bess, the fat black-and-white spaniel, dozed in a patch of sunlight, cocking a lazy ear and half an eye at any sound that might herald her mistress's return. On a scratched table was a blotter, once lint-pink, heavily scrawled with hieroglyphics. There was a dry-crusted ink-bottle and two pens with nibs twisted by hands unused to the exercise of writing. Alongside these an old-fashioned pair of brass scales gleamed in the sun.

In winter Mrs Seed lit a fire; and through the spring you could watch the progress of Ronnie's Trumpeter daffodils. Whereas a G.P.O. smells of used-up hot air and fingered metal, our post-office was permeated by delicious odours issuing from the kitchen. On Thursdays you were greeted by the savoury smell of hot-pot; Friday was fish-and-chips; Saturday, half-day, meant the crispy sizzle of roasting meat. Washday was steamy and odourless; and Tuesday brought the damp hot-clothiness of ironing. Best of all were Wednesdays when Mrs Seed baked the week's bread.

My ruminations were interrupted by the entrance and apologies of Mrs Seed herself—she had, as I guessed, been feeding the hens. In her absence I had placed my parcel on the scales and reckoned its weight. But this wouldn't do at all; spectacles had to be searched for and 'the book' consulted in professional manner. Out came the stamp-sheets, and after a long search for the one-and-fourpennies she gingerly detached one. I was about to press this carefully selected morsel on to the parcel when she cried: 'Stop! I've given you the wrong colour—you've got a one-an'-sixpenny.' Midway I hesitated. 'Oh dear, what a pity —I've licked it.'

'Never mind,' Mrs Seed took it back with a conspiratorial smile: 'It'll dry!'

At that moment a fearful dog-and-cat shindy tore the air outside, and Mrs Seed shook her head: 'It's that there Chink,' she said alluding to Miss Whittle's white bull-terrier, 'allus after Mimi. Poor cat, wi' Bonzo at one end an' Chink at t'other. One on 'em's bound ter finish 'er off.' At which Mrs Birdwhistle blew in out of the rumpus. Blowsy and friendly, she spoke in a loud voice—Mrs Seed was a little deaf—'Chinky, Chinky Chinaman —'e's grown like 'is missus. Slit eyes forever glinting through cracks—'e misses naught. Bites the kids and kills the cats. And would yer believe it,' she turned to me, 'she feeds 'im eggs. That's why she keeps 'ens—a moulty, scratchy lot. An' she keeps t'feathers ter stuff 'er pillow.' Loose breasts aswing, she leaned confidentially towards Mrs Seed: 'She'll live ter be an 'undred at this rate. A feather pillow'll keep a body breathing long after t'sense 'as gone.' Mrs Seed shrank at this, but Mrs Birdwhistle took a deep breath and went on: 'Never thee care, Liz, I'll protect 'ee from that measly broomstick over t'wall. But tell me, is that there clock right? I must catch three bus.' Mrs Seed looked anxious, considering the warped fingers on the spotted face of the wall clock. 'I dunno exactly. Ronnie says 'er do lose towards winding time, an' 'er's not bin wound fer a week.' The clock, brass pendulum bravely swinging, stuttered towards ten minutes to three, and already the bus could be heard grinding round the

B

vicarage corner after stopping at the school gate. Like a bulging grey goose Mrs Birdwhistle flapped down the steps and across the green to where the glossy red bus had slid gently as a ship into harbour.

The bus featured large in village life, bringing the children to school at ten to nine in the morning, bearing them away in the afternoon. Most of them boarded it on its return journey from Horwich, and were taken towards Adlington 'over the water' as the narrow road bridging upper and lower Rivington reservoirs was called. The few who lived in the village ran shouting into our midst, effective disturbers of the peace.

The four remaining cottages, known as Twigg End, lay away from the green under the trees to our left. In the one alongside us lived the Dapples who were to play a vital part in our future—always ready to help in emergencies. Indeed, Mr Dapple had already showed his colours by helping to decorate our house. He was even more at home in the garden—his own and ours, sweeping up leaves that first autumn, planting out during the spring. While Mrs Dapple was to smooth my thorny path of motherhood. Tall, fair, frail-looking, she was also tough, with a cool head on her shoulders. The first summer afternoon I called on her an assortment of cats and kittens were arching, prowling, or sunning themselves on the hot flags in front of her porch. Because they were all mixtures of black-and-white they were known as the Liquorice Allsorts. The largest and most handsome, Mr Basset himself, was coiled on Mrs Dapple's arm when she answered my knock. That day pink roses clambered around the fern-green door; clematis overwhelmed the trellised porch, but she was busy in the kitchen where she had been bandaging Mr Bassett's paw—he was Chink's latest victim.

Because it was Sunday Mr Dapple's saw was laid away in the woodshed, and while we were talking he came in smoking a pipe—you could smell it fifty yards away if the wind was so inclined, he stuffed it so with strong herbs. There was something about Mr Dapple, gnarled, compact, and grey, akin to an apple tree. He was well-balanced and firmly rooted. Even his hair had the greyness of apple wood, and his wind-and-weather countryman's face was keen-eyed, alert, yet serene. When he wasn't gardening he was making something: hammer and nails were seldom out of reach. Just now he turned to admire his new bird-table, tall enough to defy the most agile feline leap.

Not only birds and cats were ministered to: all the cut knees, burns and boils in the village found their way into the Dapples's kitchen. When, before long, there were seven young boys close at hand their first-aid kit was rarely out of action. Yet they made no demands on others; and as Mrs Dapple was not a one for chatting or letter-writing she seldom went to the post-office, village rendezvous and bush-telegraph exchange.

Next door to the Dapples, on their left, lived the Greens, twin brother and sister, intertwined and inseparable as oak and ivy. While he was out mending roads she stayed at home mending his socks, they had no need of friends, and were rarely seen in any but each other's company. Their christian names, Gabriel and Ivy suited them as they suited each other.

In front of these two cottages were two others whose garden walls bordered Rivington Lane. The one nearest to us, right under our beech tree, was the home of Bob Taylor, Corporation estate agent, and his young, pretty, dark-haired wife who, the summer after our arrival gave birth to red-haired twins: Peter and Paul, destined to companion our own two boys, the Seeds' two, and David Mooney from the vicarage. Here then, already, was the nucleus of the Secret Seven, who were to shake us out of a momentary peace, and provide the Dapples with endless overtime. Often enough we were to envy the Marchbanks who lived away from the village racket—up Sheephouse Lane to the left, and the Thatchers, higher up still, on the right.

Johnny Thatcher, chapel sexton and gardener to the Marchbanks, lived with his four sisters and a short-term brother-in-law in the manse. From outside this house with its grey stone roof sagging over grey stone walls and unpainted, unopened windows, looked derelict. A crippled apple tree stood guardian beside the front door long ago sealed with damp and rain-washed to no-colour. Even the back door, blistered and peeling, was opened a mere grudging crack to anyone bold enough to knock upon it. No doctor was ever called to this place of natural remedies and natural deaths.

Many a misty autumn morning we watched Martha, the second sister, slip into the spinney to scrabble for sticks, because whatever was to be seen of life up there could be seen from our back windows. Among the thinning trees, Martha, with her long, grey threadbare coat and flapping sleeves, looked like a huge moth awakened from winter sleep. Happily she and her three sisters, Hannah, the eldest, Jane and Rosie, the two younger ones, enjoyed excellent health. It was impossible to believe that they had ever been young, but when age finally overtook them they were able, in due turn, to drop to earth gently as leaves and making as little disturbance. Indeed, we heard only from Mrs Dapple months after the happenings that the two eldest had succumbed. But Mrs Seed was provoked into criticism: 'They're a proper nuisance wi' their inquests. They did ought ter call in a doctor at th'end!'

Mrs Dapple's long silence was eloquent of her discretion—because she had been called to assist the professional layer-out who had refused to tackle, single-handed, the unwashed bodies of Hannah and Martha. However, this task had enabled Mrs Dapple to throw open windows long sealed with dirt, and to flourish a vigorous broom among smuts and cobwebs.

It happened that the departure of Martha was unusually protracted—as though unwilling to leave the spinney where for so long she had been a walking shadow. No sooner was she nicely arranged, ready for the coffin, than Mrs Dapple insisted she gave a blink. 'Get away with you!' laughed her partner smoothing a practised forefinger over papery eyelids. 'And then, blow me down,' Mrs Dapple told me later, 'if Martha didn't give a great sigh an' open 'er eyes. *Weren't* we scared! I thought it wer only Lazarus as played tricks like this.'

So it was that Martha, on the brink of burial, was restored to life for another year. 'It wer th'essence o' foxglove leaves,' Johnny confided. 'I giv 'er a teaspoonful as she lay on t'bed. Must 'a set th'old ticker off again. It wer Mrs Twigg as put me up t'it.'

Mrs Twigg, by the way, was responsible for more marvels than Martha's 'sitting-up' as this incident came to be called. Her digitalis bottle had more than once resuscitated the Professor up at Sweetloves, and cured Miss Whittle of a heart-attack—a doubtful mercy. But while welcoming help from Mrs Twigg, the Thatchers refused offers of electricity and water laid on. They preferred to live and die by lamp- and candle-light, and to carry water from a spring across the road. In the manse a stand-up wash was reserved for Saturday nights before Johnny went to the village club. 'I don't 'old wi' them new-fangled tin baths,' he once told me, adding, 'an' they do say as 'ot water takes t'vitality out o' yer.' Though his sisters, who were dark-skinned, were seamed and inlaid with dirt, Johnny, blue-eyed and fair, remained fresh as apple-blossom.

After the demise of his elder sisters he was cared for by Jane, the third, and the only one who had married. So far from burgeoning out with matrimony, Jane had become almost a recluse. In her day, if you succeeded in persuading Johnny to open the back door, there would be a shuffling in the twilight kitchen as she vanished into the shadows. After her husband Matthew's death she never again ventured outside. Even in the distant past (so I was told) whenever she was seen walking the lanes with him, Jane, as though bearing the sorrows of the world, would follow, head-down, a grave's length behind. The distance between them lengthened with the years. I never saw her look up to the sun—or even a tree top. For her, life must have been all stones.

Matthew was a good chap who worked on the roads and regularly attended church, a habit which in that household required strength of character. However, Johnny seemed glad of some masculine company among those nebulous women. Certain it is the Thatchers were not the marrying sort, as Matthew must have soon discovered. And when his turn came no one could say he'd had much of a life. Anyway, the village sighed with relief when the ambulance appeared for the first and last time at their door to remove him before the breath was entirely out of his body. And we had Mr Mooney to thank for that.

After Jane died—and that laying-out, according to Mrs Dapple who had been obliged to wear a mask, was the worst ever—Johnny was reduced to the ministrations of Rosie. Though in the days of her bloom she had been the prettiest of the four, Rosie was no housewife; she had never used a needle; and her greatest attainment was a tin-opener.

In spite of all, Johnny, who knew more about Rivington than anyone else, continued to flourish and to air his opinions on the parish council where Aubrey regularly met him. Indeed, before our second Christmas here Aubrey had been persuaded on to all the local committees, apart from others connected with the mill,

the Hunt, the Conservative Party, and agricultural shows.
Through the years the number of his committees mounted to
twenty-four to form the first proverbial 'bone of contention' in
our married life. Willing and anxious to please everybody,
Aubrey could never say 'no'. (After all, he hadn't even said 'no'
to me.) However I might grumble, this serving on committees
was an effective way of getting dug in to the community.

It was at these meetings that he came to know its most powerful
member, Colonel Darley of Moorside, a grey stone house north
of Rivington, a mile away on the moors beyond Dean Wood.
Chairman of companies and Master of Hounds, the Colonel,
massively built for his forty years, and rubicund from love of
sport and port, might well have run us off our feet. But he was
restrained by a few 'independents'—Ben Haythornthwaite for
one, study farmer of Sheephouse Farm, and father of three girls;
Mr Plodder and Ronnie Seed. Even the Colonel's closest
friend, the sporting Humphrey Marchbanks, Bryony's husband,
occasionally dug in his toes and stood out against him.

In common with many villages, Rivington preferred marking
time to advancing, so that the Colonel's efforts at installing a
turbine-engine to supply church and school with electricity were
not fully appreciated. On the other hand, many people grumbled
at the inadequate water-supply. It seemed ironical that with
so much land and so many houses swallowed up to provide
Liverpool with reservoirs, the inhabitants who remained to keep
their heads above water relied on spring-water for their own,
often unreliable, supply. However, we who lived on the top side
of the green were happy enough with this arrangement: our
water is vital, clear and cold as a Scottish river—so different from
the flat, chlorinated liquid issuing from town taps. Everyone who
stays here remarks on our satiny bathwater and the excellence of
our tea.

Unfortunately the village school suffered inconveniences
(apart from earth-closets, soon remedied) unknown to us. Mr
Plodder, quietly determined, brought the matter up at a school
managers' meeting: 'Something must be done about the frogs,'
he insisted. 'Every time we turn on the taps a frog comes out—
wouldn't matter so much if it was just in the washing-up, but
whenever a child goes for a drink, plop—a frog jumps into the
tumbler.'

For once the Colonel and Mr Plodder were in agreement. 'All this water around us,' pleaded the schoolmaster, 'and we can neither swim in summer nor skate in winter. We drink out of tanks and troughs—and now the frogs.'

It would be almost true to say that the Colonel raised heaven and earth to get at the root of the trouble. At least he persuaded the Corporation to send a gang of men to dig up the road where the water-pipe runs down to the school. After blowing it clear they discovered a glutinous mass of frog-spawn in the supply tank. This was emptied and cleaned, and thereafter only an occasional newt found its way into school wash-basins. In spite of such mishaps and our general slow progress, the children here have been remarkably healthy—maybe too much cleanliness can prevent a sturdy resistance to disease.

Lacking a social conscience myself, it was social obligations, far removed from village activities, that hindered me, at first, from getting to know our neighbours in any real sense. After the usual three months then allowed for a young bride to 'settle in' I was beset with 'polite' afternoon callers. Looking back over forty years, that part of my life seems like a page from Jane Austen which began one afternoon at half-past three with a car drawing up and a well-dressed woman—she even wore white kid gloves —knocking gently on the door. Off-guard and in the disarray of old clothes, I answered her knock. We smiled politely at one another across the threshold, she from impeccable heights, and I asked her in. Trying to hide my awareness of laddered stockings, I ushered her into the drawing-room (she had given us a cut-glass decanter for a wedding-present) and did conversational duty remembering my mother's advice: '*Never* apologize if not looking your best!'

At a quarter to four I left the room to put the kettle on, but found the sulking kitchen fire quite gone out. This piece of information I felt bound to convey to my visitor because re-lighting meant scraping ashes, twirling papers, coaxing and blowing for half an hour. I needn't have worried; my caller smoothed the edges of anxiety. She was, in fact, on her way to tea with a friend. Bowing graciously in navy silk, drawing on her long gloves, she smiled and departed. That evening on the silver salver (another wedding-present) I discovered three visiting-cards—a large one for herself and two for her husband. And suddenly every wedding-present became a warning of such a visit. I, too, would have to get cards printed and look decent in the afternoons.

I can hardly believe, as I write, that in those days we had a maid, Edna, a treasure from Durham escaped from a bad husband to cook and clean for us, gratefully, for fifteen shillings a week. I was far more grateful for her services because the oil-lamps were a job in themselves; and the house, from dusty attics downwards, was unlabour-saving beyond belief. At that time, anxious to measure up to my in-laws—hunting people who went to regimental balls and dinners—I persuaded Edna to change every afternoon into a black silk dress and muslin cap and apron, answer the door and bring in tea. Day after day the old silver tray was set and shining with new silver and china. Callers arrived in ones and twos, sometimes three batches in an afternoon, so preventing my cherished afternoon walk for about six months. I determined that Edna's half-day off should be mine also. By now I had begun to dread the crunch of tyres and click-click of heels on the stone path which ran so inconveniently past our drawing-room window. (No architect should ever design such a window—between front gate and front door—which allows no time for hiding oneself behind the sofa.)

In those days I was able to housekeep for the three of us on less than two pounds a week. Milk was twopence halfpenny a pint, and a large loaf cost fourpence. I bought the cheapest bacon at fivepence, and butter at tenpence a pound. Cabbages were twopence each, apples one penny, and petrol elevenpence a gallon, so that (reckoning on the old pence) with five hundred pounds a year we were well off, and could afford an occasional five-and-sixpenny bottle of Spanish sherry.

4

A Visit to Primrose Cottage

We deceived ourselves that it was the thought of a family which prevented us leaving Fisher House. Already the place had begun to get a grip on us, and we remembered Mr Mooney's prophesy. As mentioned earlier, our first baby took root during our first autumn. Village heads nodded approvingly at my rounded condition. 'I told you so!' teased Mrs Mooney when I could no longer hoist myself into the saddle, and Mrs Taylor over the wall was pleased to see someone in the same state as herself. Like me, she was 'due' in July, but whereas I remained round and firm as a melon, she was dismayed by her fullness as early as March. No wonder—unknown to herself, she was loaded with twins.

The only disapproving glances in my direction came from Bryony who had avoided me since the days of our rides together. One day I decided to challenge her, and walked up to Primrose Cottage about tea time. It was a warm, still, June afternoon, and I found Bryony sitting on a wooden bench under an apple tree scraping carrots. 'Are those for Pegasus or you?' I asked, archly determined to start with her on a firm rein. 'Both,' she replied shortly, looking up with hostility in her blue eyes, and looking down at my enlargement. 'You're quite a stranger now, in your "interesting" condition, aren't you?'

'I came to find out why. There's no need for it.'

'No need for the baby? Well, you did try hard enough to get rid of it. I'll give you that.'

'Seriously, what's wrong with my having a baby?'

Bryony frowned and put down her scraper. 'From my point of view, of course, because it stopped our rides. But more important, when one's friends have babies they become different people— all wrapped up in the nest. And generally darned dull. As bad as people in love. I'd just got to know you, and now you go off like this.'

'Well, I'm flattered to be thought of as anything approaching a friend. But understand this, no baby will ever turn me into the "maternal type". In fact, I dislike babies—scared of them—and I dread the thought of having this one.'

'So you think. But all will be changed with the arrival. Anyway, I suppose I'd better get you some tea. Sit down.'

While she was gone I sat on the bench in the orchard behind the cottage which stood alone in the fields above Newhall Barn, part of an old farm, across Sheephouse Lane from us. This belonged, in 1336, to Robert Pilkington, Squire of Rivington, who owned all the land around here. Surrounded by gorse bushes rather than primroses, the grey stone cottage was enlivened by a yellow door. Its narrow stone-mullioned windows looked down on to a field where seven odd-shaped flat stones were flung in a diagonal path from the gate. As in all true cottages, life here was lived around the back door—also yellow—from where you stepped over moss-welded flagstones into the orchard —mostly of storm-bent damsons and barren 'crabs', described by Bryony as 'fruitless' trees. In a southern corner three bee-hives leaned against the fence.

Before long Bryony appeared carrying a tray, and I noticed how easily she moved—like a creature of open spaces. The sun made her hair glint like straw as she set down the tray on the grass between us. Pouring out two mugs of tea, she explained her unorthodox diet: 'I never eat foodless foods—white bread and sugar, cakes and biscuits—those wodges of white lint and cotton-wool which clog one's inside.' She handed me a dish of fruit and nuts. 'No wonder these countrywomen are so vast!' Airily she took a handful of hazel-nut kernels. And no wonder that she fitted so trimly into those narrow green corduroys. She continued to nibble, happily as a squirrel,—all part of the act, perhaps, to harmonize with nature. 'You're lucky to have tea today,' she went on spitting a bad nut into the grass. 'It's usually my home-brewed wine—elderberry, water, sun, and *time*—turning water into wine is quite simple after all.'

'Half the people here seem to thrive on the flowers of the field, and the other half on tea, coffee, and disinfectant.'

'The place *is* rather divided. Oddities and "ordinaries"; church and chapel, and so on. And what a cat-and-dog life smoulders under the ivy and cottage-roses—with Miss Whittle

crossing everybody, and Mrs Plodder glowering across the green
at Mrs Mooney. Warfare reflected in their pets. It's evens on
Miss Whittle's Chink and the Plodder's Bonzo as to which'll
demolish Mimi. And that reminds me, the Colonel dared to ask
me for a Field Sports Society sub. He knows jolly well I've reared
a vixen escaped from his beastly hounds! It's not the killing of
animals I object to,' she explained to my raised eyebrows, 'so
much as making them suffer in the pursuit of pleasure. Perhaps
it does the huntsman more harm than the hunted.'

'What you really object to,' I retorted, 'is people enjoying it!
The animal has to be destroyed anyhow. It's all a question of
whether to do it in cold blood or hot blood.' I turned my glance
to her canvas sandals. 'Is that why you wear those?'

'Oh, I know I'm half a hypocrite,' she admitted deftly squash-
ing a wasp with her fruit knife, 'but I do try to avoid buying
leather goods.' As I watched the death-struggle of the wasp I
thought how difficult her choices must be. Probably she was
lonely in spite of her vaunted independence. Belonging neither
to church nor chapel, she resisted all attempts to draw her into
the Women's Institute or the Mothers' Union. And she eschewed
both garden fêtes and whist-drives with their ham-and-tongue
sandwiches (white bread) and women's chatter. Bonds of all
kinds—even those of matrimony—failed to hold her. As though
reading my thoughts, she broke into them. 'You know, of course,
that Humphrey loves hunting, so in this we have to go our
separate ways. And he says he wasn't designed to live on lettuces
and nuts.'

I felt much sympathy for Humphrey who had taken to dining
out every night—often with the Colonel—and spent days away
from the cottage. But then Bryony was an artist and couldn't be
expected to behave like a normal person. At this time she was to
be seen every morning on the toft and quillit painting the church,
which she described as 'solid, static, and true to all it stands for'.
This she explained to me in her studio, a wooden shed. 'The only
unpredictable qualities of life and movement appear in the
weathercock and leaves,' she said over my shoulder as I tried to
discover the subject beneath the dominant cock and through
exuberant foliage.

Although Bryony never went to church she had a magnetic
attraction for clergymen. Rectors, the rural dean, and at least one

bishop had knocked upon that yellow door. Once admitted to house or garden they would linger in talk for hours. 'But they've not converted 'er yet,' Johnny Thatcher had grinned at me, 'an' I daresay she gives 'em summat ter chew on.'

We had hardly returned to the bench in the orchard when a black figure came through the gate and advanced towards us. 'Mr Mooney!' exclaimed Bryony jumping up, 'I must get him a deck-chair. Poor thing, how hot he must be! And he's such a nice, real person under all that black serge. A parson's get-up is a penance—silly when they're supposed to bring light.'

She picked up a chair from the studio, and went to meet him. Drops of sweat glistened on his forehead as he removed his hat, and, at her invitation, thankfully collapsed into the chair. After slinging his field-glasses over the back he pulled out a handker-chief and mopped his brow. 'I've been stalking a meadow-pipit,' he explained, 'I knew she had a second clutch, and was lucky enough to trip over her nest—a beauty with five chocolate-coloured eggs. Well, I'm delighted to find you here too,' he turned to me. 'As a matter of a fact I was about to call on you. So this time I *have* killed two birds with one stone.' Looking rather sheepish at his joke, he went on: 'I was going to ask if you'd be so kind as to open our garden-party this year?' he looked from one to the other of us unhopefully. I shook my head. 'The garden-party's in August, and the baby's due at the end of July. I shall hardly be in a fit state—in fact,' I added gleefully (and with more truth than I realized) 'it might hold back and decide to arrive on the very day!'

'Oh, I'm so sorry—how thoughtless of me to forget.' Again, he turned to Bryony, 'Couldn't you, in these very special circum-stances, Mrs Marchbanks, step in and fill the gap? It would be so kind.'

'Alas,' Bryony smiled, 'I'm not a kind person. And though I'd like to help you, the church isn't "my cup". But don't think I'm wholly irreligious. Only my idea of God doesn't fit into churches and chapels. Sometimes I wonder how he can make himself small enough to get inside.' She paused, looking upward: 'Plenty of room out here.' The vicar sighed. 'God is not confined by time and space,' he replied, repeating a well-worn answer, 'or by size. Our ideas are evolving as everything else. But we must have a meeting place. Among a group of people worship and prayer

gain in strength. . . . "Where two or three are gathered together,"
you know.' With difficulty he hoised himself out of the chair and
reached for his field-glasses. 'It's not going to be easy to find an
opener. Mrs Darley is too shy. . . .'

'How about Anna Morel—or even Rebecca?' suggested
Bryony. 'I doubt either of them saying "yes", ' he shook his head.
'For the present I'll put the problem out of mind by going in
search of a little owl.'

'What an unenviable job!' Bryony exclaimed at his retreating
figure. 'There goes a scholar and a man of vision doing his best
to round up the goats, wasting his life among stony pastures. I
only wish I could follow him, but if I had to choose it would be
the chapel rather than the church. The chapel does leave loop-
holes for individual thinking. Perhaps I am a Unitarian. I can
believe in one God—or whatever—the wholeness of life. As for
the Virgin Birth. . . .'

'That's an open question in the Church of England.'

'Then how can you say the Creed with conviction? Humphrey
went to a chapel funeral last week, and except for the Lord's
Prayer he said it was all poetry and philosophy. I like the sound
of that.'

'And do you like the sound of their bell?' I was stung into
defence. 'At least ours *rings*! I can't bear that cracked clang
from the chapel.' Indeed, I had already complained to Mr
Fletcher, chairman of the chapel committee, a blacksmith (not
harmonious) that the sound of the chapel bell on Sundays was
enough to sour the milk for a week. In such matters the buried
rivalry between church and chapel was occasionally to be heard
knocking on the coffin lid. Services clashed only on Sunday
afternoons when both bells, loud in competition, rang one against
the other across the green. But whereas the chapel bell, flat and
flurried, began its business at a quarter to three, the solemn
church bell took the air ten minutes later. Out of time, out of
tune, for five discordant minutes they wrangle-jangled at one
another. Chapel bell's *Quick! Quick! Quick!* was answered by
church bell's measured, as I told Bryony, *Go . . . to . . . Hell!*

She laughed at my description, and we both agreed that the
most ludicrous thing of all was the competitive way Johnny
Thatcher rang the bell of the empty chapel at eight o'clock every
Sunday morning while the only service at that hour was held in

church, whose bell remained silent. Had the chapel sexton felt able to ring for the church services, well, that would have been another story in another world than this.

A peaceful silence between us was snapped by a second clicking of the gate and a slim, tall, sandy-brown-haired young man coming slowly towards us. 'I'm sorry to intrude,' he began as Bryony stared at him in surprise, 'but they directed me here from the post-office. You see, I'm looking for rooms—I've got a job at the grammar school next term. Teaching English.' His voice had a lilt as though he'd crossed the border and arrived here via a northern university. Bryony indicated the deck-chair. He sat down and, like Mr Mooney, pulled out a white handkerchief and mopped his brow. He had the soft, fair, freckled skin that sweats easily, and deep blue eyes of an almost girlish cornflower-blue. Curly hair, long, white fingers and an open-necked shirt of palest blue emphasised the girlishness. 'How old are you?' said Bryony appraising him shrewdly. 'You don't look old enough to be a schoolmaster.' He said he was twenty-four—a year older than Bryony and I—though he looked about nineteen; and we felt protective towards him. However, in the circumstances and considering Humphrey (if Bryony ever considered him) Primrose Cottage seemed hardly suitable. We went through all the possible houses in the neighbourhood, and eventually alighted on Sweet-loves. He was intrigued by our sketched account of the household, so we offered to escrot him there.

On the way up the glen he exclaimed with delight at the moors and the position of the house under the shoulder of the Pike. 'It's like coming home,' he said as Bryony mounted the four high steps and knocked on the front door. Anna opened it and, pushing aside a strand of auburn hair, looked at us with surprise and dismay. Neither Bryony nor I had set foot in the house, and suddenly we felt embarrassed at confronting her with a strange young man. Bryony recovered first: 'Don't be alarmed, Miss Morel, but here is an English teacher—Mr Laycock.' They bowed and mumbled at each other. 'He's starting at the grammar school next term, and wants rooms—somewhere quiet and nearby. Well, yours are both. Would you give it a thought?'

Anna drew in her breath and turned back to where someone moved in the shadow. 'Rebecca,' she addressed the tall, dark woman now beside her, 'here's Mr Laycock, an English teacher. Can we give him lodgings?'

'A splendid idea!' Rebecca's smile gleamed with strong white teeth in a wide mouth as she came down the steps to shake hands. The two of them were about the same height, verging on six feet, and they were a handsome pair—she all glowing dark eyes and Amazon beauty; he fair, and with his Greek profile like a stripling Hermes. Rebecca turned her warming smile on us. 'So good of you to think of it—how can I thank you? And Father will be delighted; he shuts himself up too much with books. A young English scholar will do him a power of good. We're in a bit of a muddle at present, but do come in, and you,' she flashed her smile at us, 'both of you must call in sometime.'

Disappointed, we were left with no alternative but to depart. Anna accompanied us to the gate. 'I'm sorry she didn't ask you in, but perhaps she felt there were too many at once. Hardly anyone comes up here, and we get out of the habit of visitors. All the same, we'll arrange something—you'll want to see your young man ensconced.'

Once again I helped her with the awkward gate, but was too cumbrous this time to be of much use. She nodded sympathetically towards my stomach, and Bryony and I set off down the glen. 'I *do* think she might have let us have a peep,' she complained. 'Rebecca seemed very pleased, anyway. My goodness, what a smile! And what a woman! Though I hear she's what they call "odd"—another to add to our list. But now we'll be able to find out from Michael—I certainly intend to see plenty of *him*.'

After we had parted company at the bottom of our drive she called back: 'Don't leave Fisher House! It suits you, and I can't imagine you living anywhere else.'

That night there was a moon, and on the toft and quillit I stood for some minutes looking west towards woods and sea, then slowly turned to the moors stretching north and east under the unwinking Pole-star and the Plough with its seven glittering nails. In the dark and silver air the reservoirs became lakes; and the church weathercock glinted above slumbering trees. As I walked back across the green the cottage windows on the left sent out a comforting glow. To the right the vicarage poplar stood up straight as a mast. A few paces on, and there was Fisher House, its white walls crossed in the moonlight by tree shadows—an enchanted Walter-De-La-Mareish sort of house with hidden presences under its moss-padded roof.

5

Surfeit of Rats and Trees

Our moss-padded roof, alas, harboured more than hidden presences, but at that time we were too occupied with the baby's imminent arrival to notice them. Martin was already two months old at the end of our first year in Fisher House. Ideas of moving were temporarily thrust aside. We'll have our family first, we told ourselves, and then move into something more convenient. After all, here was plenty of space for children to grow up in; and our fifty-pound-a-year rent was not to be despised. Imperceptibly, week by week, we were putting down roots.

Martin's arrival in August was a most unpleasant experience. He came ten days late, feet first, after a protracted labour—much of this due to the whisky consumed to while away the long hours by the doctor who 'delivered' me. It was the nurse who saved the baby's life—and my own. Concerned at my condition, she asked, on the third day after the birth, how I felt. 'Like the football,' I told her, 'after the Preston North End Cup Final.'

All the same, when I first heard sucking noises and creaks from the Moses basket, I was filled with delight. Perhaps Bryony was right and maternity had overcome me. But even mothers are 'born and not made'. I worried incessantly about colds, draughts, and the number of blankets in cot and pram. A true mother takes all this in her stride. Yet I was blessed by an un-expectedly cow-like performance: through three babies I never had a bottle in the house, and just now 'lent a hand'—to euphemize—in the feeding of one of Mrs Taylor's twins. These ginger-headed boys, Peter and Paul, had arrived a fortnight before Martin, and their mother was at her wits' end—or, to quote Miss Whittle, 'tits' end'—to satisfy them.

Late that summer the village was enlivened by screams and shaking prams, with David Mooney and Jimmy Seed (from the post-office) both rising three and happy to add to the chorus. Miss Whittle smiled acidly when I met her: 'Well now, and fer sure yer troubles are beginning—chillun, I allus says, bring more tears 'n laughter.'

Though Edna helped me all she could, after six months I grew tired of nursery routine, and took on a Swiss *au pair* girl, Gretchen. Her wide china-blue eyes grew wider at the sight of my outsize apple pies—she could eat a whole one at a sitting. So while Martin was still living *gratis* on me, I had to cater for her enormous appetite. Thus, one freedom was gained at the expense of another. At least I had time to attend to sinister happenings under the floorboards. One day Edna called me up to the attic where she had discovered a clump of obscene-looking yellow toadstools. I called on Bob Taylor who, being father of the thriving twins, was glad to help. 'Tat for tit,' he said with a grin (we had become familiar in the circumstances) and thrust a pen-knife into a skirting-board. Immediately we were enveloped in a cloud of mustard-coloured dust. 'Aye,' he nodded, 'they thrive on mouldy wood.'

That was the beginning of many troubles: we found ourselves being consumed by dry-rot so that two floors had to be removed. From time to time a stone slate slid wearily from the sagging roof until the walls glistened with damp, and rain poured through the rafters. Mercifully the death-watch beetle had ceased its small-hours tapping in the bedroom. 'They can go ter sleep fer years,' Miss Whittle informed me, 'but one day they'll wak up an' th'ouse 'ull fall down.'

There came a Sunday morning when her prophesy seemed to be upon us. I was in the bedroom getting ready for church when a grating, crumbling noise began behind the fireplace. Trans-fixed, I listened to the sound gathering force like a mountain of shale rushing to destruction. Somewhere downstairs someone must be being buried. Where was Aubrey in this sudden awful silence? Where Gretchen? I stood in the ominous quiet for a few moments before racing downstairs. In hall, kitchen, and dining-room all was in order. Fearfully I opened the drawing-room door and refused to believe my eyes: an unlovely load of bricks and rubble sprawled across the pale blue-patterned Wilton; and the entire room was draped in a thick and sooty silence. Gradually my mind began to register certain facts: the room had been decorated only last week; we had invited the Morels for lunch; being Sunday, no workmen were to be had.

Refusing to bear such a weight alone, I ran into the garden calling Gretchen. The expression on her face as she entered the room almost made up for the disaster. Once again Bob Taylor was shaking his head: 'Yer do fair cop it at Fisher 'ouse, yer do fer sure.'

'But what's happened—is it dangerous?'

'Why, it be t'chimney feathering. It's cum toppling right down from th'attic. Yon'll be a tidy job. Mebbe two walls 'ull 'ave ter cum down. I'll tell yer wot,' he lowered his voice, 'if I was you I'd 'op it afore t'roof caves in.'

During the following six months we saw over three modern houses advertised for sale. Box-like, convenient, raw, and totally lacking in character, they were nevertheless light and spacious enough. No smothering trees to shut out the sun. In silence we disparaged each threadbare garden and the identical boxes next door—both sides, up and down the road and across the road in never-ending suburbia. We could hardly wait to get home and be reclaimed by Fisher House.

'The fact is,' I admitted wrestling with the back door key, 'I've become a slave to this place and grown a great tap-root that goes deep down under the cellar.'

Once again we hugged our good fortune in living on a water-shed, and agreed for a while longer to put up with antique range, leaking roof and dry-rot. After all, we could hear a stream from the garden, and, in spite of the trees, the feeling of open spaces around us made up for everything.

Perhaps our worst season, misnamed spring, occurred between March and May when the east winds came raging down from the Pike to roar under ill-fitting doors and rattle the window-frames. Without wedges it was impossible to sleep. We kept ourselves warm, not by sitting over fires—there was never time for that —but by ministering to them. And if summer also brought its trials with encroaching leaves and shortage of water, autumn, as Miss Whittle had foretold, brought the rats.

Trouble would begin in October with the field-mice scuttling indoors for sanctuary. Beyond the reach of any cat, they scratched and squealed in the wainscot. But one January a huge dropsical rat took refuge behind the kitchen fireplace where he grew still fatter, and became tame and bold. One morning I came downstairs to find him sitting on his haunches cleaning his whiskers in the middle of the floor. His black eyes shone with the malevolence of a Japanese inquisitor. Shocked and fascinated, I stared at him as he, pausing in his brush-up, stared back. Then, nonchalantly he cantered away to his retreat.

I raced over to the Plodders to borrow their suddenly welcome Bonzo, and after persuading Aubrey to rake the rat from his cosy-hole and leave the rest to the dog, retired to the hen-cabin. My timid return was nicely timed to meet Aubrey swinging the rat gingerly by its tail. 'It's diseased,' he remarked holding it distastefully at arm's length.

A worse incident was to come. One mild April morning a peculiar sweetish smell—like a corpse—issued from under the stairs. Though Aubrey only laughed at me, the insidious odour of rotten flesh persisted, and when we called in Bob to investigate he pulled a face in spite of Jeyes' Fluid and wide-open windows. Two days later he appeared with a mate; together they rolled back the linoleum at the foot of the stairs, and lifted the floor-boards. Immediately the whole house reeked with putrification, and I fled outdoors. After a couple of hours away I returned to be greeted by Bob: 'All over,' he grinned, 'Jim went home. Stomach turned, and no wonder. Biggest female rat I've ever seen, an' twelve young 'uns. All shining green.'

I shuddered: 'Where?' 'Bang under t'bottom stair. She'd made a big untidy nest. See!' Removing a dust-bin lid he pointed to a chewed-up mass of boys' comics.

Rats still come and go, and compared with them the cock-roaches which breed in dim corners are friendly creatures. Like-wise the woodlice—to be swept airily from basins and bowls in the back place. As for the spiders which haunt bath and sink, I wouldn't kill them for worlds. More alarming was the baby owl which arrived down our bedroom chimney one morning—a ruffled and reluctant sweep, and the bat that whirled inside at midnight to thump a soft body against the bedroom walls. In the light of Aubrey's torch the shadow of umbrella-wings was magnified at all angles—sinister, horrible as Dracula himself—driving me in terror to the bottom of the bed.

While our battle against such invaders continues, my private 'battle of the trees' eventually came to a head. But first, for twelve years on and off, I was to plead with, almost kneel to, Mr Bull, the Corporation engineer, begging to be allowed two trees down

—the whitebeam and the rowan. Each time he would drive up and stand, six-foot solid and still with his hat on, in our drawing-room. Each time my plea was overridden: 'You live on a water-shed by courtesy, and for a very low rent. We want water; and the trees attract rain.'

'And we want light and air!' I would reply despairingly. 'Are water and trees more important than people and sun? Surely even tenants have *some* right to life?'

Here (how well I knew the drill) he would jerk up his chin as he turned to go, flinging over his shoulder: 'You are not bound to stay. Indeed, we have a long waiting-list for your house.'

This struggle so tore at my being that twenty years later I wrote a poem on the subject—'Emotion' (with a vengeance) 'recollected in tranquillity'.[1] But at the time I rejoiced at the coming of autumn which, fallen leaf by fallen leaf, gave us a glimpse of the sky.

And then one summer afternoon Michael Laycock called with a parcel of books. It was so dark in the room that I had to switch on the light. 'My goodness—it's like a vault!' he exclaimed. 'Couldn't you get some trees down? Make a fight for it. Refuse to pay the rent.' His attitude spurred me on to continue the battle. But at the time his sympathy made me ask him to stay on and talk. He sat down in an armchair near the window, looking out at the trees. 'It's us or them,' I said following his gaze. 'I feel so horribly oppressed in this house, especially in summer, because the sun is everywhere but here. And in winter the draughts from these rattling windows are unbeliev-able.' He nodded understandingly. 'I can believe it,' he replied. 'Do you mind a pipe?' He set about filling and lighting it with his long, sensitive fingers and curving back thumbs—like John Gielgud's. The match flame lit up his Greek profile with its short, straight nose. Those dark, almost gentian-blue eyes with their dilated pupils were assessing me. 'All the same,' he said with an air of authority, 'you belong here—in spite of the dark and damp and trees. Somehow you must make friends with them or get them out of the way. You may even end by owning the house.'

I laughed. 'Even if the Corporation would sell, I'd never dream of buying a place like this. Our whole aim is to move to something small and modern—that would give me time to read

[1] *Prayer for Sun* (Hart-Davis).

and write, and freedom from too many chores. But enough of me. Tell me, how are things working out at Sweetloves?'

'Very well indeed. And thank you for that. And Bryony. It's an interesting set-up. I don't think I'll ever get to know the Professor. Hardly ever see him, and he never speaks to me. Did you know his name is Egbert? Most suitable for a Professor of Medieval English. He spends most of his time upstairs in his room poring over old manuscripts, translating Anglo-Saxon poetry, and eternally writing a book that is never written. Anna tells me he sits facing north, shut away from the sun in summer, companioned by an oil-lamp in winter. They call his room "the Chamber of the Midnight Oil".' Apparently the Professor had been unwell lately, and Anna had given up her teaching job to look after him. 'Is that why they've forgotten their promise to ask me up?' I enquired, curious to know more. 'Possibly. But it's not just you—they don't like visitors. Why don't you call on spec? I'm certain Anna, at least, would be glad to see you. She's lonely, I think, without her job. A very unusual, attractive person.'

Overmastered again by curiosity, I asked how he got on with her. 'Fine. I get on well with all women.' He turned the charm of his smile full upon me. 'But I'm not in love with her, if that's what you mean—though Rebecca intends that I should be.' Taken aback, I was about to rush in with meaningless words, but his eyes, laughing, mocking, held me to the truth. 'Well, I suppose it is,' I admitted, 'if I were to explore deep down.'

'Never mind exploring. You get lost that way. There's one thing I've learned from living at Sweetloves—they never pretend; they are simply themselves, so everyone else thinks them odd. Perhaps it's easier when you live alone up on the moors. No point in wearing masks. We keep those for mixing with other people.'

'You don't need to wear masks in the village,' I broke in. 'Don't you believe it. The people around this green put on masks every time they go out. Vicar and schoolmaster and postmistress —they must live up to their image of themselves. Neighbours try to show what's expected of them.'

'Surely not. Mr Mooney, for instance, isn't he his natural self with his love of birds and delving into Celtic history?'

'Possibly. But his mask is his dog-collar. And Mr Plodder. Every Day he projects his image in front of those brats so that he can keep order and drum facts into them. But "deep down", as you call it, he's another person. Maybe his ambition was to play the flute or be a ballet-dancer. Who knows?'

'Somehow I don't think the flame of genius burns in our kind, brown, sensible schoolmaster.' One by one we considered the village characters, leaving Mrs Twigg as a mystery and Miss Whittle a besom. 'But everyone's a mystery, really. What d'you make of Bryony?' I suddenly shot at him. 'Do you think she invented herself?' Michael became thoughtful. 'I believe Bryony is trying to find herself. All that vegetarian and anti-village stuff is a way through—for her—to something real. After all, the purpose of life is to discover who we are and what we are here for. And on that note of philosophy I must go.' He stood up. 'Anna, not to mention Rebecca, will be wondering where on earth I've got to. I think *we've* got quite a long way, don't you? Please come up sometime—with or without an invitation.'

I led him to the door. 'We never got on to the subject of you,' I said as we shook hands. 'Do you like your job, for instance?'

'Half and half. Generally I feel I'm getting nowhere—if we must talk of getting and going, rather than being.' His smile mocked me: 'If you really want to know, I'm a poet at heart.'

After he'd gone I felt both uplifted and mixed up, and wondered if Anna, also, found his searching blue eyes unduly attractive.

His visit, however, spurred me one bright April afternoon to go up to Sweetloves. Wondering at my temerity, I walked slowly up the glen, climbed the four steps, and knocked gently on the door. Rebecca let me in. Tall, dark, handsome in a sombre way, she resembled a cypress tree, ageless, resisting all weathers, yet with something uncertain about her. That day the house was quiet as a graveyard, and Rebecca told me that Anna was out. But she insisted on my staying for tea. It was not quite three o'clock, and I'd had a late lunch, so I pleaded: 'Only a cup please—nothing to eat.'

While she was away I stood gazing out of the sitting-room window. You could feel the surge of the moor against the house almost overpowering. I turned away to notice how the sunlight fingered blotched walls and ragged michaelmas daisies in an earthenware jug. Light strong enough to bleach an old grand-piano pushed against a damp patch which was partly hidden by a Cézanne reproduction. On the piano stood a photograph of the Professor as a young man: he wore a beard, and above his hooked nose the dark, searching eyes were those of Rebecca. Beside him, framed in silver-gilt, stood a tall fair man, delicate, almost feminine-looking, in the uniform of an army-officer. A silent half-hour went by—no doubt kettles at Sweetloves were slow—and I was wondering if this pale and gentle knight-at-arms had once waited on Rebecca when suddenly, to a clatter of dishes, the door opened and she herself stormed in behind a noisy trolley. Not tea and biscuits, but great chunks of bread and butter and, to my horror, two thick slices of fried cod. Helplessly I received my portion and played with it while she plied me with bread and butter and talk—not small but curious—concerning spiders, by which she seemed fascinated, the burnworthiness of oak and elm, and cats—this last because just now two of them, a black and a ginger, addressed respectively as the Bishop and the Shah, had padded tails-in-air into the room. Happily they proved to be opportune recipients of cod-flakes which I was able to dispense under the table without offending my hostess. Indeed, the party ended with both our plates on the floor licked shining clean. 'They save a lot of washing-up,' remarked Rebecca gazing down fondly at her pets.

Only three days later I encountered Anna in the post-office. 'I'm so sorry I was out when you called,' she began, 'and I must apologize for that extraordinary tea. . . . But do come and see me another day—I'm nearly always at home.' So saying, she disappeared, and Mrs Seed gave me a knowing smile. 'The elder one's a bit of an oddity. They say she wer jilted by 'er young man. Night before t'wedding 'e took fright an' bolted. Scared stiff if yer ask me. But she wer properly *obsessed*.' Mrs Seed dwelt on the seldom-used word. 'Never got over it. Used ter walk about fields picking wild flowers fer 'is photo. Keeps it on t'piana—so they say. All I knows fer certain is that every so often she 'as a queer turn an' goes away.' I paid for my stamps and she enlightened me still further: 'Wot wi' t'Professor locked up wi' books all day, it's no wonder they need a lodger t'elp out.'

Not very long after my conversation with Michael, Anna, no doubt prompted by him, asked me to supper. It was a strange party with Rebecca playing hostess, refusing to allow anyone to get up and hand round dishes, Michael and Anna making polite talk—masks on tonight—and the Professor sitting remote and grey at the head of the table. He was silent except when occasionally deferred to. Then he would answer absently, crumbling his bread, as though talking to shadows. You felt that he lived his life on paper, detached from human problems. Even more absently, when the second course arrived, he applied pepper vigorously as from a sugar-sifter to his applie pie till Anna snatched away his plate. After sneezing himself back into the present he apologized: 'The trouble is,' blowing his nose, 'I was born too late—several hundred years too late.'

'Well, and if you were, you're not the only one,' Rebecca soothed him. 'In this house we all live in the past. . . .' She paused, sighing towards the photograph on the piano. Anna steered back again: 'No up-to-date family would put up with it. I don't believe our kitchen sink has been renewed since the reign of George the IVth.'

Meanwhile Rebecca gathered herself up and went to the sideboard. 'Will you sample my ginger-wine?' Without waiting for an answer, she filled our glasses to the brim. The astringent, chestnut-coloured liquid stung away the fragrant aftermath of apple pie. 'Rebecca's a great one for home-made wines,' remarked Anna. 'She's learned the art from Mrs Twigg who supplies all the "enlightened" with home-brewed potions. They must be good because she's never been ill in her life.' Anna looked at Michael who shook his head disbelievingly. 'And the funny thing is,' Anna pursued, 'she never seems to get any older. She's looked about fifty for years and years—says ageing is a condition of mind, and dying a fulfilment. One day she'll float away like a leaf.'

6

Mrs Twigg

It was the Eve of All Hallows, with the leaves floated down and away, a bonfire alight on the green, and all of us bobbing for apples when suddenly a shadow took shape in our midst. Mrs Birdwhistle, her teeth fastened into a Worcester Pearmain, looked up, gave a cry, and dropped her apple with a splash into the bucket. A figure who had not been there before materialized. A woman, presumably.

'Ah!' Mrs Birdwhistle exclaimed. 'you fair lifted the skin off mi' back. Are you a spirit returned to fright us?'

'A spirit alive in the flesh,' replied Mrs Twigg, for it was she who had emerged hooded and cloaked from the shadows. 'Spirits can never die,' she soothed us, 'only bodies, like leaves piled underneath the trees. The tree is symbolic of life eternal.'

We closed in, eager to hear more. Mrs Twigg, magnetic in the firelight, gazed at Mrs Birdwhistle. 'Born under the sign of Pisces, the Fish. Sign of Christianity. If you choose you can achieve what you aspire to through intuition. While you,' she twitched her firebright eyes on me, 'are an Aquarian. Intellect stronger than intuition. But intellect is the long way round the mulberry bush. I see also,' she went on, 'that you have a child of Leo. Your husband was born under the same sign—of the Sun. Leo and Aquarius, fire and air, being opposite signs are not easy together. Those born when the sun is in Aquarius are air people. Sun in Leo is fire. You have much to learn—living with two Leos.' She smiled delightedly. 'But look upon it as a blessing. It is your *karma*. Everything happens at the right time, and for a purpose. What matters is how you meet each experience—not the experience itself.' I was silent in amazement, because she was right about our birthdates. After a pause she considered me again: 'You will have three children, one born at Christmas time.' She stopped abruptly, and I begged her to go on. She shook her head: 'It is not good to know the future—unless it is given,

as to me. And it is not often I give out so much, but I felt drawn.
Come and see me sometime. Always so much to do; always time
for everyone. Life is not cramped except by our thinking.'

By now we were all gathered in a circle around her, and
watched dumbfounded as she floated away, softly as she had
appeared. 'That was a spirit, that was,' breathed Mrs Birdwhistle
into the silence.

Mystery was Mrs Twigg's secret. Never giving herself away,
she drew people out towards her. 'She arouses our wonder in the
unknown,' Mrs Mooney decided next day. 'And she has something we all want—confidence and serenity—no wonder she
enjoys such good health.'

All the same, there were some who avoided her—Miss
Whittle's ferret eyes glinted hot red lights at mention of her
name, and Mrs Plodder folded herself in with embarrassment at
her presence. While the one felt fear, the other was discomforted.

This became evident through the default of a speaker for our
Women's Institute Group meeting—the big day on which three
neighbouring Institutes were invited. Mrs Plodder, urged on by
the committee, asked Mrs Twigg to step in and fill the gap. Mrs
Twigg grasped this opportunity for bringing light to the
uninitiated, and chose for her subject: All Things Invisible.

'So now we're going to 'ave a talk about Nothing,' said Mrs
Seed as we took our seats among an audience agog for ghost
stories. On the platform Mrs Twigg smiled her secret smile and
gazed into space. She wore a loose homespun dress of ethereal
blue, with a great garnet brooch pinned at her throat. After
being introduced by Mrs Plodder as 'Someone we all know, and
yet do not know,' she rose up and without any preliminary began
to talk about the human aura: 'I see you as physical bodies sitting
before me. . . .' Her lower lids flickered giving her eyes an upside-
down look, and the persuasive, reedy voice rustled through our
senses. 'But I can see—oh, far more—I can see into your beings.'
A few women stirred uneasily. 'You are all different colours.
Yes, all the colours of the rainbow are filling this room.
Marvellous! Her dark eyes, dark as water in a moorland tarn,
glinted over the many-coloured hats, then she turned to Mrs
Plodder, laced-up, neat and brown, and trying to make herself
smaller. 'Of course, there are some who hide their colours under
their wings.' Mrs Plodder sat rigid as a stuffed bird while Mrs

Twigg launched into astral travel: 'During sleep when our bodies are breathing and warm in bed, our astral selves travel to distant places, meeting other people. This explains the feeling we most of us experience: "I have been here before." ' Now the audience was warming up, leaning forward, mouths open—not in yawns but in interest and curiosity. When we came to astrology the whole room, with the exception of Mrs Plodder, became absorbed so that the ritual backstage rattling of tea-cups brought a sigh of disappointment instead, as so often, of relief.

Mrs Twigg, floating among the tea-sippers, was besieged by those who wanted to know more: 'Tell us about when we die. Do we meet our friends when we go?' And so on. Refusing a meat pie, she assured her listeners that life is a circle, without beginning or ending: 'That which never ends can never begin,' the most logical statement of the evening. She enlarged on reincarnation. 'I don't just think, I *know* that the human soul returns again and again to earth. And each new earth-life presents us with greater wisdom and strength to overcome greater obstacles. That is, if we've learned our lesson in the previous life.'

'Oh dear, I don't like the sound o' *that*!' demurred Mrs Bird-whistle, 'I was 'oping fer a bit of a rest. If anyone comes knocking on my coffin lid I'd tell 'em ter 'op it.' Mrs Twigg gave her a grieved look, but Mrs Mooney drew closer, asking more questions. She and I were baffled by Mrs Twigg who seemed to be a reservoir of great truths sometimes clouded with fantasy. Looking into those fathomless eyes felt like undergoing a spiritual X-ray. That she had power, perception, and intuition was never doubted. Meanwhile, tea-chat drowned further speculation. 'Funny,' remarked Mrs Mooney, 'how few people are interested in the only part of them that's going to last.'

The invisible world forgotten, members were discussing raffle tickets, a charity show, a cookery exhibition—here and now pulling a great deal more strongly than then and there. 'It's fear,' whispered Mrs Twigg into my ear. 'They are afraid of the Invisibles—mostly young souls here, but they'll come back to learn.'

We recognized Mrs Twigg as an old soul. Yet physically, as Anna had noticed, she never seemed to grow any older. Her hair remained ash-grey around a face firm as a well-stored Russet apple. In the children's eyes she had the gift of magic unimpeded by our press-button civilization. And she could still read by moonlight without spectacles. 'Although,' as Mrs Mooney crisply remarked, 'I bet she's never been put to the test of a Bible—*or* a telephone directory!' Mrs Twigg could afford to shrug at aids which would have diluted her powers of perception. Blessed with gifts of clairvoyance and telepathy, what need had she of telephone and wireless? Living ear-to-ground, so to speak, her physical senses were also quickened. She used to tell the children that she could hear the daisies grow. And if she did practice witchcraft, it was white as the daisies.

Living alone, she was not lonely; never tired or ill. And, obedient to the laws of nature and of the spirit, she was immune to discomfort and anxiety. Come peace, come war, she was fed like the ravens, sufficiently clothed as the lilies of the field. Talking of clothing, she always wore sandals—canvas for walking, and black velvet for evenings at home. Like Bryony, her most ardent follower, she avoided leather, fur, and feather, which meant killing animals and birds, but she gleaned the woods to feather her cap. Having panache, she loved plumes, jewellery, and bright colours and adorned her flowing garments with unusual stones. 'Restrictive clothing,' she would explain, 'restricts the soul with the body. I like to feel ready to fly!' This with arms upraised and loose sleeves sliding back from dark, bony wrists. She never wore gloves.

Mrs Twigg's stone cottage squatted on the shore of Anglezarke reservoir where, in wet weather, the waterfall from Yarrow comes roaring down. From here she drew her drinking water—before it had been treated, alive with bacteria—living water, as she truly said. On my first visit—it was a bright May morning—she was kneeling in her garden patch scattering the blossoms of red-chestnut into a crystal bowl of this same water. Nodding a brief 'Good morning,' she placed the bowl in the full sun so that the blossoms might soak up the ultra-violet. 'And then,' she explained, 'I'll pour the liquid into bottles, and top up with brandy.'

While I was considering the part played by the brandy, she told me that the elixir was given in drops diluted with springwater. So saying she led me indoors to the coolness of her stillroom where dozens of bottles were arranged on stone slabs. Labels written in her spidery hand told me that mustard cheers the gloomy, while aspen, surprisingly, gives courage to the timid. For people forever in two minds, the answer is scleranthus. There were cures for those who brood and for harbourers of grudges, jealousy and resentment. Such remedies which claim to cure not only symptoms but the fears and anxieties behind many diseases are recognized by doctors who explore beyond the bounds of orthodoxy. 'One of these,' said Mrs Twigg fixing me with her liquid eyes, 'is Dr Edward Bach. I have been privileged to hear him lecture. *Marvellous* man—lover of plants and animals, as well as human beings which is more difficult. (Two years previously,[1] Dr Bach had given up his bacteriological work at University College Hospital to practice homoeopathy and herbal medicine. His life was devoted to discovering the healing power in plants.)

Gifted with similar insights, Mrs Twigg became one of Dr Bach's disciples. Before long we were sitting on rush-plaited seats sipping raspberry-leaf tea while she read me passages from the master's book, *The Twelve Healers*:

> May we ever have joy and gratitude in our hearts that the great Creator of all things, in His love for us, has placed the herbs in the fields for our healing. . . . The mind being the most delicate and sensitive part of the body, shows the onset and course of disease much more definitely than the body, so the outlook of mind is chosen as the guide as to which remedy is necessary. In illness there is a change of mood from that in ordinary life, and those who are observant can notice this change often before, and sometimes long before, the disease appears, and by treatment can prevent the malady ever appearing. . . .

'I wonder why "ordinary" doctors aren't interested in prevention?'

'Ah,' Mrs Twigg smiled, 'remember, they have their living to make!'

'No need to go to the doctor's then, or to church—it's all here.' A thought struck me: 'We live surrounded by gorse bushes—is gorse a cure for anything?' Mrs Twigg turned the pages, 'Certainly,' she said, reading again:

[1] In 1930.

Gorse is for those who have given up hope and belief that more can be done for them. Under persuasion they may try different treatments, at the same time assuring those around that there is little hope of relief. [Then there's larch] for people who do not consider themselves as capable as those around them, who expect failure, and so do not make a strong enough attempt to succeed. Pine for those who blame themselves.

She handed me the book. 'There's something for everyone. Of course, it's much slower than taking drugs. But did you know that aspirin, that favourite cure-all, is a chemical imitation of the willow? The ancients knew that willow bark could cool a fever, and about a century ago some clever person saw daylight and isolated the salicylic acid it contains. Aspirin, the doctors' remedy for pain and rheumatism,' she went on scornfully, 'is no more than a mixture of acetic and salicylic acids. But you wait, it'll run into trouble.'

'It certainly upsets my tummy.'

'Whereas these herbal remedies,' Mrs Twigg pursued triumphantly, 'are pure and harmless, and only the minutest quantities are necessary.' As she spoke there was a light tap on the door, and Bryony came in wearing her moss-green trousers. Mrs Twigg motioned her to sit down on the chair occupied by Slink, the black cat. 'A shame to disturb him,' said Bryony lifting him carefully on to the rug at her feet. Unperturbed, Slink yawned and stretched, his luminous eyes, yellow as gorse-bloom, fixed on a barn-owl huddled inside a book-shelf. 'I'm trying to train him to keep away from Nelson' (the owl had one blind eye) 'and Peter,' Mrs Twigg explained. Peter, a rabbit rescued from a trap, was asleep in a box by the fire. Both invalids were tormented by the cat, and for once Mrs Twigg could not 'see a way to overcome such primitive urges'. Slink was fascinated by the immediate twitchings of fur and feather. 'And I've encouraged him to be vegetarian,' she sighed, 'but the group-soul of the Cat is too powerful. So far as they've evolved predators will be predators.'

After considering Mrs Twigg's dilemma Bryony said that she had come for a remedy—if that were possible—for a cancer of the breast. 'It's for an aunt of mine. She has a "thing" about going to hospital and having operations.'

'I should think so, indeed! I've cured more than one cancer—simply by complete rest in bed, and nothing but fruit-juices. Rest the patient; starve the growth. Few people believe me; fewer still have the patience and faith to put it to the test. It may well take three years. I'll come and see your aunt if she wishes.' Here I dared to chip in: 'My father is a doctor. He has a copy of Wesley's *Primitive Physic*[1] which claims a breast-cancer cured by frequent applications of poppy water mixed with honey and roses. Afterwards the water alone completed the cure. Perhaps the patient drank it and went to sleep for three years.'

Mrs Twigg, discounting knowledge outside her range, answered shortly: 'Your reach is higher than your grasp. Those who aim to be prominent, but don't know where they're going should take elixir of wild oat.' Stung in turn, I replied milkily: 'Have you sown wild oats, Mrs Twigg?' Bryony laughed, but Mrs Twigg ignored me. Her jade ear-rings twitching, she returned Edward Bach to the shelf, and we felt it was time to go.

'You really mustn't twit Mrs Twigg,' Bryony reproached me on the way home. 'People on her level don't see things our way. It's because we feel insecure that we have to bore holes in life—to see how funny it is from the other side.'

---

[1] Published 1755.

isher House and Aubrey

2a   The author with her sons, Martin and Richard, walking towards the Green

2b   The Green in summer

Rivington Pike is a lonely place on a weekday (seen from the south)

The Pike on Good Friday (from the north)

4a   Ploughing Rivington's fields under the Pike

4b   Hopeful start for the Holcombe Hunt

Lower Barn of Anglo-Saxon origin, renovated in the present century
by Lord Leverhulme

Waiting for the party. Lower Barn, 1910

6a   The Church

6b   The Chapel

Walking to the Green past Mill Hill Cottages on a hot summer day

The Green in November, ready for Bonfire Night

8   Typical of the south Lancashire countryside: the Pike and Rivington
Reservoir—lying to the south of Rivington village

7

A Taste of Hunting

Harmony restored between Bryony and me, we had started riding together again after Martin's birth. It soon became clear that one of the subjects she was twisted up about was hunting. So that when I told her I was going to have my first day out with hounds, she accused me of being weak-kneed in not refusing to follow a husband's example. 'I wouldn't dream of betraying my principles just because Humphrey chooses to dress up and jog up and down after a wretched hare!' she exclaimed indignantly. 'Your principles are not mine,' I retorted, 'and you can't imagine the pressures our husbands are under in the mill while we're out cantering in the sun. All boxed up with problems and prices and snags in the yarn.' Like Aubrey, Humphrey was engaged in textiles, and being fine-spinners they were threatened by foreign competition. 'In any case, weak-kneed is hardly the epithet for hunting folk.' At this point she dug her heels into Pegasus and galloped away from me.

Well, she'd objected to the baby, and got used to it. She would have to get used to this idea which Aubrey had suggested to me some time ago. Sometimes I think that hunting saved his life when one by one, the family mills, pride of his life, were eventually closed or taken over. From Monday morning till Friday night he was ground down, harried, forced into corners, but on Saturdays he became a new man. Hunting absorbed every Saturday of his life from October till March.

He used to ride one of his father's horses, and went to meets with the Colonel and Humphrey Marchbanks, who shared a box. That was before hounds came over to our country. After years of unambitious hacking the idea of hunting struck me like the challenge of the Matterhorn to a mere rambler. Some compulsive desire for excitement and danger made me accept it—in spite of Bryony's disapproval.

My début was fixed for the meet at Affetside, apex of the

c

stone-wall country hunted by the Holcombe Harriers. Then came misgivings. Not only had I never been over a jump, I would have to ride a strange horse—there was no room for Mingo in the Colonel's box. After a sleepless night I struggled into a new hunting-coat and boots; and hacking to the meet with my father-in-law I longed to turn back home. Astride my lively chestnut mare, Tango, wearing an uncomfortable bowler, it felt like the end of the world. Prayers for frost or fog had gone unanswered: the sun shone relentlessly on the dark little inn from where, half an hour before the meet, horse-boxes were to be seen lumbering up the hill. Farmers' sons and daughters on rough ponies cantered across fields and jumped walls. My father-in-law, the Hunt Secretary, swore at them for cutting up the grass.

Riders appeared in twos and threes, and presently the Colonel's box creaked alongside the inn and shuddered to a halt. Ten minutes later he himself, accompanied by Humphrey and Aubrey, drove up in his green Bentley. Striding away from the car the Colonel, scarlet-coated, top-hatted, was to become a superman, deferred to and addressed as Master. To-day, however, precise details of hunting procedure were blurred by my preoccupations when my father-in-law shouted: 'That mare'll take care of you—you've only to sit on 'er!' Whereupon the four men disappeared into the pub for a stirrup-cup—to emerge within minutes, horribly glowing, pulling on gloves with a conquistadorial air.

Horses were being unboxed and stamping down ramps to the road where they stood impatiently grinding their bits. Father-in-law mounted his huge, bony chestnut, Oojah with the string-halt, which had been walked up and down by a groom. Then came his companion-in-cups, Colonel Hardcastle, ex-Master, who resembled a full-bellied figure from John Leech. By now he needed helping on to a mounting-block in order to ascend his even vaster Royal Flush—over seventeen hands. This was a coal-black who had once been used for a State funeral. It was easy to imagine purple plumes and the trappings of death. Was this an omen? Aubrey on Fritz, a brown thoroughbred, always took his own line across country—to pacify farmers—and was rarely to be seen.

As in a dream I saw hounds streaming with waving sterns around huntsmen and whips. Heard the hunting-horn, bugle-call to arms, as we moved off, a straining, knotted bunch brushing knees and stirrups in the narrow lane, thrusting through puddles on a cinder-track. There was no sign of Aubrey. Not a friend was in sight. We surged through a gate into a wide field where horses leapt forward to be pulled up suddenly while huntsmen and hounds charged ahead. Praying that they would never find, I looked anxiously around for gaps. Humphrey Marchbanks drew alongside. 'Don't worry,' he sympathized, 'That little mare knows everything. You've only to sit tight—she jumps big and safe as houses. Ah,' he broke off as one couple 'spoke' in the distance, 'They've got on to something. . . .'

I never felt so alone in my life. How unimaginative hunting men can be, I thought as I was swept along with the rest, and, indeed, in front of the rest by my prick-eared hot-head. With hounds in full cry we squelched through gaps and open gateways. All around people were jumping—but not I. No jumping for me today. After all, I consoled myself, if we get into a field we must be able to get out—even if it means turning back. How little I knew of the way of a horse with hounds!

Still no sign of Aubrey. Briefly I glimpsed my father-in-law's bulky figure on his mountainous Oojah—more like a flying camel than a horse—dwarfing a four-foot wall. As that wall rushed nearer and nearer, all injunctions to throw my heart over first were lost—my heart was fields behind and safe at home. Shrinking from this unwelcome obstacle, I sat back in the saddle and pulled at the reins in a futile attempt to avoid the unavoidable. Naturally I was left behind, received a smart rap on the backside from Tango's hefty leap, and landed beautifully in a patch of bog. Within seconds helping hands were pulling me upright, presenting me with a muddy bowler and giving me a leg-up. I had to admit that hunting-folk were practical, objective and kind. 'Nasty cat-jump, that!' Humphrey shouted into my left ear. 'Give her her head next time!'

Galloping over the rough in the wake of stable-companion Oojah, Tango had me pasted with mud and while pounding downhill I lost a stirrup. At the bottom through one streaming eye—the other had caught a fly—loomed an even craggier wall, loose boulders alongside, of which, again, Oojah's Gulliver-stride made nothing. There was no turning back; sawing at Tango's mouth I tried to check her career and was just sitting pretty when she gave a huge spring from a standstill. My somersault was seen by the Master himself: 'You *must* be fit!' he shouted good-naturedly. 'Bounced like a rubber ball!'

By the end of the day I had come to terms with Tango, hunting, and life itself. Undaunted, even, by a solid wooden bar serving for a gate—the last bar between myself and freedom. On the way home Aubrey, followed by brothers and sisters, sailed over this obstacle for fun. Then one and all they turned to look back at me. Closing my eyes, I gave Tango her head, and she flew the bar like a blackbird. So I learned how it feels to have wings. This, then, was the delight of galloping across country, which is all that hunting has ever meant to me.

At that time, having no bias on the subject, I continued to hunt while Bryony continued to jibe at my unenlightenment. Not only Bryony but the Morels and Michael—'ignorant intellectuals' according to the Colonel and Humphrey—were opposed to this 'cruel sport'. Whatever such people thought, the Hunt went on, and the Holcombe Harriers came over to our country when the land around the kennels at Ramsbottom became dense with housing estates. The advent of hounds caused quite a stir among farmers, countryfolk, and so-called 'gentry' alike.

September would be heralded by hunt meetings at the Yew Tree—a pub about two miles away over the water. The Colonel, being Master, took the reins, with Aubrey, Humphrey and five others to discuss interminable matters. Their chief concern was the conciliation of farmers—not all were co-operative like Ben Haythornthwaite. Many were the dances and hunt suppers given to soften objections to a cavalcade galloping over cherished land till it seemed that the pursuit of such pleasure was far more arduous than merely working. However, the Colonel contrived to turn these meetings into social occasions from which Aubrey would arrive home glowing with whisky and well-being at about one in the morning.

Everyone in the village turned out to see the Hunt, including the Mooneys, who were 'neutral', and Miss Whittle who thrived on disapproval. Bryony, an obvious absentee, scorned the whole paraphernalia of horses, hounds, boxes, scarlet coats and top-hats in pursuit of a defenceless animal. Aubrey laughed off her barbed comments. 'If you only knew, she's longing to hunt herself—

just for the ride. I'm sorry for Humphrey—nothing like hunting
for getting the malice out of your system.'

He himself was proud of his family connection with the
Holcombe Hunt—the only pack of harriers in England permitted
to wear scarlet. This privilege was granted at nearby Hoghton
Tower by no less a person than James I, who, during this same
visit, knighted the sirloin of beef—kingly gestures which have
added pride and glamour to the Hunt.

8

Bonds and Knots

Life in a country village in the 1930s, when married women with young children rarely went out to work, was neighbourly. Rivington housewives, with the exception of Mrs Dapple, school caretaker, were occupied with family, garden, village activities and chatter. The only two on the fringe of such occupations were Bryony and myself. While she was absorbed in her painting, I soon found that running a house with a baby, social life, riding and hunting provided insufficient scope for mental energy. I longed for a wider purpose, a deeper involvement in life. And like many another, lacking any sort of training, I wanted to write. So far, I had achieved no more than a few articles and poems in print. Hunting-folk rarely talk books; and now that Martin was walking and talking, there were children's tea-parties to be given and gone to. These were a bore, though perhaps not so bad as the many dinner-parties we were already involved with. Aubrey, unlike me, was a social being and by now his willing geniality had landed him on dozens of committees. When I demurred at his frequent absences, he defended himself: 'Someone's got to run the affairs of the parish.'

'And of the Hunt, the cotton industry, the Conservative Party, schools, and agricultural shows,' I rubbed it in. 'Why not take on a few yourself?' This with a hasty good-bye kiss.

Alas, I am not a committee woman, and the evenings I spent alone at home with the boys seemed endless. One night after he'd gone to a Yeomanry Annual Dinner I went to bed and read till half past one. By two o'clock there could have been a puncture, by half past an accident. At three I got up, put on my dressing-gown, ran down the drive and along Rivington Lane. I must have looked like a creature demented as I danced into the middle of the road. 'Well, you *are* a silly!' Aubrey greeted me as he drew up alongside Lower Barn, a quarter of a mile from our house.

He was happy with his many commitments and acquaintances

—never anyone too close. Most of all he enjoyed the company of farmers and his mill spinners at hot-pot suppers, social evenings, and bowling matches. Congenial by nature and universally loved, he was at his best in company.

Mrs Mooney's complaint was the opposite of mine: 'You don't know how lucky you are to have a husband who goes out— mine stays in all day, *and* every evening except for the church council meetings. I never have the place to myself. No one gets it quite right, but you and I are lucky compared with some.' She nodded in the direction of the Marchbanks. On the one occasion Bryony had mentioned the subject of marriage we were trotting side by side, and she spoke contemptuously: 'One puts up with it,' she said shortening her reins and sitting forward. 'And as for sex—well, I get *my* fun this way!'

Bryony also affected to dislike children, and when, almost shame-faced, for the second time, I confessed that another baby was on the way, she was indignant. 'What, again? I thought you only meant to have one.'

'Oh no, an only child's a bad thing. We've decided to call this one Shirley.'

'Bet it's a boy.'

'Not again! This one must be, *is*, a girl.' To protect myself from disappointment I re-named 'it', due at the end of November, Andrew—for St Andrew's Day. When the time came the baby, master of the situation, refused to emerge in spite of violent inducements in a nursing-home. After several enemas and injections of quinine I was returned home a non-starter, and went instead for long ineffectual walks in the snow. The day before Christmas Eve I plodded six miles in Wellingtons through snow-drifts, up hills, and over stone walls, and early next morning was obliged to retire again to the nursing-home. At three in the afternoon I 'came round' to hear church bells ringing while flakes of snow whirled feather-soft outside my window. Presently the nurse appeared with a sprig of mistletoe. 'It's a boy!' she announced holding the mistletoe above my head. 'And don't tell me again you wanted a girl—this is a lucky baby, born in a caul. According to the sailors he'll never be drowned.'

No washing up for me that Christmas. But thereafter at this time I was to be doubly busy with a birthday party on Christmas Eve when we used to light the candles on the tree alongside those on the cake. Because the day of St Nicholas (second choice of name) was long past when he arrived, we called the boy Richard Noël. He grew through the usual stages into a healthy five-year-old so that we were surprised by Mrs Twigg's reaction on first seeing him: 'You don't know how fortunate you are to have a child like that! *Such* a pity to feed him on meat.'

Richard's life story was to have a profound effect on our lives. One early result of his coming was to give me a strong affection for the end of the year, so that the sight of Aubrey wheeling the last michaelmas daisies past the drawing-room window gave me a feeling of fulfilment mixed with promise.

Lingering over the last flowers, as over a last love, I now welcome the third summer—of St Martin—stolen from the warmth of September. Martinmas. The name rings the changes through days of bronze and days of damp, with copper suns and trodden leaves enriching the afternoons, while the latter Sundays of Trinity are ticking away into Advent. And now there's a feeling of expectancy, as though anything might happen. How different from the bleak and hollow days that come so grudgingly to light on the heels of Christmas, which also rings differently since Richard was born.

What I enjoyed most in those small days of December was to walk across the green about tea time before curtains were drawn, and to look into the cottage windows. Each one displayed a tree sparkling with frost and coloured balls. At this hour, with everyone indoors, all was quiet; and through the dusk the black finger of the vicarage poplar pointed to a star. Then the spirit of Christmas came alive. Beyond the rush of glittering shops and crowded streets, the excitement and spending, was a shining stillness, bright with promise, more hopeful than any tinselled tree.

In the January after Richard's birth Edna left, and I engaged, through an agency, a pretty Italian girl who claimed to be a good cook. She proved to be a good deal more than that. Tiny but dynamic, Violetta, as she was called, arrived one midnight when Richard was being fed. 'I do not like babies,' she said pursing her small mouth and wrinkling her nose. 'Never any for me.' A strange remark for anyone so brimming with sex-appeal.

When she'd been with us a week or so Violetta, after producing a delicious dinner, took to sitting in the kitchen with her head laid on the table beside the radio tuned-in to Milan. And there for hours she remained, slow tears zig-zagging down her face and on to the check cloth. She smoked incessantly and wouldn't go to bed. Late one night, hearing a Strauss waltz issuing from the kitchen, I went downstairs to remonstrate with her: 'Really, Violetta, you can't sit here all night filling the place with smoke!' Raising a tear-stained face, she stubbed a cigarette into the butter. 'Oh, oh,' she wailed, 'I could do with love again!' The fruits of love were what she was reaping. After five months she confessed, again through tears and smoke, that she was pregnant. 'The doctor gave me something and promised it would be all right,' she wept, 'but it was not so.' She hung her head, and only then did I realize the significance of that copious apron. 'But how have you kept it hidden? You must be seven months gone.' Further confessions included the purchase of a maternity corset (in my name) at an expensive shop. There was nothing further to be said except: 'You can't stay here.' But Violetta refused to return home, refused to leave.

Reckoning on two months' grace, I was shaken one Sunday morning two weeks later while sitting in the drawing-room happily contemplating the sunshine outside. This while Aubrey, after church, had gone to the Yew Tree, and a faint sizzle of roast beef permeated the air. On all levels life seemed good. When suddenly Gretchen burst into the room. 'Oh, please come upstairs—*quick*! It's Violetta. She's in the bath. She won't get out. She says she's going to have the baby in your house, then *you* can look after it.'

Together we raced upstairs and into the bathroom. Violetta, enormous by now, was slippery as a whale. As we tugged and struggled to land her from the thrashing water, there came a knocking on the front door. Gretchen ran down to answer it, and I, left alone, had the wit to pull out the plug. I was in the act of trying to pull Violetta—now heavily in labour—out of the receding water when Gretchen reappeared, 'It's Mr Mooney,' she said, her blue eyes round with apprehension. 'Well, he'll have to help,' I replied, 'but first help me—one tug together, and the fish is landed.' Dripping and moaning, Violetta stood on the mat refusing to get dressed. I flung an overcoat around her; and when she collapsed on a chair shrieking at the onset of another pain, I ran downstairs to beg Mr Mooney's help. Together we manoeuvred her down the stairs and into the Baby Austin—no easy task.

In fact, the performance could be truthfully described as a narrow squeeze. The baby, a boy, was born half an hour later— in hospital and before Aubrey arrived home happily late for lunch.

I was fortunate in having a husband impervious to such comings and goings. Imperturbable, he continued to dig the garden. I can see him now in an old wind-jammer digging through an autumn afternoon, wheelbarrow beside him piled with the rusty refuse of summer. Carefully his rhythmic spade bites into the earth around the michaelmas daisies still purple with the last colour of the year. Then in leisurely manner he takes off his wind-jammer and arranges it around the sundial. Meanwhile the garden robin, which has been hopping on the fringe of his work, snatching at worms, has come to rest on the haft of his spade. Signal for a pause. He rummages in his pockets, lights a pipe, and puffing with match-box as bellows, contemplates the robin on the fresh, dark patch of earth at his feet.

Watching him that day was to learn the wisdom to be found in his gardening with its pauses for reflection. I opened the window and sat on the ledge taking the sun. It was very still: the scratch of a leaf unclasping itself; a fragment of bird-song intensified the silence. This was something Aubrey knew instinctively because, in the best sense, he is a simple man, and like Adam before the Fall, carries a sort of childhood with him. He was digging again now; never hurrying, he always seemed to get so much done.

Meanwhile, Violetta had her baby adopted, and returned to us for a spell spoiling us with her savoury spaghettis and pizzas. It was too good to last: within three months she had yielded to the persuasion of a farmer, and in no time was again in love— happily so, because she was to be married.

Discontent was temporarily subdued by the clamour of two young boys, with the urge to write quenched by shouts and laughter and running feet. Indeed, a new life began the day Jimmy and Tommy Seed from the post-office discovered that they could climb the wall into our garden—a discovery which broke through all social and domestic barriers. These two were inevitably joined by two others, Peter and Paul, the red-haired twin sons of the Taylors who, as already mentioned, lived on our

left under the beech tree at the bottom of the garden. In no time
the six of them, along with the Mooney's boy, David, formed
themselves into the Fisher House Club, based in a hen-cabin in
our back-yard. When the orange flag with the black rabbit flew
high above the bracken the Gang was in session, and anything
might happen.

There was a tent for fair weather; the saddle-room for foul;
and a fire for both. On fine days sausages were fried in the open
and washed down with cocoa. Sometimes the Gang, mobilized
into the Secret Seven, was armed with bows and arrows; sometimes with air-guns. Always Fisher House was beleagured.
Occasionally our boys would disappear on bicycles, leaving a
blessed calm in their wake until, after a prolonged absence, relief
would give way to uneasiness and finally to anxiety. 'Isn't it
funny,' I said, 'how the things you grumble at become a necessary
part of your life?'

Neighbours were involved in these goings-on. Miss Whittle,
for instance, objected to the camp-fires which shot sparks on to
her thatch. And it was woe unto anyone who sent a cricket-ball
tingling through her kitchen window. On one such occasion her
white bull-terrier, Chink, received a crack on the nose; and she
threatened to call the police. But the boys shouted that Chink
was the Enemy of the People who bit the village babies and
killed its cats.

Those long lyrical summer evenings were drawn out until
dusk; and Mrs Mooney complained that David, the eldest of the
Gang, never got his homework done. Along with the fun went
inevitable feuds. Sometimes 'outside' children would join in to
threaten the sanctity of the Seven. Armed with bamboo canes,
knives, and pistols, they whirled around the house decapitating
flowers and shouting into the shadows. I'll swear that our back
door is still hot from the rapping of village knuckles.

Yet when eventually quiet descended upon the house with the
boys at school, I found myself uncreative in the strangely unwelcome freedom. Instead of an upsurge of energy I felt depleted,
and could only fill my life with empty things. Writing was a
lonely job which needed the stimulation of other writers, and
poems of frustration tended towards egocentricity. I took up
French and the piano again, and tramped the moors as though
towards some purpose hitherto unrevealed.

9

Interlude up the Pike

By now I knew almost every blade of grass around Rivington, yet I'd never been up the Pike which, with Winter Hill and Noon Hill, forms the moorland ridge to the east of the village. Though Rivington Pike, famous pilgrimage for hikers from miles around, looked too trodden and out-at-elbows to be inviting, Johnny Thatcher was determined that I should climb it—if only to see Lord Leverhulme's bungalow situated just below the top. 'The *second* bungalow,' he insisted, 'the one your aunt didn't burn down!' He could never resist mentioning this outrage committed by my aunt at the height of her suffragette campaign.

For years the Pike has also been an attraction for visitors from many counties. On Good Friday it seems that everyone from south Lancashire turns out to climb up to the beacon tower on its summit. Here, on this day, 1,192 feet up, is a fair, complete with stalls and merry-go-round. Until quite recently nearly everyone brought a hard-boiled egg—for the traditional egg-roll on Easter Monday from the top to the bungalow grounds below.

Johnny had already told me how, towards the end of last century, the land between Rivington and Horwich had been bought and tamed into Lever Park by William Hesketh Lever— his middle name after Aubrey's great-grandfather, Thomas Manley Hesketh, who founded the family firm of fine-spinners, T. M. Hesketh and Sons. As a matter of family interest, this Thomas Hesketh had made his money out of sugar and soap, and had for years aspired to turn soft soap into hard, a feat of metamorphosis eventually achieved by a bright young employee named Lever. After this the two men became close friends so that young Lever called his son after the Hesketh who had backed and befriended him. Today it is a matter of historical interest that this son, even brighter than his father, became Sir William Lever and finally Lord Leverhulme, Soap King of Port Sunlight. His bungalow on the Pike with its exotic gardens, was another expression of his enterprise, and when I first climbed up to the place I marvelled at the ingenuity which had coaxed alien trees and flowering shrubs from this stubborn hillside. His Midas-touch had quarried rock-gardens, rose-gardens, and tennis-courts from recalcitrant soil. And not content with cultivating gardens 1,000 feet up, he turned the land below into an out-door zoo—long before Whipsnade was thought of. Johnny, one of the keepers, never tired of telling me how, while helping with the Shetland ponies, South American ostriches, and various breeds of deer, he was in charge of the kangaroos. One of these, Jacko, bred and born on the place, was his especial care.

Many a summer morning in Sheephouse Lane Johnny described his relationship with this youngster. 'We used ter 'ave boxing matches—'im an' me,' he said. 'Kep'mi fit all right. Then cum a day when t'boxing wer real; 'e fair gave me a leather-ing. I shouted fer mi life, but only ter t'wind. An' then, when e'd knocked me flat in t'grass another keeper appeared and giv 'im wot for. My, didn't I say mi prayers! I wer black an' blue fer a month, but still alive ter tell t'tale.'

Though all was now a riot of neglect, there were unfamiliar blossoms woven into tangled borders, a bronze Cupid pouring water into a matted lily-pond, and flights of steps leading up to a stone loggia. It was a hot June day, so I looked for a shady place to sit down. Behind a pillar a man was already ensconced in the best position. His back was towards me, and a thin blue spire of pipe smoke flavoured the still air. I stopped, and Michael—for it was he—turned towards me as though expecting to find me there. 'Come and sit here,' he said. 'Isn't it wonderful?' He knocked out his pipe and laid it on a stone ledge. 'It's funny you should come just now because I happened to be thinking of you.' I didn't answer, and we sat in silence gazing down at the smoky plain. 'Fancy building that!' he exclaimed at last pointing to the replica of the ruinous Liverpool Castle huddled at the water's edge below us. 'A rich man's folly to feed the hungry. Lever-hulme had a powerful social conscience. He'd known poverty himself as a boy, so that after the war when his men were unemployed he made work for them by setting them to build a ruin.'

'You've certainly done your homework on local history.'

'I like to weave myself into a place and its people. You know, you yourself are very much a part of it—and your house with its trees. I think you'll find it very difficult to leave.'

'Don't say that. I hate the idea of being shackled to a place and taken for granted:

Men may come and men may go
But I go on for ever.'

'And do men come and go?' His dark blue eyes searched mine intimately. 'Do they tell you how beautiful you are? If not, I'm telling you now.'

'Don't be idiotic! And that's no way to talk to me.'

'Dear, dear . . . I'm just talking to a young woman in the context of a lovely day. We happen to be in it together.' Feeling a fool, I picked at a grey medallion of lichen on a stone. Michael was silent for a while, and then: 'Tell me, how d'you like Bryony—honest?' Contrarily I wasn't pleased by this switch away from myself. 'She's peculiar,' I said crossly, 'and we've been over this before.'

'But nicely peculiar, wouldn't you say?'

'If you really want to know, that eccentric behaviour is a pose. She likes to be different from everyone else. As a person she's not a patch on Humphrey. . . .'

'But they're not suited. It must be frustrating for such an attractive girl to be yoked for life to the wrong person—that is, if you believe in the lifetime yoke.'

'Which I suppose you don't?' The last fragment of lichen was dislodged leaving a patch of bare stone. 'On the whole, I do.' He searched my face again. 'But I think it works better with a little latitude—marriage, the single theme without variations, must be intolerable. That's why it so often ends in discord. In some marriages three are better than two.'

'You seem to have observed a lot from the outside. Perhaps you see yourself as the cementing third party?'

'It might be a useful way into the network—the best way of learning to avoid pitfalls.'

'And once in, you'd slip through the net and leave the two of them to tie up the gap,' I said angrily. But he was laughing at me: 'If you knew how attractive you look when you're angry—your eyes sparkle like blue frost. Come on,' he stood up, 'let's explore the gardens. I've never seen the bungalow, have you?'

Relieved at this diversion I got up, and together we climbed
another flight of steps to the tennis-lawn where black squares and
rectangles marked the activity of turf-thieves. Since Leverhulme's
time the garden had been neglected, and the bungalow taken
over by Magee's, the brewers. Solidly built of stone, this
bungalow, like its original, was circular, well-fenced against
vandals, so that we couldn't peep through the windows. Instead,
we climbed up through persistent bushes to the top road. Michael
was no walker, and I strode in front of him, not caring if
occasional branches whipped back across his face. 'It's like following an ibex,' he panted, mopping his brow when at last we stood
in the clear. 'You smoke too much and take too little exercise.'
Looking westwards towards the sea I was able to forget his
presence and insidious charm. Below stretched the plain—sage-
green fields and scrubby woods in the foreground; grey pastures
around Wigan's slag-heaps and coal-mines. Just now the cooling-
towers of Warrington and Kearsley stood up yellow as Grecian
pillars in a shaft of sun. To the north the Ribble curved around
Preston enclosing Courtauld's immense twin chimneys, I followed
it to the horizon where the sea shone like sheet-metal, and turning
north again beyond Morecambe Bay I could see Black Combe
rising blue as a grape, and beyond, the Langdale Pikes, faint and
unfocused with distance.

Michael, blind to the Langdales, was looking at his watch. 'All
this, and you're only thinking of getting back!' I exclaimed.
'Do mountains, the countryside, nature, mean nothing to you?'

'I'm very fond of nature, when it comes to human nature,' he
replied, 'for all its deviations and deceits.' He was pointing to
the gate-house behind us. I gave it my grudging attention because
this last outpost of civilization was unique in that it enabled a
man and his wife to live across the road from each other while
under the same roof. The drive ran right though its middle, so
that if you wished to reach the sitting-room from the kitchen you
were obliged to walk upstairs, cross a bridge, and walk downstairs to the other half of the house. The two bedrooms were like-
wise divided. No house could have better suited its occupants, the
Bickerstaffes, who spent most of their lives crossing each other
without the aid of bridges. Mr Bicker, as we called him, occupied
the north bedroom; his wife the south—to steal the sun.

'A house divided against itself,' I thought aloud. 'On the contrary,' Michael replied, 'an ingenious pattern for married life. When you'd had a row you could keep apart. When in love you could stay apart without ever getting stale.'

'Then you'd miss the whole point—rubbing together.'

'An expression I find quite distressing.'

'You're impossible!' I turned away from him to stride uphill. It was a relief to leave the last bush for the wilderness proper. Here nature's stranglehold on a man-made paradise revealed a relentless power at work to return order back to original chaos. After half an hour's scramble I was standing on the Pike summit, leaning against its beacon tower. Michael, slipping on loose stones made slow progress. Ten minutes later he joined me, blowing like a broken-winded horse, unable to reproach me for the climb. Pulling out another spotless white handkerchief, he again mopped his face before flopping down beside me. Up here the Almighty will is not disputed: eastward lies the moorland and westward lies the sea. To the north-east Noon Hill with its cromlech is a near neighbour. There, three hundred years ago, those tough-minded dissenters climbed to their well-earned Sabbath worship. A long slow ridge carries the eye gently to the top of Winter Hill. But the eye is deceived: those knots of coarse grass trip you into lurking bogs and mossy cushions. This is treacherous no-man's land of which Dr Johnson might have exclaimed (as he did to Boswell on the Isle of Mull) 'Indeed sir, a dolorous country!' I said it aloud, and Michael nodded vigorously: 'I'm with you there. For God's sake let's get back into civilization.'

A wild blue wind was flapping around the tower, snatching away all words. Soon we were pushing downhill through a tangle of undergrowth, negotiating steps and twisting paths which dived through bushes and dark tunnels of interlocked branches. Down, down, we forced a passage from one garden to another, hardly noticing that the sun was expanding like a red globe towards the sea. We had been out for hours; now it must be well past supper time. Eventually we found ourselves in a jungle of rhododendron, plunging down labyrinthine avenues where startled magpies and jays rattled angrily out of cover.

'Don't you dare do this to me again!' Michael shouted as I forced my way down through thick branches. In a pause between rustling and crackling I heard the waterfall: 'Listen! We can't be far away now.' Gay and over-confident I plunged forward, tripped over a root, and landed in a bed of rotted leaves. In trying to get up my right ankle hurt abominably, and when Michael pushed his way through I was almost weeping with pain and vexation. 'Well!' he looked unbelieving. 'So the ibex has fallen.'

'You don't need to be so cocky, and you might help.' He pulled me up, but I couldn't put my right foot to the ground. 'D'you want carrying?' he asked doubtfully, then slung his arm across my back, gripping my left shoulder so that I could hop on my left foot. We made awkward progress till I felt faint and had to sit down. Michael looked anxious, but pulled me up again insisting that we get back before dark. 'And you've got a beautifully muddy cheek,' he said pulling out yet another clean handkerchief, wiping my face, and kissing me lightly. 'Not necessary,' I said leaning against a tree. 'Not necessary, but it helps things along. There's no pleasure like one which leaves you unsatisfied.' I was silent, and in silence we continued down through the failing light.

By the time we reached Sweetloves it must have been after ten o'clock. Rebecca opened the door. 'You—both of you!' she gasped. 'What on earth have you been up to?'

'To be exact, we've been up the Pike,' Michael grinned. 'Well, your supper's ruined,' she said crossly, and then noticed my dishevelled state. 'You're hurt! So *that* explains it. Won't you come in?' But it didn't explain much to Anna who was in the sitting-room reading by the dim light of a lamp. Our reception was extremely chill. She refused to look at Michael who employed all his tact and charm to explain our chance meeting, the exhausting climb, and my accident. Perhaps it was my woebegone expression that thawed her finally, for she set about lighting a fire of damp wood, and setting a kettle among the smoke. We were grateful for the long-delayed cups of tea sipped while the cats settled themselves inside the brass fender.

With harmony restored, it was Anna herself who suggested the inevitable—that Michael accompany me home. Our arrival at Fisher House half an hour later was, as Michael put it, 'a very different cup of tea.' Gretchen, all sympathy and consternation, let us in. 'I'm *so* glad to see you safe! Mr Hesketh had to go to a meeting, so I gave him supper,' she explained. I sighed with relief and collapsed into an arm-chair. 'You angel. I do hope he wasn't worried?'

'Oh no, he was in a big hurry. Late home from work, and late for the meeting. He said you'd be off on one of your long walks.'

By the time Aubrey arrived home I'd had a bath and was reading in bed. He came into the room rosy and slightly shame-faced after several pints of beer. The meeting, held at the Yew Tree, had been about an agricultural show, and Aubrey could never resist the farmers' suggestions for another song, and another round more than he wanted. In his anxiety to avo'd questions from me he asked none himself.

Limping about the next day I found myself asking questions as to Michael's intentions—if, indeed, he had any. His flirtatious manner with me seemed odd in view of Anna's strong disapproval of our adventure, and of the intimate glances and tone of voice he had used towards her at that supper party. She, with Rebecca's encouragement, was certainly looking in his direction. Living under the same roof, sharing a taste for literature, and with the door of opportunity pushed wide open, what stood in the way? The answer was not long in coming.

A few weeks later I was having tea with Bryony when Michael called in and joined us. It was the first time I had seen him since that day on the Pike, but he had obviously been seeing a good deal of her. You could feel the communication between them by their silences rather than by what was said. The proprietory way she poured out his tea, knowing that he liked two lumps of sugar; the looks exchanged. No grated carrots today. They spoke of the 'Dads' (Church Amateur Dramatic Society) which Bryony, in spite of anti-church views, had recently joined because Michael was a member. It seemed natural that they should take leading parts; and before long they were lost to me in discussion of the play, the style of their performance. He responded to her with the sensitive pliability her egotism demanded, and she seemed to break into flower before my eyes, opening out as to the sun.

In the midst of this duologue Humphrey arrived unexpectedly. 'Sorry to interrupt.' He shook hands with me and Michael, and gave Bryony a token kiss on her forehead. Coolly she handed him a cup of tea as he sat on the wooden bench, refusing the deck-chair offered by Michael. 'Nice to see you both here,' he stirred his tea not looking at either of them. 'I daresay Bryony gets a bit lonely—can't paint all day. And I'm away a lot.' Tall and trim, with his dark eyes and dark, shining hair, he resembled a well-groomed thoroughbred. His precise and disciplined actions gave the impression of a training too perfect to break down. Whereas Michael understood women and was a man before being a gentleman, Humphrey, public-school and public spirit, belonged to the world of men and affairs. Just now he bolted two sandwiches and remarked on the weather. Then, feeling unwelcome, he swallowed his cold tea, stood up, and returned cup and saucer to the tray. 'Sorry to have to leave you so soon, but I must get changed. Going out this evening—save you cooking.' This to Bryony with a deprecatory smile, and to us: 'Do stay on awhile. Such a lovely afternoon.' He walked briskly away.

Bryony relaxed and smiled at Michael who took out a handkerchief and mopped his brow beaded with sweat. They sat there looking at one another.

Humphrey's sudden departure had made me feel uncomfortable for him, uncomfortable to be sitting there. I got up ignoring Bryony's threadbare plea for me to stay on, and said good-bye. Crossing the green, feeling ruffled as a cat in a north wind, I determined to avoid future encounters with Michael, and from now on to walk alone.

In fact, the uncomprehending saw my habit of long, lonely walks as a waste of time and energy. But solitary walking is the best way of recharging batteries, and receiving ideas. Ideas, fragments of poetry 'happen' when you're not thinking. The gentle rhythm of walking, the peace and 'awayness' of the countryside lull the busy conscious mind out of action as you come to your real self in harmony with the universe. On the practical level these walks showed me every footpath and every climbable fence in the neighbourhood.

One of my favourite haunts was Dean Wood, the glen whose stream bordered the land south of Moorside—a paradise forbidden to all but the Darleys. Often I climbed over the wall, and crept through the bushes out of sight from the house, then walked among smooth grey-trunked beeches and stunted oaks along the narrow track above the ravine to the waterfall at the head of the glen. Here you had to push your way through sapling silver-birches and rowans foaming with blossom in spring, coral-beaded as early as August.

One hot day the following May, feeling safe among such company, I took off my clothes and sat under the waterfall—a less romantic performance than it sounds because a waterfall has the power to suck you in against the rock. And getting dry with scratchy fronds of bracken is not to be recommended. That was the first day I ever saw anyone in the wood. Through the leaves on my return journey I spied Bryony and Michael clambering out over the wall ahead. Waiting till they'd gone, I went forward to the place they had left. There at my feet was a circle of flattened bluebells, the juicy leaves pressed white and fresh against the earth.

Blackberrry time provided evidence more positive. In Rivington we are all avaricious blackberry pickers, and one afternoon, shamelessly stripping the brambles of luscious black-beaded fruit, I almost fell over the pair of them on the wrong side of the wall. Ignoring Bryony's rumpled hair and crumpled blouse, I pretended to be engrossed by the condition of my paper-bag. 'If I don't hurry this thing'll burst before I get home.' I lifted an obstructive briar, and stumbled past feeling as embarrassed as Michael looked. He stood up, brushed back his hair, and pulled out the inevitable white handkerchief to mop his brow. For once he had nothing to say, but Bryony was amused, exultant, even. 'Make yourself a good pie out of your stolen fruit!' she sang out as I climbed awkwardly over the wall. There was no denying, we were all three trespassers in Dean Wood.

10

The Great Snow

After this episode Bryony and Michael were often seen walking together, which caused comment in the neighbourhood, and sharpened the edge of Miss Whittle's tongue: 'They thinks as going out openly is cover—but 'oo knows wot cover they 'ave in t'open miles away on them moors?' Before answering that question, I must return to life in the village which, however quiet, was never at a stand.

One evening setting out across the green, I was dismayed to see a section of turf cut out and measured, as though for garden plots. Ronnie Seed, passing by, told me of the idea of flowerbeds —to occupy the children out of school, and enliven the village. No one, apparently, visualized the dismal return to shaggy and unkempt patches. This led to my letter in the *Bolton Evening News* lamenting the spoilation of one of south Lancashire's last village greens, scene of maypole, morris-dancers, and stocks. Miraculously, on the evening the paper came out the sods were replaced after nightfall. This was my first link with the paper whose staff I was later to join. But that was not until the war years changed the pattern of our lives.

Oddly enough, it was the outbreak of war in 1939 which gave us a real chance to consider leaving Fisher House. Threats of air-raids made us decide that I should take the boys back to my old home. Only then, after a mere eight years, did I feel the pull of the place—actually weeping as I took down the curtains, fearing that we might never return here to live. In fact, after three months we were back, and all thoughts of removal were submerged under war-time restrictions.

The set-backs which began in January, 1940, however, had nothing to do with the war, and even united us as a village. At eight o'clock one morning Martin came shouting into our bedroom: 'It's been snowing so hard I can't get out of the back door!' The implications of this statement broke through immediately—no school, no milk, no bus. Nothing but wet socks and shovelling. We ran downstairs to find the wide kitchen window reduced to a series of port-holes opening on to Arctic fields. A great drift had shouldered itself, lintel-high, against the door. This was going to be a long, weary dig-out. After an uneasy breakfast we collected every shovel in the house, and by lunchtime had succeeded in reaching the garage—only to discover another drift, at least twenty-foot high, piled against the outer doors. The drive was obliterated; tree-tops sprouted like bushes from an uneven white bed, while the high walls of Sheephouse Lane were invisible. We could just see the top windows of the manse—like eyes peering through a white muffler. Outside all was numb and silent, inside the telephone was dead.

No question of reaching our neighbours: we had not the energy to dig further just now. For the next two days we lived off our own steam, opening tins, sawing logs, and digging a daily stint. Each night the snow froze hard as granite and the stars glittered above a static world. Magic outside and misery within: the main pipes were frozen up; the lavatory glugged unresponsively; and a reluctant trickle oozed from one tap. On the third day we walked wall-high on packed snow to the incongruously named green—now ringing with the sound of shovels and spades. In front of the post-office Mr Seed and his boys had cleared a circle slowly expanding to meet the Mooney's patch across the road. Mrs Mooney, a red scarf knotted over fiery hair, greeted us cheerfully: 'We're out of bread. How about helping me to pull the sledge into Horwich?' Already David Mooney and his younger sister, Eileen, were launching it on to the frozen road.

We conferred on the green and decided that for once the men should stay at home and dig while Mrs Mooney and I adventured to the shops. Everyone was in need of something—groceries, meat, vegetables. And Miss Whittle was demanding a drum of paraffin. At that moment Mrs Dapple, ever-wise virgin, appeared among us with a tray of hot scones. 'I've always a score o' flour in stock,' she explained to our wondering eyes.

Expectant as Arctic explorers, Mrs Mooney and I set out. 'It's like *Alice Through the Looking-Glass!*' she exclaimed as the wide roof of Lower Barn along Rivington Lane appeared like Noah's Ark above the snows of Mount Ararat. Adjacent to this, the fifteenth-century Great House was literally 'up to its eyes'.

Eventually we reached the shops bustling with war-time camaraderie—strangers spoke to one another and exchanged snow stories, while townspeople, fascinated by our plight, crowded round asking for details of the snowbound village.

For three months the frost continued. Day by day the sun shone over a diamanté countryside. Ponds froze solid as glass eyes in lashes of stiffened reeds; and icicles, each one thick as a child's arm, tinkled in place of the Yarrow waterfall. But Mrs Twigg was not perturbed. When we called on her with some provisions she had a crackling fire, and seemed to be living on air. In answer to our questions she began to explain the secret of existence without food : 'It's all a matter of slowing down breathing and raising vibrations. An empty larder's no worry to me. And I can put myself to sleep for a week!' Listening to her I felt myself an inferior being of 'too, too solid flesh'. But I must leave Mrs Twigg beside the frozen fall, and return to the village which in the absence of the snow-plough remained for nine days without a road.

For the children this was paradise—long, sparkling hours of no school. Blue day after blue day the air rang with sounds of skating and tobogganing. Only Miss Whittle complained, because a cannonball of snow shattered her bedroom window. As for Mr Plodder, he put on skates and, behold, our solid schoolmaster was transformed. All wings and fire, he flashed over the ice with the grace of Mercury himself. Was this the familiar brown-study figure bent over a desk and soberly addressing the blackboard? Curving through parabolas, spinning, gliding, turning, he took on a new dimension, inspiring his pupils to achieve figures of eight before undreamed of. Michael's assessment of him had been right: mask forgotten, he had come to his real self to incite my admiration: 'He should have been a champion skater!' This stung his wife into snapping back: 'That's what he wanted to be before we were married, but his parents warned him off it. And so did I. "We can't live on ice," I said.' Mrs Plodder's tone was frigid.

When eventually the snow-plough arrived—with the school bus in its wake—a barrier of more than ice had been melted between Mr Plodder and his pupils.

Death in the Snow

Though our road was clear, I wondered, rather belatedly, how they were faring at Sweetloves. While electricity had come to the village, neither this nor telephone wires had travelled so far up the fell. Spring water was laid on only in the kitchen where a cavernous range devoured vast quantities of fuel. Sweetloves remained a house of lamps and shadows and storms. Its inhabitants put up with draughts, outside plumbing, and ghosts. Yet in summer the wild garden of unkempt perennials was a rag-bag of many colours: hollyhocks, sunflowers, and larkspur sheltered against stone walls, and cottage-roses scratched a living from impoverished soil. At the back Rebecca had even nurtured a few reluctant vegetables into being; and on the south side, between banks of bluebells, the stream dashed and sparkled down the glen.

Winter up there was another matter: with roof snow-thatched, stream in chains, and road obliterated, Sweetloves was isolated from the world below. They ran out of paraffin and tea —deficits made good at the post-office where, during a hard season, Anna was only to be seen on urgent business. We heard of cold suppers by candlelight and early to bed to keep warm. Yet now, with the longest, coldest winter blanketing the entire countryside, we were wholly concerned for our own comfort.

Indeed, I felt guilty that in our efforts to dig ourselves out we had spared no more than a thought for the Sweetloves household. On the tenth day Mrs Seed told me that Mr Laycock, for the past week, had been walking over the drifts to arrive at school an hour late. The clearance of our road was no use to them anyway, and I determined to go up and see how they fared.

By now the packed snow was hard and slippery as marble. Though digging had become impossible, walking in the fields was comparatively easy. Crunching on and up through sparkling air felt like the start of a Swiss mountaineering expedition. Then,

with the house at last in view, there came a faint sound like glass
being hammered. Very curious, I crossed over to the railings
above the glen, and looked down. There, immediately below,
kneeling beside the frozen stream in a flame-coloured pullover,
was Anna. Hacking intently at the ice she didn't hear my call.
Only when I slid down the bank beside her did she turn round to
sit back on her heels. 'Not a drop of water in the house!' she
greeted me. 'Everything's frozen up and Father's ill in bed. No
coal, and the wood's nearly finished. We've even drunk the last
drop of ginger-wine.' She laughed at my consternation and told
me that Rebecca had plodded like a pack-horse into Horwich for
food, paraffin, and the doctor. 'Good thing Michael's gone to
work. His usefulness as hacker and hewer was being outweighed
by his appetite.'

I was stunned by this bulletin, yet could do no more than offer
to help carry buckets. 'Thank you. They do say that ice weighs
heavier than water.'

It was far colder in the house than outside, and as we set down
the buckets in the kitchen the fire fluttered and spat like a
cornered animal. The two cats, fluffed as tea-cosies, got up unwillingly, yawned, stretched, and moved out of the warmest
patch. Anna disappeared into the back-yard and returned clutching some green branches. With these unhopeful offerings she
tried to coax a reluctant flame. 'We'll never melt the ice at this
rate,' she sighed getting down on her knees and blowing into the
smoke, 'and Father's waiting for a hot drink.' The kettle contain-
ing the last drop of water sulked, as only a watched pot can, on
its bed of twigs.

At this moment Rebecca arrived, dumped a sack of parcels on
the floor, and looked grimly around. 'Only one thing to be
done,' she said, her voice shrill with intensity. 'One of the chairs
must go.' She picked up the axe from a corner and ran her
finger over the blade. 'Oh no,' pleaded Anna, 'it would upset
Father so much—you know how he loves his spindle-backs. They
were a wedding-present.'

'At this rate he'll never come downstairs to sit on them again.'
Rebecca's determination was overriding. 'That kettle would boil
quicker in the snow,' she frowned. 'D'you realize Father's
temperature is a hundred and four? I'm not having the doctor
arrive to find him *frozen* out of his fever.'

We drew back and watched while she brought one of the servers and laid it on its back on the stone floor. Then, picking up the axe, she took careful aim at the backbones. The accurate blade bit into the seat and severed arms and legs. This done, she placed the red velvet cushion under the Bishop, who graciously accepted it, and one by one, flung the 'limbs' into the fire. Aided by varnish and years of polishing, they leapt into life and activated the kettle until the lid rattled and steam issued forth. Tea was brewed; a hot-water-bottle filled; and Rebecca hurried upstairs. Anna and I waited in uneasy silence, listening to muffled creakings and footsteps above. Presently Rebecca's firm tread reassured us. 'Well!' she exclaimed snapping open the door, 'That chair has drawn the line between life and death.'

Next day Mrs Mooney and I loaded the sledge with groceries, paraffin, and a bottle of rum. By now we were practised huskies, and this time we had two assistants, David and Martin, who ran alongside singing us up the glen:

> Fifteen men on a dead man's chest,
> Yo ho ho and a bottle of rum!

The air was so still not a twig stirred; and before long we could see the Professor's night-shirts hanging stiff and lifeless on the Sweetloves' line. Ordering the boys home, I knocked on the door. After a long pause it opened grudgingly and with a shudder. Anna nodded to us to go inside, and helped us unload in the kitchen. I knew that matters were worse. 'I'm sorry I can't even offer you a cup of tea,' she said at last, 'Father has pneumonia.' At that moment Rebecca came in looking grey and crumpled, as though she had slept in her clothes. Wearily she pumped up the primus-stove remarking that the doctor had been and gone. 'And now there's no reason why you shouldn't have a cup of tea,' she said fetching the tea-pot. 'The doctor will have to come tomorrow and every day till he's better. And that means walking. No hope of a road for weeks. Otherwise he'd have had Father in hospital.'

The house was oppressively quiet; and the glare of sun and snow outside intensified a sense of foreboding. The Bishop and Shah had abandoned the comfortless fire-grate for the bubbling paraffin-stove whose sound, combined with the tick-tack of the grandfather-clock, gave some sort of assurance. Rebecca filled yet another hot-water-bottle and went upstairs.

On our silent way down the glen we became aware of a subtle change in the atmosphere. 'The chain is breaking,' Mrs Mooney remarked. And, sure enough, by tea-time a ruffle of feathery cloud appeared round the sun. The weathercock swung from north to south-east, and Johnny Thatcher, coming through the chapel gate, looked up at the sky. 'More snow on the way,' he prophesied. In the village there was a metaphorical tightening of belts and nursing of fires. Mats were laid alongside draughty doors; and before supper when I went out for coal and wood, I heard a small wind whistling through the branches.

It gathered force during the night; and next morning we awoke to hear it moaning and whining through every crevice and keyhole—the sort of wind that penetrates the pores of bricks and gets through to the bone. Holding my breath, I zipped back the curtains, and there again was the snow—thistledown flakes whirling and eddying aslant the trees. This was different from the first fall, fat as goose-feathers. Though so fine and swift this was relentless finger-work, padding roofs and eaves and window-frames, felting ledges and footpaths; masking, once more, the entire countryside.

When I emptied the ashes grit stung my eyes; and I got a savage cuff from the south-easter. The whole business of digging out and dragging sledges began again. Keeping alive and warm became a full-time job. On the fourth day the wind dropped, leaving us becalmed as a snow-scene water-colour. As before, Mrs Mooney and I acted the parts of postmen, milkmen, and errand-boys. After one of these performances, while delivering goods at the post-office, we heard Mrs Seed's account of three cars and the bus buried in a snow drift. But worst of all was the calamity following a service in chapel on the night of the snow. The congregation of about seven adventurous members along with the minister had been unable to get home. 'Road blocked an' no bus.' A note of half-triumph at what she had been spared quickened Mrs Seed's description. 'Couldn't even get out o't'gate. 'ad ter go back an' sit in them boxes wi' naught ter warm 'em but 'ymn-books!'

While we were listening entranced, adding imaginary details, the door pinged and in came Anna, a bundle of yellow oil-skins. 'What a relief to find you here!' She stamped the snow from her Wellingtons. 'We've had a terrible time—Dr Gray couldn't get through, and Father got worse,' she spoke in gasps. 'We took turns sitting with him night and day. And last night, about ten o'clock, he died.'

Mrs Seed shook her head and led her to a chair by the kitchen fire. Then as she busied herself brewing tea Mrs Mooney went out to fetch the vicar. Within moments they were both back, and Mr Mooney suggested that the three of us accompany Anna home.

The recent snow had obliterated the track, forcing us across the fields—now hard and shining as quartz. I shall never forget that journey up to the blind, forbidding house. At last we found ourselves in the chilly sitting-room discussing funeral arrangements. It was a bizarre situation: the five of us in a ring of lamp-light with the cats lurking in the shadows. Outside the snow, upstairs the body. And the burning question: how to convey it down the icy glen? Burial, at the moment, was unthinkable. Suddenly unable to bear the tension any longer, Rebecca broke in: 'We could lay him out in the snow for weeks.' Twisted between concern and laughter, we looked away from one another until Mr Mooney came to the rescue. 'Such a thing *has* happened before. A young mountaineer was once trapped in a glacier, and thirty years later his son discovered the body—perfectly preserved, and younger than himself.'

'But as things are now,' Rebecca pursued, 'we can't wait for a road.'

Fortunately the Corporation met the situation by ordering twenty men with spades to dig a path from the churchyard up to Sweetloves. The whole village took part in this epic, observing the diggers spadeful by spadeful on their arduous journey. Bets were laid as to whether they would make it in the four days allowed till the day proposed for the funeral. Further delay was inadvisable because by then the Professor would have been dead a week. Mrs Twigg was optimistic. 'I knew this was going to happen,' she nodded with a far-seeing smile. 'I saw the Angel of Death flying up the glen the night before he died.'

From under her cloak she produced a packet of camomile leaves which she pushed across the counter to Mrs Seed—for this meeting took place at the post-office. Whereupon Mrs Seed bent down and from under the counter brought up in exchange two bottles of milk and a loaf. 'Thank you! Thank you!' Mrs

Twigg stowed away these more substantial goods. 'Owing to the weather my stores are lower than usual though, as you know, I am well able to go without a bite for days. It's a matter of control, rising to a higher plane. But then, not everybody is ready.' Whirling her purple cloak around her she smiled on our unbelief and disappeared. 'Isn't it funny,' said Mrs Mooney, who had followed me in, as we dawdled down the steps, 'how she seems to float away—gone before you can answer, leaving you all in a puzzle?'

'I certainly never met anyone like her. And I can't imagine her ever being married. By the way, was there ever a Mr Twigg?'

'Ah,' Mrs Mooney smiled, 'perhaps he never was. Perhaps she breathed on him and he disappeared—like the dew.' We gazed fascinated after the retreating figure.

Meanwhile the snake-like track lengthened up the hill. A blizzard just now would wreck everything; and a sudden thaw would be equally disastrous. In Johnny Thatcher's words: 'It 'ud be enough ter jerk 'im out o' t'coffin—wi' bearers slipping an' stumbling down t'hill.'

Apprehension grew as we followed the diggers' progress, and in the wartime absence of weather reports kept our eyes on the sky and the weathercock. So far the barometer remained steady.

The funeral was timed for two o'clock tomorrow, and three of the diggers had gone down with 'flu. As for their seventeen fellows, they worked on like slaves in a chain-gang. The higher up the hill the harder the snow with the temperature falling below zero every night. By the light of the moon they laboured on. Ronnie Seed and Bob Taylor brought storm-lanterns because, as Bob remarked, 'Never trust t'moon.' Nearly everyone battled up the glen to encourage the diggers and make them food-offerings—potato pie from Mrs Dapple; hot-pot from the vicar-age. Others provided sausages, sandwiches, and the moses of sweet tea—all drawn up by sledge. 'Pity it's too steep ter fetch 'im down on 't,' observed Johnny. That night the weathercock again slug round to the south-east, and the locals prophesied more snow.

At noon next day the first spades clanged against Sweetloves' front door step as though to summon the sisters who duly appeared, both attired in long black garments. They thanked the men for their magnificent performance. 'Coffin's on t'way up,' said Ronnie respectfully removing his cap.

Down on the green the children were making a snowman. Instead of the usual scarlet muffler, Martin gave him a black tie while David Mooney insisted on crowning him with his father's mortar-board. In the hot midday sun the snow, yielding as sugar-icing, was ideal for an occupation which diverted us from count-ing the minutes. But when at a quarter to two there was still no sign of the cortège, we hovered uneasily in and out of doors. Several neighbours, including the Darleys, Humphrey March-banks, and the Haythornthwaites, had gathered on the green to pay their respects. At the last moment Bryony, fair hair flying, ran to join us. 'It's ter be 'oped she'll cover 'er 'ead in church,' muttered Miss Whittle.

By now Mrs Seed, deputy bell-ringer in the absence of her husband, had her hand cupped behind her better ear straining for the pre-arranged signal—an owl-hoot from Bob. At last it came, sustained and shrill, and she hurried away to the church. Everything went to time, as in a play. We had just succeeded in halting Operation Snowman when the funeral bell tolled, and the slow procession, 'bush-telegraphed' down the hill, appeared in sight. The coffin swayed past us on the bearers' shoulders; and we could hear the rhythmic crunch from six pairs of nailed boots. Behind followed the sisters in black, and Michael bareheaded. It was like a scene from Chekhov. Tall and pale, black lace scarf afloat, Rebecca might have been Masha 'in mourning for her life'.

Silently we watched the procession as it approached the vicar-age. At the exact moment the vicar, in a crisp white surplice, emerged from the gate. He stepped forward to take his place in front of the coffin, and the first snowflake alighted like a feather on his dark head.

One by one we moved forward and followed single-file up the path to the lych-gate. Here it was frozen like glass, and two of the bearers slipped so that the home-plaited wreath of holly and ivy fell off the coffin. Michael stepped forward, picked it up, and held it uncertainly while the bearers recovered their balance. In church Mr Mooney excelled himself—he was at his inspired best when giving a funeral address—until we felt we were at a thanks-giving service for the Professor's release from dark existence.

Returning down the path we joined the vicar and the two sisters standing with bowed heads by the graveside. Snow, beginning to fall in earnest, clung to the whitening coffin as it was lowered, scraping the iron earth. 'Ashes to ashes, dust to dust', the vicar intoned, 'and snow to snow', he might have added as the sisters threw handfuls into the grave.

We moved away downhill, and looking back I saw the three of them slowly transformed from black to white—remote, unreal as figures in a glass-bell snowstorm. I found myself under the lych-gate beside Michael. 'I'm afraid it's been a shallow burial,' he remarked drily, 'how they managed without a drill I can't imagine.' Bryony, on his other side, laughed. Her eyes were only for him, and I knew she wanted me to move on.

Because Sweetloves was inaccessible I had invited the few mourners to Fisher House for refreshments. That must have been one of the strangest gatherings ever held, of personalities as diverse as Colonel Darley, ruddy and prosperous with twirled moustache, and Mrs Twigg, hooded, cloaked, and murmuring of crossed vibrations. The Plodders, uneasy in both camps, stood together and looked out of the window at the thickening snow. Mrs P., as usual, avoided Mrs Mooney: you could feel the swords crossing between them, sharp-edged from a duel over a Mothers' Union outing. And there was Humphrey handing round sandwiches and trying to smooth over rough edges. Home on leave, he was obviously enjoying a soldier's life. As always, groomed and glossy from shining black hair to shining shoes, he was today at his best, speaking to you as if you deserved special attention. It was impossible not to like him; impossible to know him. He held you courteously, though firmly, at arm's length, and never talked about himself. Probably no one, certainly no woman, had ever penetrated that impeccable surface.

He was too much of a gentleman to notice Bryony and Michael magnetized in the sort of intimate conversation of which he himself would have been incapable. Intimacy of any kind, you felt, he would regard as slightly indecent, whereas Bryony at that moment, oblivious of everyone except her companion, was laughing into his eyes, catching every remark and throwing another back. Sparks flew between them so that they were unaware of the arrival—awaited by the rest of us—of the vicar and the two sisters.

This was the signal for Aubrey to open a bottle of port which made Mrs Plodder start as though a gun had gone off. But the warm, red wine and clinking glasses relieved the tension. 'Here's to the Professor! May he rest in peace!' proposed the Colonel tossing off a glassful at a gulp. If he could have seen the pain on Anna's face he might have swallowed back his words with the wine. Ignoring his lack of feeling I went up to her and tried to offer some comfort. Dubiously, in the following silence, we sipped, Mrs Plodder taking hers as though it were medicine. Suddenly Mrs Twigg held up her glass to the light, peered through it, and remarked that the Professor's passing at that moment had been ordained. 'I can see him now,' she said in a faraway voice, 'he is browsing through celestial libraries. Soon his book will be written, and bound in black and gold.'

No one responded, and in the awkward pause Aubrey re-filled glasses. Gradually the company became talkative, and conversation descended, to quote Mrs Twigg, 'to a very earthy level'.

On the other hand, spirits equally uncelestial rose; and the Colonel drank three more glasses. Seeing the 'squire of the neighbourhood' at his most approachable, I dared to ask him a favour: '*Would* you approach the Corporation on our behalf, and ask if they'll take some of our trees down?' Though I have not dwelt on this, the subject of our garden trees had by now become almost an obsession. While no flowers would grow in their shade, moss flourished on the lawn beneath which their roots intertwined. Damp trickled into the roof and ran down the walls. In autumn gutters and drains became choked with leaves. 'You're seeing Fisher House at its brightest,' I went on to the suddenly defensive Colonel, 'because it's winter. But in summer we're walled in with leaves—you can touch them from the bedroom window, and the branches scratch the glass like finger-nails. Please, couldn't you put in a word for us?'

'Not a hope,' the Colonel replied briskly, his mind snapped shut. 'The Corporation's object is to preserve trees—especially whackers like yours.' Airily he waved towards them. 'They attract rain; and water's more important to the Corporation than tenants. Can't pay 'em anyway, to let you have this place for fifty pounds a year. Believe me, they'll have the house down before the trees.'

'But just these two,' I pointed to the whitebeam and the

rowan. 'They make us feel like prisoners. . . .' Before I could finish Mrs Twigg turned on me: 'Don't you dare have those trees down! There's healing in their leaves. And a tree suffers pain when it's felled.' Reproach darkened her dark eyes. 'Have you never heard the spirit of a tree groan and cry out as it crashes to the ground?' This outburst attracted Mrs Mooney's attention. 'It's true,' she nodded agreement. 'Besides, you should know that the rowan gave Rivington its first name—Rowanton, as it used to be called, the village of the mountain-ash. And the rowan keeps out evil spirits—we need it here with the moors haunted by witches.'

By now everyone was listening, and the vicar interposed: 'A tree has a spirit as surely as every living cell has a soul. Not only human beings and animals, but plants, too, have a kind of consciousness.'

'Oh come,' retorted the Colonel, 'if that is so, it must be almost as cruel to cut up cabbages as to slaughter pigs.'

'But it *is* true!' Rebecca cried out, 'Trees are living beings.'

The Colonel cleared his throat, and the Plodders, who had looked more and more embarrassed at this turn in the talk, said hasty good-byes. The next to go was Mrs Twigg. On the doorstep she saluted both whitebeam and rowan before turning to me: 'And you, think peace and light into the trees—they'll turn into friends and bless you.' So saying, she tapped first the one and then the other with her stick and took herself off.

Though I, too, love trees (when not crushed against a house) from now on I determined to cross spells with Mrs Twigg. When I returned to the drawing-room the guests had divided again. The Colonel was answering the vicar on the subject of altar candles. 'I'm in favour, as you know. By any means let us have light in dark places.' He smiled rosily in the afterglow of port. 'And what about light in this dark house?' I demanded crossly, but he refused to be drawn.

Anna was talking to Mrs Darley, small and grey and quick in her movements as a flycatcher, while Rebecca, suddenly resembling a buzzard, was circling above Michael and Bryony, determined to swoop down upon their conversation. Feeling the shadow of her wing, they retreated for shelter behind the Colonel's back.

Bryony, sparkling away for Michael, was like a firework too

D

long laid away in the dark, and now suddenly lighted and bursting into life. In spite of her fairness, slim figure and expressive eyes, she was not beautiful: nose and chin too sharp, eyebrows too thick, and legs like spindles—usually hidden by trousers. But today she wore a blue suit which emphasised the colour of her eyes to a dark, almost navy, blue. Mrs Mooney insisted that this was a sign of being over-sexed. 'I never trust people with eyes that colour,' she had said, 'and her husband is *not* the one for her. Anyway, she's going to enjoy the war as much as he does—only more so!'

12

War Days and Jobs

If the war years in Rivington have seemed like comedy, the medal's dark side domestically was the black-out, two ounces of butter and tea a week; a gallon and quarter of petrol, which reduced life to the essentials of collecting food and keeping warm. Five miles away from a munitions factory, we suffered no more than a land-mine and a handful of bombs. Only the raid on Manchester really shook us. Three nights before Christmas 1940 we awoke to a purposeful dull thudding that grew loud and louder than a thunderstorm. We sat up in bed, considered the air-raid shelter, and stayed where we were. The house shuddered and slates fell, but the boys never woke.

Aubrey, less fortunate than his brothers who were called up, was made responsible for six mills, already on the brink of failure due to the recession in textiles. Apart from this loaded responsibility, which killed his father, he was in charge of the local Home Guard, which meant four nights a week on duty—one all night session from which he returned grey-faced and uncomplaining, at six a.m. All this, more exacting than any form of conscription, sowed the seeds of a subsequent breakdown. As for me, I cycled to the shops, errand-boy's carrier loaded, vegetable bags bumping either side the handlebars.

By now Gretchen had returned to neutral Switzerland, so that household chores were added to W.V.S. work and, three times a week, waiting-on and washing-up, with two helpers, for two hundred and seventy war-workers in a British Restaurant.

Outweighing such comparative trivialities was our anxiety for Richard's health. When he was five years old he developed the first of a series of ear abscesses which meant almost no school for two years. He had four operations—three for mastoid. Week after week, by bicycle and bus, I went to see him in hospital where he lay white-faced, head swathed in bandages. But he never complained, and each time I opened the door turned towards me with the shadow of a smile. His nurse adored him and boasted: 'Never murmurs when we do his dressings, and the "Hurricane" pilot next door has to have an anaesthetic.'

During one of many convalescences we bought him a black Shetland pony, Monty, an animal fiery and obdurate as his namesake, which no one but Richard could manage. Many a morning the pair of them would trot away and stay out for hours, thus causing as much anxiety as the operations. But when, eventually, he arrived back late remonstrance melted beneath his smile. 'You mustn't ever worry about me,' he said on one such occasion. 'Whatever happens, I shall always be all right.'

At that time we had an 'evacuee', Charlie from Salford, a year older than Martin, billeted on us because of the blitz. He settled down happily, but his nerve-racked mother was forever coming over—to inspect his food, his bed, and to complain. She shouted habitually, and stayed on late into the evening, rooted in our drawing-room till I was driven almost crazy.

And so I learned subtler pains than those of actual danger— overwork, anxiety, and a sense of futility. With most of the men away we women welcomed even 'Make-Do-And-Mend' parties at the vicarage, our only form of entertainment. Talk inevitably revolved around rationing, the black-out, and evacuees. We discussed the Morel's Stephen, who stole the teaspoons and turned out to be a kleptomaniac, whereas Mrs Mooney's ten-year-old made a habit of flinging Mimi, the white cat, into the raintub. Perhaps Mrs Darley, fastidious, prim, and childless, suffered most from two bed-wetters. 'And they don't even stop at wetting!' she had complained to the billeting-officer. As far as Rivington was concerned the Evacuation (so aptly named) proved to be a failure. But at least we learned that children from city streets grow bored and rebellious in the country where there is no cinema or sweet-shop round the corner. No bustle of traffic to fill the intolerable quiet.

Bryony's war-effort was concentrated on her garden which doubled its production of fruit, vegetables, and honey—a boon to children deprived of sweets. Later, when a local undertaker lost two of his men to the Forces, she surprised us by offering to drive for him, and on one occasion actually took the wheel of the hearse up to Rivington Church. 'But not,' as she drily remarked, 'for one of *our* inhabitants!' This because of the scramble on the part of outsiders to 'get in' to our much bespoken graveyard. At least this activity provided her with a car—an asset previously scorned. After the funeral just mentioned, unknown to the undertaker, she drove the hearse at high speed to Wigan station—to meet Michael's train from Euston. Called up belatedly, he was already coming home on leave from an indeterminate assignment with the R.A.S.C. Not surprisingly it was Miss Whittle, walking along Rivington Lane, who spotted him beside Bryony in the hearse. 'Next time,' she grimly remarked, 'let's 'ope she'll 'ave 'im be'ind 'er in t'box!'

On one pretext or another Michael wangled frequent leaves which were spent largely in Bryony's company—much to Rebecca's chagrin. 'He sees far too much of that young woman,' she complained. 'Here am I looking after him, making him a home and nourishing meals, and all he can think of is chasing after her. No good will come of it, and people will talk. Why can't he spend the evenings with us?' she went on, fondling the Shah's ears. 'Surely Anna is good enough company?'

Mention of Michael's name made Mrs Plodder's mouth crease into disapproval, while Mrs Mooney voiced general opinion: 'It's up to her to end it. He goes for married women because he wants to sow without reaping.' Being in the army, however tenuously, seemed to have increased Michael's confidence and with it his personal magnetism. How was it that for all his involvement with Bryony he could always make me feel, when in his company, that I was the one who mattered? One afternoon, as he lingered over his good-bye, I cut him short: 'Don't bother to come again when your leaves are so short—it must be difficult to fit everyone in.' His gentian-blue eyes glowed: 'You *can't* be jealous! Don't you realize you're unique? And, besides, I never feel the same way for two people. I happen to like you.'

With our lives so dislocated there was little time for writing, though sometimes the pressure of duties and events drove me up to the attic for a few moments' quiet. Moments spent in trying to come to myself. Alas, my thoughts butterflied—to the stove; letters unanswered; the job ahead. I was jarred by a dog barking, a knocking on the front door. And when the telephone shrilled like a fire-alarm it was a relief to be relieved of uncreativity.

Besides, at such a time it seemed wrong to be engrossed with what everyone regarded—with some reason—as unnecessary.

However, before long I was immersed in a real job which, with routine work, prevented any sort of intrusion into my private and social life. It happened that in 1942 Frank Singleton, well-known writer and journalist (and one-time president of the Cambridge Union) asked me to run the woman's page of the *Bolton Evening News* of which he was then editor—having left London for his native town. This surprise offer, due no doubt to wartime shortage of staff, proved a most rewarding experience. If I imagined I could write good prose Frank soon disillusioned me. His Pygmalion-complex drove him to teach me the hard way of trial and error and biting criticism. Laboured-over articles would be returned: 'I don't want "fine writing" or hard reading.' He sent me out to interview important townswomen and report on female activities such as church bazaars and lads' clubs. I struggled with recipes for acorn coffee, wartime Christmas pudding, and cures for pimples and dandruff—Mrs Twigg came in useful here. But it seemed I could never satisfy the editor. Many an evening as I cycled home, weighed down with shopping and a sense of failure, I vowed to give up. Later I came to bless that difficult initiation.

Returning home after a day's work I had to sit down and write every evening—a task that nobody took seriously. Fortunately at this time many household chores were lifted from me by a young woman in her late twenties. Her name was Irene, and true to her name she brought peace in the home. An English graduate, she had a weak heart which prevented her from teaching in schools, so she came here to help with the boys and especially to give Richard lessons—no easy job because he was in and out of hospital, and needed attention in all ways. The mastoid scars kept breaking down, and he was plagued with abscesses. Without Irene, who washed and cooked and painted in her spare time, I could never have continued my job. She was a rare person —the sort of artist who will get down and scrub floors. All this was too demanding for her willing, but erratic, heart, so that after the General Election in May 1945—a thrilling day of vote-counting over the ticker-tape—I gave up my not very successful attempt at journalism and took to free-lancing at home.

Richard's recovery was slow: like a mountaineer on screes,

only one step was gained after climbing up three. But gradually health returned, and by the following spring he was riding again. He had outgrown Monty so we found him a beautiful grey Welsh-Arab, Windri. Mingo, now eighteen, but amazingly rejuvenated by the war years at grass, proved an excellent companion ride. Each morning, like prisoners released, we cantered between singing hedgerows and galloped on the moors. These rides were always accompanied by Bobbin, our black-and-white Lakeland sheepdog whose habit of leaping down from high walls in front of the ponies gave us many a scare. Braced by the exercise and stinging air, Richard was soon out in the hunting-field, taking everything in his stride, flying over obstacles that daunted us older ones whose lives were worth so many years less. Though imaginative, he was without fear, carrrying with him a sort of inviolability which recalled Mrs Twigg's: 'You don't know how lucky you are to have a boy like that.' She deplored our dependence on doctors and drugs, and advised a vegetarian diet. But I wouldn't listen. Even when, later, we sent him away to a school (which happened to be vegetarian) and his abscesses cleared up completely, I refused to be convinced.

Most of our neighbours had taken on work connected with the war. The Dapples spent every evening at the ambulance post; Mr Plodder and Ronnie Seed were air-raid wardens, while their wives and Mrs Mooney were involved with the W.V.S. At Sweetloves, Rebecca was entangled in lengths of khaki knitting —we heard later that they used her scarves for bandaging the tails of cavalry horses. 'Holding the fort!' she would exclaim dropping a row of stitches as she rose thankfully to greet me. All visitors were welcome in her loneliness. Since the Professor's death Anna had been teaching in Horwich, so that Rebecca was left many a long, grey hour with the cats, the hungry kitchen fire, and her knitting. As for the men, Colonel Darley had been reclaimed by the War Office, and Humphrey, as mentioned, was happy to be away—serving with the Yeomanry, which Aubrey would have loved more than anything. Both men belonged to the Duke of Lancaster's (Territorials), moppers-up of so many peace-time evenings.

A happening which brightened our war years resulted from an act of God, in the form of a freak storm which one night rocked the house. Too sleepy to get up and see what might be blowing off or blowing in, I stayed where I was. In the morning a feeling of light in the room made me jump out of bed and zip back the curtains. I stood for some moments gazing up and down incredulous. There, stretched full-length along the path below, leafy head foaming with blossom, wiry roots thrusting through the garden wall and gate, the whitebeam lay prostrate. 'Well!' I could only exclaim, calling Aubrey to my side, 'I just don't believe it!'

In no time I was ringing up Mr Bull: 'What you've refused me for twelve years, God has achieved in a night. Come and take away your tree!'

Life itself is a story impossible to believe when you come to write it down. Two months later, that very summer, the rowan developed a disease and died. While the Corporation men were busy sawing through its powdery trunk, I overheard one of them muttering to his mate as he nodded in the direction of the house: 'I bet yer she's a witch.'

Gleefully I shook invisible hands with Mrs Twigg. But this was my round. Living at last with the midday sun felt like living in a new house, and made me vow that our next home must have west windows unobscured—a path of sunlight leading towards a mellow old age.

On the adverse side came a letter for Irene. Her mother was dying, and she must return home to nurse her. Amid sighs and tears—on both sides—she left, and we cast around for an alternative. There were only the Miss Mossops, retired teachers, who lived not a mile away. I haven't yet spoken of these grey, moth-like sisters[1] simply because they were never to be seen—their fear of catching cold prevented them from taking the fresh air, except in a heatwave. At the onset of autumn these two made a ritual of stuffing keyholes and cracks, bolstering doors and windows against draughts until their whole existence was resolved into a war against colds and damp. Rather than expose their underclothes to the air they slept upon them at night, and every morning stripped the sheets off the beds and sat upon them whenever possible. Throughout the Great Snow they had stayed in bed, oil-lamps burning, feeding like squirrels on stores guaranteed to last from December till May. When the vicar called to remark on their non-attendance at church the elder

[1] See *Lancashire Memories* by Louisa Potter.

sister had held up her hands in protest: 'Really, vicar, the place is like a vault. Only our deaths could bring us there!'

Even so, I dared to call myself to ask the younger and brighter Miss Mossop if she would undertake Richard's education. Her hesitation was overridden by her sister's warning: 'Think, Priscilla, before you speak. Young boys are the most powerful carriers of germs. I doubt if we could survive them.' And on second thoughts I doubted if Richard could have survived those sealed windows and the vapo-cresolene lamp ever burning against infection.

So he went back to the village school and learned a few rudiments of arithmetic. But he learned far more on days of truancy from which he'd return pockets bulging with country treasures. One afternoon I arrived home to find him on Windri performing a figure of eight round the drawing-room sofa till the good old Wilton was printed with hoofmarks.

13

Both Sides of the Fence

Richard's enthusiasm for riding was rivalled by Martin's dislike of it. In vain Aubrey tried to persuade him to a leg-up on Windri. Never attracted to country pursuits, his interest was in news and newspapers. Since the age of seven at the village school he would run home, fling down his books, and demand the *Daily Mail*. Sitting in an arm-chair, unperturbed by shouts from the green, he would read the paper—every word of it, even the share index. (Perhaps this habit sowed the seeds of the Tory town councillor he was to become.) And when the Holcombe Hunt, for the first time after the war, met on the green, he retired to the attic with the *Geographical Magazine*. Indeed, here was a cuckoo in the nest.

Needless to say, we three others were mounted—Richard on Windri, Aubrey on the Colonel's second horse, I on Mingo—nearly crazy with excitement at the sounds of the Hunt after years of abstinence. I hoped I should be able to restrain her sufficiently to keep an eye on Richard, because once Aubrey was astride his powerful chestnut he was rarely to be seen by the ruck of the Hunt. Preferring to take his own line, he was liable to disappear—to scout the land or soothe an irate farmer over whose winter wheat someone had trampled.

On hunting days Aubrey belonged to a world far removed from business and domestic cares. He became entirely himself and wholly independent until I used to think he was completely happy only in the hunting field, not merely because he loved the sport, but because the whole set-up, the camaraderie of farmers, members, and followers was in his blood.

On this particular day we were giving the stirrup-cup. Several horse-boxes had already crunched up past the post-office to park outside the chapel gate; others were unloading below our garden wall. Groups of children on ponies had hacked out and were now trotting back and forth across the green. The Colonel and

Humphrey (even their horses were stable companions) had arrived impressively mounted on a pair of greys. This was their day and their country; like a couple of imperialists they cast around our scant community for someone to hold their foaming fidgetting thoroughbreds. Very soon the Colonel's eye settled on the Seed boys who were delighted to oblige for easy half-crowns. Whereupon the gentlemen dismounted and, splendid in scarlet, white breeches, top-hats and spurs, advanced towards our silver tray (cleaned up for the occasion) upon which many glasses of port winked in the November sunshine. Mrs Darley, a timid shadow, flitted in the Colonel's wake and refused the cup. Too nervous to ride herself, she would show willing by coming to the meet, and then, as soon as they moved off, speedily evaporated.

Just now our all-too-small silver tray was beseiged by top-hats and scarlet coats. Toasts of 'Good hunting!' and 'Good health!' were sung into the sunshine. Anti-hunt opinions could never diminish the excitement of the hunting scenes, colourful as a country fair arrived in our village.

Meanwhile children ran among the horses causing chaos, while Mrs Seed, mounted on her front steps, had no eyes for anyone but her own two boys clinging to their impatient charges. Mrs Mooney came alongside Mingo. 'People on horseback seem so superior,' she smiled up at me. At that moment Jimmy Seed abandoned his reins to Tommy, and dashed across the green. He had caught sight of his beloved Sally Haythornthwaite, the prettiest girl in the school with whom he secretly exchanged kisses, and who blew hot, blew cold towards him according to mood.

Two hunt servants were unbolting the hound-box. The ramp clattered down and a murmur of approval greeted the twenty-two couple of the bitch pack as they poured out, a mottle of black and white and tan, to nose the grass, sterns waving in anticipation. Horses neighed and stamped; there was a creak of saddlery, clink of bits, when loud and clear the magical hunting-horn bugled across the green—a sound that must quicken the dullest pulse and heart-beat. Riders gathered their reins and settled into the saddle; spectators drew back. 'Hounds please!' called the huntsman lowering the horn from his lips as he led the pack through the crowd. In thunderous cavalcade we trotted behind him over the water.

They drew the farmland of Anderton Hall while we remained

in the road watching huntsman, whips, and hounds working over the fields. Presently the huntsman disappeared, and from the far side of Anderton woods bugle-notes rang out. Ten minutes went by and horses began to fidget. Windri, his Welsh-Arab blood in a ferment, took a wisp out of someone's tail earning Richard a cold look. They were going to draw blank after all. When suddenly Joyful, a first-season bitch, 'spoke'; the pack got on her line, took it up and filled the autumn air with wild music. They were off. Hounds streamed away across fields lettuce-green in a shaft of sunlight, over the brown corduroy plough-land, and down and out of sight into the valley known as Abysinnia. Alongside the stream here was a favourite series of posts and rails—lovingly erected for the Hunt by Aubrey. Mingo knew them well; I shouted over my shoulder to Richard and gave him a lead. And then, looking back, I saw Windri spreading over them, clearing imaginary ditches until he actually overtook me. Windri's cosmopolitan blood must have been on the boil because when a Pony Club boy, Alan Shaw, riding his crazy pony Crackerjack, bolted in front, he plunged, snorted and dashed into the wake of Crackerjack who never even rose at the next fence. Crashing into it he came down in front of Windri who, being quick and springy, leapt over boy and pony and all. Richard lost his stirrups, but with the aid of Windri's flying mane managed to right himself. Anxiously I galloped beside him, but soon we were free of the railed-in valley, free as air, streaking up the Nab—a brackeny-heathery hill pitted with holes and crossed by formidable stone walls.

Away over the top hounds were still giving tongue; we galloped on and up, following sheep-tracks between clumps of bilberry and gorse. The moorland air, alive with music, rushed past our ears. Ahead, the scarlet coats of huntsmen and whips bobbed over walls and ditches and out of sight. The primitive urge to follow, follow, follow the music is something of the blood —such exultation the Bryonys of this world know nothing of, or have forgotten. Choosing the lowest part of the wall ahead, I gave Richard a lead. By now he and his pony were one, Windri negotiating awkward grips and ditches more expertly than the thoroughbreds who were shown hounds solely in order to qualify for point-to-point races. I rejoiced to see him giving a lead to one of these polished beauties who had jibbed at a nasty huddle of broken-down wall. No need to worry about him. Whereupon I gave Mingo her head—the only way to ride an animal who knows the game. She shot over the next wall like a bullet, made a beautiful landing, and streaked down the bumpy hill with far more confidence than her rider. In this rough country cobs and ponies are the thing: instinct seems to warn them of holes; and being small, they are handy and more manoeuvrable. I overtook several top-hats, and, no more than putty in my pony's control, inadvertently jumped a gap in front of the Master. He cautioned me against overriding hounds.

All this while hounds were in full cry. Tingling with excitement I galloped alongside the second whip. 'Game pony!' he shouted as we cleared a stream together. Halfway up the next hill they checked outside a spinney. Richard, flushed and elated, cantered up a few moments before the Master who roared at us: 'What d'you mean pushing in front like that? If those ponies are uncontrollable, they can damn well go home!'

Colonel Darley in the hunting-field was not the same person as the well-bred and genial host of Moorside. At this moment, blotched with anger, he looked ready to burst with the effort of restraining himself from shouting 'Bloody Hell!' which, I suppose, is what we deserved.

Hounds were feathering, but they'd lost the scent. The huntsman ordered the whips to call them in; he'd decided to draw the side of the moor above Picaddilly—our countryside rejoices in resounding names—an extension of Rivington Moor and typical of the area: bumping miles of bracken and bent interrupted by peat-bogs and dashing streams. Unfeatured country crossed by the familiar walls of millstone-grit. Obediently we trotted behind with the stragglers; on the road now, through the village of White Coppice, last outpost on the fringe of a desolate moorland. The stony track rose steeply from the valley where rowan and birch trees border the stream. Up here only a scrubby oak or two and a scatter of thorns scratch a living.

Above and behind us to the left was a patch of forbidden country, about five hundred acres belonging to the Marshalls of Hailstorm Hall. Forbidden to the Hunt because Gerald Marshall, the only son, had once been ordered off the field. This incident had occurred the season his mother turned out on an aged police-horse guaranteed to display the maximum mettle with the minimum risk. Though terrified of hunting, Mrs Marshall wore the full regalia of top-hat and veil with side-saddle habit. Violets, artificial eyelashes, and a wig completed her get-up. For her, a fall would have been unthinkable. Nevertheless, the unthinkable happened. (The Marshalls were generous subscribers.) Several gentlemen, including the Master, dismounted in their concern to smooth over the débâcle, and shield its indignity from curious eyes. After the two incidentes the Hunt took every possible precaution of avoiding Marshall territory.

For some reason on this particular day the hare made Hailstorm Hall her centre. Round and round the garden she ran, exuberant hounds on her scent—the first three couples soon to be joined by the whole pack which took up the line in unison. In vain, huntsman and whips strove to whip them off; helpless, Master and Field watched from the valley. Beyond recall they streamed around the threatening shoulder of Hailstorm Hill. The crescendo of hound-music, mounting to a Wagnerian chorus of triumph thrilled us who heard it with horrid foreboding. Suddenly, like a whip, a shot cracked the air. 'Now we're for it!' the Master spoke to Aubrey who had just ridden up. Three more shots in rapid succession were followed by ominous silence. Rigid in our saddles we stared up the bleak hillside.

After a long interval three red coats bobbing in the midst of the pack were to be seen moving down the fell. The huntsman rode up to the Master and mumbled a few words in his ear. He whistled in dismay and turned to a knot of us gathered anxiously nearby. 'Old Marshall's shot three hounds. Killed two.' Enormous consternation moved the Field. To injure hounds in any way was sacrilege unheard of. 'I'll call up the RSPCA!' he hissed, grinding his teeth. 'Do him in for cruelty to hounds.'

Richard, who had been listening intently, turned to the impeccably plaited maiden beside him. 'But the RSPCA is for cruelty to *all* animals. Couldn't we be had up for cruelty to hares?' The Plaited One who wore a Pony Club badge (she was a niece of the Master) stiffened her back. 'Don't be silly,' she replied sharply, 'hunting's quite different; it's a sport. To shoot hounds deliberately—well, I never heard of anything so revolting in my life!'

After an uneasy interval they found again well to the north of White Coppice; and flushed the fresh hare from a spinney. Half a dozen cultivated fields provided the best rail-and-ditch jumping of the day. Aubrey, expert at short cuts, had taken charge of Richard because Windri was outpaced on the flat. Here was an opportunity to let my speedy Mingo have another fling. Like a spring released, she scudded across the level land, rose at her fences, and landed with the resilience of a rubber ball. We were soon heading for Brindle Brook—at its widest a notorious hunt pitfall. By now, unless hounds doubled back, it was the Brook for us or blue funk in front of the Field. Nearer, nearer, with every stride . . . I saw huntsman, whips, and Master safely over followed by Humphrey and a couple of aspirants for the races. Mingo disliked water and open ditches but there was no stopping her now. Her blood was up and I hoped for the best. 'O God, let us clear it!' I prayed as the brook curved wide and silver before us. No one who has not ridden a polo-pony will appreciate that lightning swerve at full gallop: one moment we were heading for the water; the next I was neatly deposited in the rushes while Mingo, reins dangling, charged wildly in the opposite direction. The timely arrival of Aubrey and Richard spared me the indignity of being mounted by one of the stragglers.

Much subdued, I found myself cantering sedately beside Richard when, with a sudden pounding of hooves, Alan Shaw's Crackerjack came thrusting between us to jump sideways in front of the Plaited One at the next fence. She shouted at Alan, fear and fury reddening her speech beyond Pony Club etiquette. However, at the next rail Crackerjack dug his toes in and flung down his head pitching Alan over his ears and into the ditch. 'Serve you right, you filthy cad!' sang the maiden flashing by.

The hare, cornered in an angle of wall, ran back. She was too late; the pack closed in upon her like a Rugby scrum. As the huntsman flung himself from his horse and whipped off the hounds, she screamed—an almost human cry, like a baby's. He bent down to rescue the sodden remains from gulping jaws. Drawing a knife from his pocket he hacked off mask and pads, and with a yelp of animal triumph flung the small carcase into the air. The hounds devoured it within seconds. Wondering which sound was the more hideous—the animal cry of the huntsman or the baby cry of the hare, I felt myself swept back through the centuries to witness some primitive ritual of blood sacrifice. The old man's shooting of the hounds seemed by contrast no more than a ludicrous comedy.

Lost in thought I hadn't noticed the huntsman approaching Richard. 'It's yer first kill,' he was saying, 'yer must be blooded a full member o'th'unt. 'Richard hesitated. 'Dismount, can't you?' the Plaited One said scornfully. 'This is part of the game.' Obediently he did as he was told, and the huntsman daubed his forehead with blood from the horribly dripping mask. Smiling broadly he thrust the Thing into Richard's hands. Bewildered, Richard frowned with distaste. 'What shall I do with it?' 'Shove it in your pocket. You can have it mounted, silly!' His companion spoke impatiently. 'And hurry up or we'll be left behind.' She moved away; and I found a clean handkerchief. Richard was dangling the oozing trophy by an ear. 'You take it,' he said. Even more reluctantly I thrust the object into my pocket.

Suddenly the glory had gone out of the day. I realized one could only enjoy hunting in hot blood. Returned to thinking, it was unthinkable. And yet Aubrey, kindest of men, saw nothing amiss. And most hunting people are good-natured and friendly. Perhaps their sport purges them of baser instincts—the lusts for human destruction and cruelty, in which case many a fox or hare must have acted as scapegoat. Whether this is a bad means justified by a good end I don't know. All I do know is that the end of hunting is not pretty. More than one Diana has confided to me: 'I can't bear to see the kill—that's when I move off.' But one cannot ignore the masculine view that animals must be killed anyhow, often in crueller ways than hunting, and therefore why not, in heaven's name, make a sport of the inevitable.

That day the sustained note of the call-off came as a relief to everyone; and the ride home was subdued and silent. Later in the evening I went into the kitchen to find Richard burning something in the stove. It was the hare's mask. 'Do you really enjoy hunting, Mummy?' he asked pushing the sizzling mass deep into the embers. I found myself landed on both sides of the fence. 'Of course I do,' I replied, 'except for the kill.'

'But isn't hunting *for* the kill?' he persisted.

'Most people hunt for the ride. They don't think about the kill.' And anyway, the hares would have to be shot if they weren't hunted. Sometimes they get away half-dead and take days to die —and that's far worse,' I concluded somewhat lamely.

14

The Headless Cross Boggart

I decided there was no answer to the ethics of hunting when a few days later Rebecca came knocking on our door. She wouldn't come inside but stood there, hatless and distrait, complaining that a hare was regularly visiting their kitchen-garden, and had already done a lot of damage—would the hounds please dispose of it? Whereupon my views became even more blurred. 'But I thought you disapproved of the Hunt?' I challenged her. 'Oh yes, we do,' she replied, 'when it's just for sport. But when the animal actually steals our food, that's different. We rely on our vegetables for the winter. And only this morning at eight o'clock I looked out of the window, and there was a huge hare standing on its hind legs and eating our Brussels sprouts to its heart's content.'

'Oh come, Rebecca,' I couldn't resist teasing her, 'and *now* who's splitting hairs?' Even Anna, more anti-hunt than her sister, agreed that this vegetable-loving hare must be destroyed. 'We have to set traps for moles and rats in self-defence. That's a proper reason for killing,' she insisted when I next met her. 'After all, it's the motive that matters.'

'And the motive is food—for human consumption,' I replied. After all, self-preservation is a first instinct, and it's linked with killing animals. Stick to your Brussels sprouts by all means, but remember to count the cost. Next time the hounds are over Aubrey will see that they draw these fields—and don't forget to pull your curtains!'

Though Bryony's garden was similarly raided, she persuaded Humphrey to spend a large sum on wire-netting. 'And what's more,' he later confided to Aubrey, 'when that pet vixen of hers bit me on the ankle, she was far more concerned over *its* health than mine.'

Fortunately, at this point, we became involved in another kind of hunt, wholly unconcrete, which raised quite different questions.

This was the the tracking of the Headless Cross Boggart, our local ghost, long regarded as legend, and soon proved to have a real foundation. We all knew Headless Cross, a crude stone signpost bearing directions to Wigan (spelt with two *g*s) Bolton and Blackburn (Blagburn) above the lower quarters and legs of a man. This monument stands on a triangle of grass—once a village green—in Grimeford Lane between Horwich and Adlington, and about a mile from Rivington.

The story of the cross passed down to us concerned a Roman Catholic priest, Father Bennett, who lived in the sixteenth century, and used to have charge of the Lady-chapel then standing in the valley which is now flooded by Lower Rivington reservoir. During the Reformation the chapel fell into disuse, and Father Bennett, certain that it would be wrecked and plundered, determined to hide the valuables—a silver cross, a pair of gold candlesticks, and some richly jewelled chalices—in the underground tunnel connecting his house with the chapel and also with the convent at Roscoe Low (now a farm) in Grimeford Lane.

Some people came to think that in the act of carrying these treasures to their hiding-place he had been overcome and suffocated. Others believed that he had been murdered by robbers or a rival priest with eyes on the loot. Whatever happened, the treasures disappeared along with the good Father who was never seen again. Actually, he was not found to be missing until the evening after the New Year when it was his custom to dispense bread to the poor of the neighbourhood—an occasion for rejoicing and dancing. When he failed to appear at the usual hour, there was great consternation. Questions were asked and a search-party organized. Six members of the landed gentry from Rivington and Anderton rode out in all directions combing moorland and woods. Finally one of them, Dick Fisher of Rivington, volunteered to report to Cardinal Allen of Rossall, thirty miles away. The Cardinal could have nothing more than concern to offer—by now there must have been little hope, and at this time Roman Catholic churches throughout the land were being wrecked, and their priests brutally murdered.

After the interview Dick galloped much of the way home. As he reined in his horse near the convent, he was overjoyed to see a familiar figure—surely there was Father Bennett himself crossing the green to his house? Urging his tired horse forward, Dick now recognized the famous leopard-skin cloak by which the Father was so well known. Trotting within a few yards of the priest Dick raised his cap and shouted a welcome. In that instant the figure, hand on his front gate, disappeared.

So much is history. But when Maurice Birchall, a local taxi-driver, told Mrs Mooney that on the previous New Year's Eve, driving past Headless Cross, he had seen what he eventually decided must have been a ghost, she couldn't contain her excitement. She ran across the road to share it with me. It happened that particular night that Maurice was booked to drive a young couple home to Adlington from a dance in Horwich. The fog was so thick that he was obliged to hug the right-hand verge, head and shoulders out of the window. As he rounded the corner near the grass triangle where the cross stands he saw, to quote his own words: 'The wickedest-looking old man wi' little glittering snake's eyes.' He went on to describe how this daemon who wore 'A sort o' green mouldy cloak an' a square black 'at' had backed away from the headlights into the hedge. At the time Maurice was convinced that this was a real man 'up to no good'. At any rate, the sight brought him out in a sweat so that he returned home with his passengers by the main road.

Because he was afraid of being laughed at he kept this story to himself for a while, only confiding in his aged uncle, an authority on local history. 'Why man,' his uncle had exclaimed in delight, 'thou'st seen nobbut th'eadless Cross Boggart!'

Maurice was troubled; he couldn't get the incident out of mind. Eventually he told the whole story to Mrs Mooney—the best and most sympathetic of listeners. He still maintained that what he had seen was a man and not a ghost, but she agreed with his uncle, and suggested that there might be some connection with the Father Bennett story. Perhaps the ghost was actually the murdered priest. Because there was no living link, no historical record, she determined to try other means of finding out, especially when she discovered that Maurice wasn't the only one who had seen this apparition. One afternoon she came over and sat down on the sofa with a portentous air. 'Well,' she began, 'don't laugh, but I've found a medium who may be able to answer our questions.'

'A medium?' I echoed, stupified. 'But how d'you know he isn't a fraud?'

'He's the chef at the Albion in Manchester,' she replied, adding to my doubts. 'Only came over from South America a few months ago, and speaks broken English. I heard of him through the editor of the *Psychic News*—a thoroughly reliable man. Patrick knows him well. Anyway, he told us that this medium, Garcia, really has the "seeing eye" and quite remarkable powers. And naturally he knows nothing of our district or history . . .' she broke off before my unbelieving stare. 'I know you're a sceptic, but you may get a big surprise. And now I'm going to ask you something. I've been wondering whether we could persuade him to come to the vicarage.'

So it was arranged; and Mr Mooney volunteered to meet him and Mr Smith, the *Psychic News* editor, in Horwich because both men were strangers to this district. Besides, Mr Mooney wanted to drive them past the Millstone, a nearby inn, and Headless Cross—to give Garcia a chance of tuning-in. I shall never forget that February afternoon, grey with mist and drizzle, when the car arrived and the three men, coat collars up against the wet, hurried past the sitting-room window. Garcia, huge and dark, filled the passage hallway while Mr Smith, diminuitive on one side, Mr Mooney on the other, divested him of his coat and hat. In the sitting-room Mrs Mooney, the Morels, and Miss Fogg, a spiritualist from Adlington who had begged to be let in, were ringed expectantly in the firelight. 'Ah, dis atmosphere good!' exclaimed Garcia striding into the room and rubbing his hands. 'Many peoples here. Many, many peoples.' He smiled broadly and bumped himself down in the large chair open-armed to receive him. 'De air is, how do you say, busy? Verra, verra busy.' We asked if he'd like the curtains drawn, but he shook his head. 'No funny business for me.'

Whereupon, after a brief silence, he took a huge breath, deflated, took another, sank deeper into his chair, stretched out his long legs, slightly apart, and let his head fall forward on to his chest. Deep, deep silence. Miss Fogg's eyes closed as her bosom, flashing diamanté, swelled in a sigh. My diaphragm quivered in a nervous desire to giggle. Garcia groaned; his long arms dangled outside the plump arms of the chair, fingers nearly touching the floor. Nonsense, I was thinking, and felt embarrassed and uneasy when suddenly a voice, loud and clear, proceeded through

Garcia's lips. Yet it was not Garcia's voice. Not only the accent but also the tone was different.

To begin with, names, incidents, vague and unspecified—after all, Johns, Edwards and Marys must have come and gone many times through these doors. Esther (the name of John Fisher's wife) was a little more definite. And then, loud and clear, David. David Lloyd George, the voice announced, had often visited Sir William Hesketh Lever at his home on Rivington Pike. Ah, I thought, he's looked up local history. My budding incredulity froze instantly—especially when he spelled out in full the name of William Hesketh Lever. (Mediums are not to be envied: we disbelieve when they are vague; distrust when too specific.) Feeling his way, Garcia came to the ghost of Headless Cross. The wicked old man seen by Maurice, we heard, was an Italian foundling, Guillimo Blanco (William White) brought up as a priest, who all his life had tried to trace his parentage—a search not ended by death. Every year on the night of St Sylvester his spirit returned to haunt the neighbourhood where he had lived and worked. 'Why does he return every New Year's Eve?' Mrs Mooney put in at this point. 'He can't find his parents here, that's certain.' There was an expectant pause. Garcia's chin sank lower. He groaned and spoke more slowly, deliberately. 'A deed of darkness binds him to earth.' He stopped, groping. Another long pause broken only by the creaking of Miss Fogg's stays. 'And something has been moved. Something is in its wrong place. It worries him. He will return until this is restored.'

(We discovered later that this something referred to the top half of the cross which Lord Leverhulme had transported to his bungalow grounds—to lend them an air of antiquity.)

The voice told us that during his lifetime Blanco had been associated with Bishop Thomas Penswick who himself died three years after Blanco's death. I was ridiculing all this as make-believe when we were told that in the Liverpool church of St Nicholas and Our Lady are two plaques bearing the names White and Penswick. And so what, I asked myself when suddenly the voice took a new tone and dropped into the here-and-now: 'It was Eric Marsh who saw him first.'

Now Eric Marsh lived in one of the cottages opposte Headless Cross. How could Garcia have come to know of him? When questioned later Eric was bewildered and dumb—his family was

Roman Catholic, opposed to ghost stories; and he had been severely scolded for once daring to mention the subject. We were convinced that the boy had never seen or heard of Garcia, Mr Smith, or anyone interested in the Boggart.

To return to Garcia, slumped in his chair and breathing heavily in unison with Miss Fogg. After a stertorous interlude he 'came to', opening his eyes and sitting upright. The rest of us, not knowing where to look, looked away. Only Miss Fogg was at ease, as though she'd just landed happily home from a visit abroad. Mrs Mooney, the first to speak, challenged him. 'If you don't mind my saying so, I think you've got the name of the church wrong. It's plain St Nicholas—not "Our Lady"—near the pier-head. I ought to know because I know the place.' Garcia shook his head, disclaiming all knowledge of information given from beyond himself. In order to verify the story, the Mooneys and Mr Smith suggested taking Garcia along with them to Liverpool.

I could hardly wait to hear the result of this expedition, and at nine o'clock the morning after was knocking on the vicarage door to find Mrs Mooney bubbling over with excitement. 'Come inside,' she said, 'there's too much to tell on the doorstep.'

She herself had taken charge of the party and directed it to the pier-head tram. 'We sat on the top-deck,' she explained, 'and were half-way to St Nicholas's church when Garcia's Voice "came through" ordering us to get off and go back on our tracks—to Russell Street, and there, he said, next to Reece's Dairy and behind the Adelphi Hotel we'd find the church we were looking for. Well, I could hardly believe my ears. I was sure there was no such place!'

However, they did as they were told, and after boarding a tram going the other way, followed directions till they came to an insignificant church beside the dairy. This was the Roman Catholic pro-Cathedral of St Nicholas and Our Lady. Once inside, the three of them (Garcia had dissociated himself) were soon gazing up in astonishment at two brass plaques. 'And would you believe it?' Mrs Mooney's voice rose an octave. 'There, bang in front of us, were the names and dates of William White and Thomas Penswick!'

With curiosity inflamed, she next made for the library and found a copy of *Lancashire Churches and Crosses*. In this she discovered the name Penswick, Bishop Thomas, d. 1836, followed by an account of his life which described how he used to travel up and down the countryside blessing wayside crosses, our Headless Cross among them.

Two others who had seen the ghost were the Morels. At Sweetloves one afternoon Anna described how she and Rebecca were returning home from a party in Grimeford Lane: 'Again it was New Year's Eve, which *does* happen to be the day of St Sylvester,' she said, 'when by the light of our torches we saw the cloaked figure of a priest.'

'Yes, it's true,' Rebecca put in, 'I took particular notice that he wore a biretta; and there was a cold, evil feeling about him. Maurice Birchall was quite right.'

So that was why they had wanted to be present at the seance. 'As to that,' Anna tuned-in, 'I don't know what to think. We heard nothing about the Father Bennett murder, and yet so many things fit with this later story. D'you think Garcia could have looked up *Lancashire Crosses*? But very odd about Eric Marsh—the most convincing piece of evidence to me.'

Mrs Mooney, thinking the same, invited Garcia once more, and again he spoke of the dark deed committed by Blanco. Though he did not use the word 'murder' this seemed the most likely explanation. Anyway, the ghost appeared again on New Year's Eve, 1946. Some months after this Lord Leverhulme restored the top part of the figure to its rightful place, and Guillimo Blanco—if indeed it was he—was seen no more.

Mrs Mooney believed that Leverhulme was misguided in such interference in matters outside his scope. 'Fancy lifting a monument so loaded with history up to his modern bungalow!' she had protested. 'No wonder the spirits were disturbed.' But she wouldn't have had them otherwise, for without doubt she was 'psychic'; and there was nothing phoney in her sense of presences real though unseen.

As to the identity of the Boggart, we were left guessing, but Mrs Mooney was convinced by Garcia's revelations that the apparition was indeed the said Guillimo Blanco, and had nothing to do with Father Bennett. Whereas the Morels believed 'It' was Father Bennett's murderer. 'And who's to know he didn't return to earth a second time,' Anna reasoned, 'as Blanco—Black in the guise of White—to the scene of his crime? Uneasy or evil spirits

must come back again and again—to try to work out their destiny.
Reincarnation is the only theory that makes sense of life.'

'And that,' responded Rebecca, 'is a very good reason for
opposing capital punishment. If we kill a murderer before his
time is up, he will return to repeat his crime. Leave him his life,
and there's hope for him. For myself I believe the apparition
was the murderer. If this time was his second appearance, the
story fits.'

While Anna and Rebecca were engrossed in the Boggart story,
Michael was scornful, even contemptuous. During the time of
the appearances the sisters asked me up for a cup of tea and a
discussion. We were in full swing when Michael came into the
room. 'Still on with the ghost story?' he said flinging down his
books. 'If you ask me, what you saw was no more than a flesh-
and-blood priest. Why shouldn't he also have been out to a
party? Even priests are human.' He strode impatiently about the
room. 'For my part, I find real life situations more rewarding,
and there's a big one blowing up at the very moment around the
village school.' He turned to Anna: 'You've not forgotten the
meeting this evening?'

'Of course not!' she answered sharply. In silence she collected
her books and left the room.

Michael had shut his mind against the ghost, and at the same
time seemed to barricade himself against Anna. Just now coolness
was hardening into antagonism. After she had gone he turned
away and warmed his hands in front of the fire. Recently elected
to the village school managers' committee, he took the job
seriously—it was the first time the village had taken him seriously
—and he meant to prove his worth. With Anna, already an
established member, he carried on endless arguments and discussions as to the best methods of teaching infants. If the school
were to close just now he would lose his newly-won prestige; and
no doubt a crisis was developing. He ran his fingers through his
wet hair—it was raining hard—and Rebecca, for the first time
noticing that his shoes and jacket were soaked, exclaimed in dismay: 'You'll get your death—going out in all weathers with no
hat and those flimsy shoes! We don't want any more ghosts
around here.'

She hurried out of the room to fetch his slippers, and on
returning knelt down and blew into the fire while he changed

wet shoes for dry and proceeded to fill his pipe with greater care than usual. The smoke rising from it mingled with the wood-smoke from Rebecca's crackling sticks. Satisfied, she sat back on her heels looking up intently at his turned-away face. He was getting spoilt, taking such devotion for granted. Not that Anna fussed him; now she had a job she was reconciled to being avail-able—a good companion who, if less accessible, might have been more appreciated.

Oblivious of Anna's absence, Michael drew on his pipe and continued staring into the fire. He hardly noticed Rebecca bring-ing him a cup of tea. Waiting on him had become a necessary part of her life. 'What's the big day-dream?' she inquired indicat-ing the cup by his side. With an effort he switched off: 'It's the meeting this evening,' he frowned. 'Anything could happen.' As he spoke Anna came in. 'Going to be tricky tonight,' he glanced towards her. 'We can't do much against the Ministry with only twenty children.'

'But they're such *scattered* children! Think of the Bickerstaffes on the Pike—how could they get to any other school?' And the Browns from Windy Rannets, and the Nab's Farm children. They've all got to be educated somehow. And can you imagine the Ministry providing taxis for them?'

'Surely they're not thinking of *closing* the school?' I looked from one to the other. 'More than thinking,' Michael replied, 'they're going into action against us this evening. And they always win.'

'That's a splendid line to take,' Anna mocked. 'If you'd any-thing about you, you'd attack. Anyway, if you won't I will!'

'The trouble with you is you don't know when you're beaten.'

'Don't I? Well, that's just where you're wrong!' With a lift of the chin, eyes alight, she stood there half-challenging, half-con-temptuous, his dismissal of the ghost story still rankling. His mouth set in a stubborn line he said nothing. Rebecca's dark eyes gleamed approval, and I slipped away unnoticed.

15

Village School Saved and a Cottage Destroyed

With the rain blowing into my face I ran home down the dripping glen. What argument, I wondered, might prevail against Authority. For four hundred years the school had been the hub of village life. If it were to be closed now not only the children and parents would suffer, the Plodders would leave, and the Dapples, as caretakers, would be out of work. For half a lifetime they had cleaned and polished, fed the stove and washed dishes. How many times had they swept up when windows were broken, how many flies-in-the-eye had Mrs Dapple removed?

I found Aubrey, who was chairman of the committee, imprisoned in the drawing-room with Mr Plodder. Once inside the door Mr P. was inclined to stay on talking 'shop'. This evening, with Mr Black, a member of the Education Committee, to face he was too disturbed to notice my warning clatter of dishes. 'They think of us as a liability,' he shook his head as I came into the room, 'but somehow we must plead, argue, persuade them to the contrary.'

'Don't worry,' I tried to soothe him, 'we're all on your side. But first we must have supper.' Even after this I had to shoo him to the front door. Not that we weren't equally concerned. Since we came to Rivington there had never been more than twenty-eight pupils in the school so that it was almost a family affair, and a family garden where each child was given a plot of land. Here in the spring they scattered seeds from hopefully coloured packets. All shared in planting and weeding the vegetable patch; and while the boys grew potatoes and cabbages, the girls cultivated herbs, which enlivened my stews and hot-pots. It was a Beatrix Potter sort of garden: you half expected to see Peter Rabbit in blue jacket with brass buttons advancing between cabbages. Out here the children learned as much as in the classrooms. One day Jenny Bickerstaffe examining a hole in the wall, discovered a coal-tit's nest with eight eggs which, in spite of daily examination, eventually hatched out. Thrushes and blackbirds built trustfully in the rhododendrons; every oak and sycamore was a personality, while a fallen ash trunk, ideal for jumping competitions, served also as a reading desk.

Miss Jackson introduced the children to the poems of John Clare. A favourite was *Little Trotty Wagtail* because of the pied wagtail which daily visited the yard to the tune of:

Little trotty wagtail you nimble all about
And in the dimpling water-pudge you waddle in and out. . .

Arithmetic was a practical subject: if you wanted to find the area of a flagstone you went into the yard and measured it. While poetry and painting were learned from life. The lore of the seasons, cosmic rhythm and harmony—all were unconsciously absorbed. No need to consider man in relationship to his environment: Wordsworth himself could have wished for nothing better. Indeed, 'modern' methods of education were practised here forty years ago.

In this atmosphere Martin thrived, and Richard, wiser than we knew, regarded school as a playground for recovery. All the eight children of the village were spending their early days here, apart from half a dozen further afield, a handful over the water, and the three young Bickerstaffes up on the Pike. No wonder there was apprehension at the threat of closing.

Aubrey, trying to smooth the jagged atmosphere of the committee room, introduced Mr Black with his usual courtesy and geniality. Square of jaw and shoulder, tall and dark and spectacled, Mr Black stood up. Nothing oblique or subtle in his approach: to him the world was black and white. After commenting briefly on the age and usefulness of Rivington Primary School he coughed and changed tune. 'But, ladies and gentlemen, all this is in the past. Times change.' He picked up a sheaf of papers and read out forms and figures to prove us a financial millstone. 'I'm afraid it just isn't economically possible to run a school for twenty children. There's no alternative but to close it. Very sorry.'

He sat down in a clashing silence, dynamic with cross-currents. Suddenly Michael stood up. 'First of all,' he challenged, 'I'd like to ask what *are* the alternatives if the school is closed?' While

Mr Black was suggesting Horwich and Adlington, I felt Anna on my left and the Colonel on my right charging Michael with explosive so that his reply rang with authority: 'Very well! Then the Ministry will have to provide taxis to collect the children from three farms, not to mention the family who live at the gatehouse on the Pike. Imagine a taxi struggling up that river-bed to take three children to school! And in winter returning them through frost and fog and snow. It's not feasible.'

No one spoke; Aubrey studied his notes; Mr Black gazed at the clock as Michael, swept along by our feelings, continued: 'And another thing, this school is unique—it dates back four hundred years and stands on the site of one of the first grammar schools in the country. Tradition apart, it's got more of real value to give than the most modern school in town—indvidual attention. Why,' he turned towards the headmaster and junior teacher, 'Mr Plodder and Miss Jackson here know every child as a person. Know their family background and difficulties. This is vitally important in a class of young children of different ages.' He sat down to a chorus of 'Hear! Hear!'

Mr Black cleared his throat. 'Maybe. But that sort of thing's not possible these days. Doesn't pay.'

'But it *does* pay!' Anna was on her feet, green eyes bright with anger. 'In the people it turns out. People are more important than pence and pounds. Every child here *matters!*'

'I completely agree,' gruffed the Colonel, 'our school does an excellent job—being in the country; lessons under the threes; gardening; nature walks and so on. Produces individuals, not a bunch of nondescripts. Builds character, personality. . .' he was almost about to break into the old school song when Anna grounded the argument: 'A great deal more will be lost than gained in closing. A school is necessary in this scattered area. And next year, very likely, there'll be more children. What will you do then?'

The discussion mounted, each one of us adding a brick to the pile till Mr Black was walled-in and talked out. The Committee was unanimously agreed to put the matter before a higher authority.

Such an issue could not be settled all at once. We waited in suspense while letters flew back and forth between county and headquarters. Outsiders brought in to review the situation were tramped to the farthest farms, driven uncomfortably up to the gate-house. Perhaps the ideas of running taxis in such a region swayed the balance. Whatever it was, one morning came formal notice of reprieve.

Rejoicing at this good news was expressed loudly and colourfully on Bonfire Night. In any case, the fifth of November in Rivington is guaranteed to blow away—or blow up—any small feud that might have arisen. The uninhibited burning and firework-throwing has a cathartic effect like smashing china or even hunting. Willy-nilly every household is purged of 'burnables', a salutary process reminiscent of a Mexican village custom of burning all household possessions every fifty years. Even in our village we may not lay up for ourselves earthly treasure; and moth (if not rust) has small chance of corrupting.

For this annual clean sweep we bless our pagan bonfire on the green midway between church and chapel—bristling token of complete reconciliation. This year on the afternoon of the fourth the soft, damp air crackled with the sound of sticks and children's voices as branches and stakes were arranged round the steadily mounting pile. As much care goes into this operation as into the making of a haystack. Aubrey had brought some skips, beautifully oily from the mill, and Harry Thistlewaite, who lived two miles away, supplied tea-chests, tinder-dry from his grocer's shop.

If this ritual turns grown-ups into children, it also turns Roman Catholics into heretics. The Thistlethwaite family who went to Mass every Sunday were its most ardent supporters, supplying fuel, food for the party afterwards, and unflagging enthusiasm. Even Mr Mooney, for once stripped of his dog-collar, was to be seen sleeves rolled up wheeling barrow-loads of sweepings through the vicarage gate. Everyone in the vilage brought an offering—as though we were building a nest for the burning of the phoenix. The Mooneys and Plodders, working in harmony, were soon joined by Johnny Thatcher and Mr Dapple, dragging between them a bundle of wood—an advance on last year when Johnny had drawn back, fearing that sparks from the fire might singe his beloved chapel chestnuts. The Seeds, Taylors, and Mrs Birdwhistle, having for months denied the rag-and-bone man, offered every available remnant.

Inevitably there was one defaulter—Miss Whittle who remained angrily indoors after denouncing the wicked custom of burning money while more than half the world was starving. And because for once Chink was reduced to cowering under the table, she accused us of cruelty to animals. Mrs Dapple and Mrs Seed were kept indoors for a different reason; they were baking parkin and boiling toffee. When I opened the back door of the post-office at four o'clock I was wrapped in the warm smell of treacle which led me into the kitchen to discover Mrs Seed in the act of pouring the dark, gleaming liquid, molten as lava, into a tin. Soon it would set like rock for her to hammer into jagged pieces. Just now she was bending down and drawing out of the oven a tray of delectable parkin spiced with ginger and flecked with oatmeal—like Harris tweed. Accurately as a mathematician drawing squares, she flicked across and down the shining surface with a knife.

Before it was dusk the bonfire pile had reached an impressive height; the men thought it unwise to add another twig, and were lighting pipes in agreement when David and Eileen Mooney, Martin and Richard, and the Seed boys came struggling round the vicarage corner with a sofa salvaged from the props of the 'Cads'. After setting it down on the green they ran into the post-office to borrow Mrs Seed's step-ladders. Propping these against the pile, David persuaded his father to mount. Together, aided by Mr Dapple, they balanced the sofa, legs-in-air, on top.

Mrs Plodder always made the guy; and at bonfire time she was at her best, good-tempered and co-operative—as if sticking pins into a guy relieved her feelings and enabled her to see good in everybody—even Mrs Mooney. But she was jealous of her puppet; no one was allowed to see it until the moment for burning. At six o'clock the following evening the door of School House opened and the guy was displayed at the top of the steps. This year he was indecently human with jerking limbs, gaping mouth and white face. As he lay sprawled at the bottom of the steps he looked like a drunk thrown out. At the sight of this tragi-comic figure the children, brandishing sparklers, darted about the green like fire-flies. The lighting was timed for six-thirty, and just now parents were appearing two by two—Mooneys, Seeds, Dapples, and Taylors, Harry Thistlethwaite, the good Catholic, drove up with five children, while Johnny and Rosie Thatcher came hurrying from the manse. A moment later Ben tipped his wife and three daughters out of his jeep while he followed with a hay-fork because his job was to pitch the guy. Latecomers included Michael twisting a scarf round his neck and saying 'Good evening' to the vicar, while from the opposite end of the green Bryony and Humphrey emerged together from the shadows.

The only two who avoided each other were Sally Haythorn-thwaite, Ben's youngest and prettiest daughter, and Jimmy Seed. Their budding boy-and-girl friendship had seemed all set for blossom when suddenly Jimmy found himself fallen from her favour. While he added to the bonfire with simulated ardour, she hovered between lamplight and shadows, never far from the mobile figure of David Mooney. Whether or not he was conscious of the fact, he was the sole target of her wild brown eyes. 'Our Sal's looking up,' Mrs Haythornthwaite confided out of Mrs Seed's half-hearing. As usual the Darleys hadn't turned out tonight. Mrs Darley was terrified of the bangs, and the Colonel felt his dignity might be threatend by such communal jollification.

Richard, expert fire-lighter from the 'Secret Seven' days, helped Ronnie Seed to pour paraffin around the base of the bonfire while Mr Mooney rattled a box of matches. More stragglers ran to the scene, and visitors flung themselves out of last-minute cars. Solemnly Mr Mooney bent down, struck a match and, as though performing a baptism, brushed a strand of oiled straw. Immediately a muscular tongue of flame licked the dry sticks until the whole pile roared like a lion into life. Children shouted and darted in and out of the light; grown-ups gasped and drew back. In a few moments the sofa was ringed with fire, and the guy, like a figure in Dante's Inferno, stiffened, sat upright, and toppled forward on to his burning throne.

Now was the moment to set off the fireworks. In a moment the sky above the green glittered like the Planetarium. Globes of red and orange broke into shivering fragments; a rocket whipped into space, paused, and dropped slow green stars. Roman candles whisked coloured balls, ephemeral as bubbles, while silver fountains, sunflowers, golden rain, flared and fell in dizzy succession. Luminous snowstorms arose in the darkness till we were dazzled and dazed with surprises. Mrs Seed and Mrs Birdwhistle were handing round treacle toffee, while the boys scooped black uneatable potatoes from the furnace. After this brief interval crackerjacks and bangers hidden like snakes in the grass, caused shrieks of alarm and scared the younger children away.

Aubrey pinned catherine-wheels to a row of sticks where, slow to catch fire, they suddenly whirled into life, revolving like tigers' eyes and shedding luminous tears. These, with a final volley of rockets and Roman candles, signalled the end of the show. The half-pleasing acrid smell of gunpowder hung in the air while the bonfire coiled itself into a burning nest of rock-pythons—to twist and smoulder through the night. Mr Dapple lit his pipe: that meant supper.

By the time we crowded into the Sunday school Mrs Seed and Mrs Dapple had placed hot-pots and potato pies flanked by parkin on a long table. Unexpectedly Mrs Twigg arrived carrying a holdall from which she produced several bottles of elderberry wine. This crowned the evening: Aubrey ran home for a corkscrew and returned to find that Humphrey had beaten him by a bottle-neck. The popping corks made a welcome sound after the explosion of fireworks; and everyone grew merrier and more flushed than was warranted for by the innocent elderberry. 'This is vintage wine,' Mrs Twigg assured us. Vintage or no, I guessed it was laced with brandy like her famous herbal cures. Sally had slipped herself in unnoticed beside David—her well-begun conquest already half won. And there across the table was Bryony glowing with pleasure between Humphrey and Michael. Humphrey seemed to go out of his way to be agreeable to Michael—as though relieved for someone to share his wife's vitality. Wonderingly I recalled Ben Haythornthwaite's account of meeting Humphrey at the Yew Tree on some hunting matter when over a pint Humphrey had confessed: 'The fact is, I can't satisfy her, so if she fancies the young schoolmaster, well, here's good luck to him!' Having got that off his chest he downed a second pint and turned for home in high good humour.

Mrs Twigg was talking into my other ear: 'I don't care to watch the bonfire; it smacks too much of witch-burning. There's more behind these rituals than you people realize—a subconscious expression of the race memory. Burning away prejudices and resentment, venting them on a guy just as people used to burn heretics and martyrs.'

Her words were drowning the rising noise of the room, and I let them run off my back. With Mrs Twigg I felt something of an earth-worm in the presence of a glow-worm—or a fire-fly. At that moment Mrs Mooney leaned across the table and came to my rescue: 'D'you remember what Goethe said about us not being able to remain long in the conscious state? According to him we must always be plunging back into the Unconscious to find our living roots.'

'Aah,' nodded Mrs Twigg as though she had read Goethe before we were born.

Meanwhile the mass subconscious had surged up into song and dance. Chairs were scraped back while Humphrey and Michael guided the unprotesting Bryony to the piano-stool. The two men led her into 'John Peel', 'Little Brown Jug', and 'Uncle Tom Cobley'. Everybody gathered round and started singing, except Mrs Twigg who, with an understanding smile at such childish revels, twirled her cloak around her, gathered up her holdall, and floated into the night.

By an unfortunate coincidence Miss Whittle, who shunned Bonfire Night, became the victim of one of the small fires which invariably followed the Fifth. At this season fire got into the blood of the village boys, so that next day when Johnny Thatcher lighted several piles of chestnut leaves—rusty offerings from the chapel—they decided to keep one of them going all night. After the village purge there was little left to burn. Then David Mooney suggested dismantling the vicarage summer-house. Unknown to his parents he led his companions to this woeful object whose thatch was ragged as the yew tree overhead. By the light of a storm-lantern they quickly dismembered it and flung planks and timbers on the fire. 'Mum'll be glad to see the end of this,' David encouraged them on their last journey through the back gate. The Taylor twins added a sackful of wood-shavings, our own boys the dregs of paraffin. 'It'll go up like a house on fire!' laughed Richard striking a match. On the instant his words came true, and the boys ran back in alarm as the vigorous north-wester fanned the flames. The fire blazed towards Miss Whittle's cottage and, to cut a short story shorter, what she had long feared was come upon her. Sparks crackled down the thatch, driving her outside in her nightie. Barefoot, grey hair flying, she darted into the post-office shrieking for the fire-brigade. Within moments the entire village was assembled—this time to gape upon calamity in not unpleasurable alarm. Chink, also evicted, was

E

barking in terror, snapping at every ankle. For once his owner's shrill curses were justified.

United in awed and thrilling silence, we stood entranced as mouthful by mouthful the thatch was devoured and the chimney-stack fell. It was like a dream until the urgent fire-engine bell rattled us back to reality. Firemen were running around, finding taps and fixing hoses. In no time long muscular jets of spray were battling with the flames. Water and fire wrestling together. While the cottage was stripped to the rafters, runnels of water rushed down beside it. Suddenly activity ceased, and the drama was reduced to a singed and smoking silence. 'Neat little job and just in time!' exclaimed a hefty fireman. Hardly had he spoken than a hideous shriek, inhuman and prolonged, split the air. 'God Almighty, the dead are raised up!' cried Mrs Birdwhistle voicing our alarm. The dead were not, indeed, raised, but added to. Miss Whittle could have never devised a sweeter revenge on David Mooney because in this moment the blood of Mimi, the white cat, was on his head. Chink's blinded eye was a small price to pay for such victory. Miss Whittle was even reconciled to the loss of homestead and hens.

The Corporation were more than grateful for the providential gutting of this sagging property, and were promising the tenant a brand-new bungalow of red brick 'on the boundary'—as we called the nondescript half-built-up area beyond our pale. Another benefactor was the insurance company who was to compensate Miss Whittle for loss of property—not to mention dignity. In fact, the sixth of November turned out to be her day: dreams of a new carpet, furniture, and roof were to materialize as Miss Fogg had foretold. All in all, it was David's fire that set her up for longer life than she might otherwise have been granted to grumble at. And curiously enough, next day as we watched her triumphant departure by taxi, arrayed in Mrs Seed's summer hat and coat, we felt an unexpected sense of loss—as though she were taking away from the village a strand of colour, decidedly red. 'Never worry,' smiled Mrs Seed at my half-regret, 'that's not the last we've seen of 'er.'

Indeed, before next year was out Miss Whittle had left her nondescript bungalow for a cottage and the more colourful gossip of Rivington.

16

The Garden-Party

Before the village school had been fought for and saved by its managers, members of the parochial church council were at war on the subject of altar candles. As already mentioned, Colonel Darley was in favour, so that when Mr Mooney appealed to him he came out robustly for 'elevating the church in keeping with its long history.' At this Ben Haythornthwaite, glowing from sun and rain, interrupted: 'Hold hard, Colonel, that 'istory goes back ter popish times—we want none o' that 'ere.' The Colonel bristled: 'I would be the the last to suggest such a thing. What we need here is more light—church a damn sight too dark—excuse me, vicar—and if candles on the altar are offensive, then so are flowers, scattering pollen and hay-fever all over the place.'

'Hear! Hear!' agreed Humphry Marchbanks, but another farmer supported Ben: 'Keep t'church plain an' good an' "low".' Whereupon the vicar turned to Mr Plodder: 'So far, you have been silent. May we hear your views?'

'I'm afraid my views are not quite in focus. But I can see one thing clear enough. Candles will upset the older folk, and they form the biggest part of the congregation.'

'High time, then, to give the youngsters something new and bright. Half the old folk will be gone in five years—some in less,' replied the Colonel. Finally a vote was taken, and the candles got in by one—Humphrey returned from the war with a D.S.O. tipping the balance.

Meanwhile, with church bells throughout the country ringing in the first Sunday of peace, the vicar preached on 'Light after darkness' and introduced two modest candles as symbols. His idea very nearly worked for all that Mrs Plodder, a Methodist under the skin, accused the Mooneys of Papist sympathies. Had it not been for the Garden-Party Row the candles might have burned on unchallenged.

Unfortunately, as it turned out, this year Eileen Mooney had been selected by the Sunday school committee as Rose Queen in preference to Mrs Plodder's favourite, Sally Haythornthwaite. Indeed, Sally, tall and dusty, had grown to be the most beautiful girl for miles around. Protected by a surfeit of boy-friends, she had unwittingly captured Jimmy Seed's heart while reserving her own for higher game, and was the envy of her two older sisters. In her rôle of Sunday school teacher Mrs Plodder always chose the dresses for the Queen and attendants. This year, to get her own back, she abandoned the traditional white for the Queen, and insisted that she should wear the same colour as her retinue. Because Eileen was red-haired as her mother, Mrs Plodder decided on blancmange-pink—so that she would be ill-suited and undistinguished from the others. When Mrs Mooney objected that the Queen always wore white, Mrs Plodder retorted that this year, in celebration of victory (if not peace) tradition was being flouted.

The true reason for this was Mrs Plodder's annoyance at her rival's habit of chatting to her husband after school. Often enough these two wasted as much as ten minutes in conversation outside the vicarage gate. Mrs Seed was sympathetic: "e needs a live-wire across 'is path now an' then. 'E's earthed soon enough at 'ome.'

Other small flares were being lighted in the anti-candle-ite camp: "Tain't fitting fer t'vicar's daughter ter be Queen,' and ' "Light after darkness", indeed!' But the rest of us welcomed the candles, and ignored black looks from Plodders and Haythornthwaites. The rift between the church divided was far sharper than the accepted division between church and chapel. Even the animals reflected these differences: on the Friday before the party the Plodder's terrier, Bonzo, took a length out of Mimi's tail, and we almost heard the rattle of drums. To make things worse, the vicar hadn't prayed for a fine day, and everyone knew that rain on the garden-party meant disaster. Mr Mooney, who preferred to leave the weather in the hands of the Almighty, was criticized. And Miss Whittle, who never went to church and never missed a garden-party, objected to the fortune-teller: 'No good'll coom ter t'church from palm-crossed silver.' Even Mrs Seed was upset because David Mooney, rather than her own two boys, was in charge of the bran-tub.

At the last moment the official opener gave back-word, so the vicar knocked on our door, and begged me to fill the gap. Unable to refuse I said Yes, and then helped Mrs Mooney set out games on the vicarage tennis-court—darts, hoop-la, skittles, and roulette: 'Mrs P's certain to object to this.' And this was the moment, the words not dry on her tongue, that Bonzo leapt over the wall and attacked Mimi. 'And to think,' said Mrs Mooney bitterly, 'we throw open our garden for the benefit of the parish!'

By now the redoubtable Mothers had set up two stalls and improvised a small tent for the fortune-teller—none other than Miss Fogg, the medium, who weighed seventeen stone, and was reputed to go into trances. Bets were laid as to whether this flimsy tent would accommodate her considerable person. 'Depends on 'ow much ectoplasm she gives off!' laughed Mrs Birdwhistle. Presently David and Eileen, carrying bats, balls, hoops, and a clothes-line, appeared. 'Wot's that for?' someone inquired. 'For a tug-of-war between church and chapel,' replied David smartly.

Three o'clock on the Great Day. And clouds gathering imperceptibly towards the moment of opening, timed for fifteen minutes after the arrival of the three o'clock bus. Suddenly a wind got up and the sky darkened. Miss Jackson, Sunday school assistant, with the dancers she had so patiently coached fidgetted in the shadows, while Mr Plodder hovered around the harmonium on which he was to play the opening hymn. The moment I appeared at the opener's table—on the terrace above the lawn—he lunged into it with 'Now Thank We All Our God' before I hurried through my stand-in speech. The vicar's prayer and his thanks to me were even more hurried—after an anxious glance at the threatening sky.

Already eight small girls in rainbow net, escaped from Miss Jackson's quiver, had begun twirling rose-hoops to music. Last year's Queen walked solemnly up the terrace steps and bowed before me as I took off her gold crown replacing it by a smaller one of silver. 'Woolworth's!' Miss Whittle whispered loudly into the pause. Whereupon the harmonium with laboured breath undid its stays, and expanded into the 'Bridal March.' The heralds blew their trumpets, and Eileen, followed by two stumbling pages, came forward. Flushed to an unbecoming salmon-pink, she knelt on a purple cushion while I took up the gold crown and placed it carefully as a hot dish upon her fiery curls. Everyone clapped. And now we were let loose among the stalls with the usual exhortation to spend all we had. I bought tea-towels from the Mothers' Union, and Mrs Mooney in her upset gave me wrong change. Behind was Mrs Haythornthwaite, bridling from compliments about Sally's appearance. 'Not such a good day,' she observed tossing her head like a sprightly mare, and rolling her eyes upwards. 'Shouldn't be surprised if we have a storm. It'll be the first wet garden-party in *my* memory.'

She stumped away towards the click of wooden balls on the tennis-court. By now a scramble of women had stripped the drapery stall; groceries there were none; and every child was sucking an iced lollie. Even Eileen, deserted by her retinue, had allowed herself to be tempted by an ice-cream cornet which she licked tentatively like a deer trying a new shoot. Instantly Mrs Plodder was on her track: 'Have you forgotten your manners? And your promise as Queen not to suck ice-creams in that costume?'

This was the match that lighted the dry straw. 'Leave the child alone!' Mrs Mooney's hazel eyes glinted warningly. 'You've done your best already to ruin her day, dressing her like a doll in pink.'

'Pink indeed!' flared the other. 'Why shouldn't I choose pink, You steal *all* the colours.'

The words were out, and the two women, bristling like cats, faced one another. Mercifully Aubrey, the peace-maker sprung from nowhere, stepped between them, and guided Mrs Plodder away to her husband who took her home. Mrs Mooney stayed to brave the afternoon out—bowls, hoop-la and all. The tide was already turning in her favour: balls, bats, hoops and rings were handed to her with deference. And at roulette she couldn't lose. The bran-tub, abandoned by David, was held by the Seed boys, and when Sally came for a dip Jimmy dived in and handed her a parcel: 'Specially for you!'

All was smooth when Mrs Benson, one of the Mothers, stumbled out of the fortune-teller's tent. 'Oh!' she exclaimed. 'Do go in an' see to 'er. She's gone off—breathing that 'eavy I can't wake 'er up.' The women queuing outside bunched around listening in pleasurable alarm, while Mrs Mooney lifted the tent-flap as if it were a coffin lid. And there was Miss Fogg, arms hanging loose, head lolling as she bulged through the wicker-work chair. Her diamanté-loaded bosom swelled and contracted as though worked by a pair of bellows. 'Are you all right?' As Mrs Mooney spoke the huge body shuddered; and with a jangle of ear-rings Miss Fogg threw up her head. Opening her eyes she looked at us from far away: 'The Spirit bloweth where it listeth. I am in Other Hands.' In spite of this she was persuaded into the vicar's study. After settling her there with the next client Mrs Mooney put her ear to the keyhole. Presently Miss Fogg's marzipan voice came through: 'Big money coming your way. A wedding and a surprise. . . .' The vicar's wife straightened up with relief: 'So long as she keeps it at *that* level!'

I was watching the roulette players when a heavy, ominous drop of rain splashed roundly on to the board. 'What did I say?' Mrs Haythornthwaite almost neighed in excitement. 'Bad pennies from heaven!' The first drops were followed by a cascade; and in a skirt-lifting whirl of wind the stalls were disbanded. There was a frenzied scutter for the tea-tent, now flapping and straining at its ropes like a ship.

In the midst of this clatter Mr Plodder appeared, sat down, and munched his way unperturbed through ham sandwiches. Then, wiping his mouth he stood up to make a speech, but his words were drowned in a truly pentecostal wind, while lightning tongues of fire jagged the sky. A crack of thunder caused shrieks of alarm. Crowded together like sheep in the fold, we were obliged to remain for half-an-hour while the tent rocked in the storm.

Next day was the first Sunday that Mrs Plodder had ever given matins a miss. Mr P. went alone and heard the vicar announcing an increase over last year's garden-party takings. The church was full—people like hearing their efforts praised from the chancel steps. During the first lesson the versatile Ronnie Seed, organist as well as verger, audibly encouraged Tommy to 'pump more wind into 'er'. The resulting crescendo and accelerando left us behind in the psalms, singing hesitant and high, while he roared ahead like the Lion of Judah; but in the first hymn we refused to give way and Fought the Good Fight clinging tenaciously to the end of each line till Ronnie capitulated. When the vicar mounted the pulpit steps, the congregation was ready for another 'Light of the World' sermon. Meanwhile the altar candles burned steadily.

But even as Tommy Seed snuffed them to wisps of smoke, Mrs Haythornthwaite under the lych-gate was shaking her beflowered hat at his mother: "Tain't fitting fer Rivington. Candles put ideas

into folk's 'eads. Would yer believe it, after Communion last
Sunday that Mr Laycock, 'e could 'ardly wait ter get out o' church
ter light a cigarette.' Mrs Seed's tulle bows quivered in divided
sympathy. 'Dearie me,' she hesitated. 'P'raps t'Army's done it. Any
road, we can be thankful 'e didn't light up at the altar!'

On the ever-burning subject of altar candles we remained divided, so that the matter was again brought up at the next meeting.
Mr Plodder spoke first: 'Might I suggest that we light the candelabra instead? Being suspended from the centre of the nave it
could give no offence. Might be seen as a middle way—tolerance,
you know.'

'Ridiculous hair-splitting!' barked the Colonel. 'If candles are
acceptable in one position why not in another? In any case, the
people sitting in front would have to twist their necks around like
giraffes to see 'em.'

'Ridiculous or not, the candles will make trouble. Underground
murmurs can mount to a storm.'

'What exactly do you mean?'

'So far only the usual complaints. We always get them. Someone objects that the vicar won't allow her to take hold of the chalice
at Communion. "He hangs on to it," she says, "so I can hardly
wet my lips!"'

'It's very "low" to want to hold the chalice yourself,' interposed
Humphrey. 'And now you're being a high-church snob!' I teased
him. 'For my part, I prefer to be given the chalice—there's a sort
of grace in the act, as if it belonged to everybody, and not just to
the parson.'

'Never mind t'chalice,' Ben Haythornthwaite broke in, 'we're
'ere ter discuss candles. An' I'm telling thee I'm not alone'—he
indicated two farmers who growled agreement—'It's no good 'ere,
isn't 'igh church practice, and if them candles stays on th' altar,
us'll walk out.' When the Colonel called him small-minded and
reactionary, Ben retorted: 'Us country folk is a sight nearer God
in a field 'n cluttered wi ritual. We've got t'sun through t'east
window. Wot more d'you want?'

At that moment someone clattered through the door. It was
Ronnie Seed. 'Sorry, sir, t'interrupt,' he addressed the vicar, 'but
the missus was 'aving a look round t'church before locking up,
an' sithee.' Dramatically he unrolled a crumpled object and

flapped it like a flag in the face of the meeting. It was the altar-cloth with two great holes burned in it.

Eventually the argument was settled by the candelabra—to be lighted on feast-days only. There it still hangs, shining symbol of the middle way, the golden mean.

17

Wash-Days and Days at the Pool

After such factions common to any village, Rivington settles back
on its keel like a well-balanced ship. On a blue-and-white Monday
morning soon after this particular storm several strings of washing
were to be seen flapping like bunting in the wind. Mrs Dapple,
as usual, had been the most ambitious with blankets and curtains
as well as innumerable 'smalls'. But then she had the best position
for her line fixed by Mr Dapple on the common land behind their
cottage. She was always two hours in advance of me I thought
ruefully when pegging out on a much-mended rope. Somehow I
could never acquire this 'pegging out' knack; I had instead a
faculty for dropping the 'whitest whites' and treading them into
the grass. Nor, lacking a counterpart of Mr Dapple, did I ever
learn to fix a line. Today my tea-cloth had lapped itself around the
laburnum trunk; the prop had let me down so that three pillow-
slips trailed on the ground, while the birds made targets of the
sheets. Much discouraged, I flicked off a few flies and started un-
pegging.

By this time Mrs Seed, another early-riser, was already gathering in her second crop of 'coloureds'. And there over the wall, Mrs
Plodder, hands on hips, was standing back to admire her 'whites'
flying like wild-geese in a gale. It came to me then that the collec-
tive noun for washing is 'skein' or 'pride'. A pride of Mrs Plodder's
pyjamas; a skein of his shirts.

The only house, our side of the green, devoid of a washing-line
was the manse whose story was told in dust-grey curtains. Mrs
Plodder with her scouring Methodist conscience declared that the
whole place should be fumigated: 'I don't believe those curtains
have been washed since they were hung forty years ago!'

No one could imagine Rosie, the youngest Thatcher, having a
wash-day, but as the household received so many gift-parcels of
clothing, we concluded that they wore these garments till they
dropped off—or were eaten off. To look at Rosie you'd think

she had been born in a coal-shed, yet whenever I knocked in passing to see if she needed anything—even soap—she would stand at the door laughing my fears away, the rudest possible picture of health.

During her sister Jane's last illness I called one day with some beef-tea. After a long interval Rosie was peering at me like a field-mouse through a crack in the door. When I inquired about the invalid she answered quickly: 'Doing nicely, thank you!' And then, fearful at having to open the door wide enough to receive my offering, she reached out a skinny hand and snatched it in her haste for me to be gone.

On one of her rare visits to the post-office—she preferred to forfeit her pension unless accompanied by Johnny—Mrs Seed was sympathizing with her predicament: 'Such a big 'ouse ter keep up fer the two o' yer. 'Ow many bedrooms 'ave yer?' Rosie gazed back blankly for a moment before replying: 'Bedrooms? Oh, dearie me, I've no idea. Never counted 'em!' If the truth were known the family never used the bedrooms until the day they took to their death-beds. Maybe there was only one such bed upon which, in due course, each member took first, and at the same time last, turn. One can imagine Rosie, after Jane's departure, bolting the door of the 'death-chamber' and refusing thereafter to climb the stairs. At any rate, she and Johnny spent the nights in the kitchen sitting the fire out until dawn when she crept into the spinney to gather sticks.

From this sooty background Johnny, our wisest and best-loved character, emerged clean as a spring morning to trim hedges and sweep leaves. Regularly as a swallow he appeared every April to prune our roses. Like Mrs Twigg he had 'the green' in his finger-tips, and like many a countryman, he was a poet at heart. Over a pint of beer or a pile of leaves he would spin verses till the ruinous farms and deserted lead-mines rang with life. But I could never get him to talk about his sisters.

So much for the manse with its blue finger of smoke and domed chestunut tree. Around the neglected garden the wilderness has taken over; bracken, willow-herb, and nettles creep higher against the hedge every year. But at sunset the blind house comes to life with the grey stone glowing and windows catching fire as though the sun itself, and not its reflection, were setting in the glass.

About a hundred yards below, divided from the manse by

bracken and garden-plots, stands School House, square and forbidding and Victorian—though well-cared for outside as in. No
slate would be allowed to fall from this roof; no sun permitted to
fade the carpets through discreetly curtained windows. Though
no one could look in, Mrs Plodder could look out. And little
escaped her eye.

Now reconciled to village undercurrents, she was intrigued—
as we all were—to watch Michael so often crossing the green
towards Primrose Cottage. If any incident of this *sub rosa*
relationship escaped her Miss Whittle could always fill the gap.
Not that Mrs Plodder deigned to discuss such a thing with Miss
Whittle. Conclusions were reached in roundabout ways. For
instance, if Mrs P. had been out and chanced to meet her on the
green, she might casually enquire: 'Anything fresh? Anyone
interesting been up?' At which Miss Whittle, catching on like
kindling wood, might produce sparks. As happened one spring
evening with: 'Nothing much—only I just caught sight o' Mrs
Marchbanks an' Mr Laycock setting off through t'wicket-gate this
afternoon. They wer carrying bathing-towels.' Which startling
piece of information was beyond even Mrs Plodder's power to
withhold. The two of them might well have been making for the
Lead Mines Valley and Green Withins beck which, like all the
water around here, was sacred to Liverpool Corporation Waterworks. They might well be prosecuted. Unable to walk so far herself, Mrs P. dropped hints: 'Perhaps you might have seen them
on your long walks?'

Already I was feeling guilty. I had myself bathed many times in
the 'Forbidden Pool' two miles up on the moors beyond Dean
Wood. My one concern, so different from that of Mrs Plodder,
was that these two might have discovered it. I had certainly met
them several times walking in the valley, a wild, desolate cleft
where the beck dashes over rocks, frothy and brown as beer. One
day they had been kneeling beside the stream as though looking
for something. When I drew near Bryony straightened up and
greeted me without embarrassment: 'Look!' she exclaimed holding out her palm to show me a scatter of what seemed to be tiny
cinders. 'Galena.' She bent down, picked up a stone and ground
a fragment of the stuff on a slab of rock. The glittering slate-blue
powder sparkled in the sun; as I admired it she told me that
when the mines were being worked, more than two centuries ago,

Josiah Wedgewood had himself come up here to examine the pigeon-blue galena from which, it was said, he produced his famous Wedgwood blue. While she was speaking Michael busied himself cramming pieces into a matchbox. 'For the geology class,' he grinned, 'this is a strictly educational outing. You wouldn't believe the botany specimens we've collected. Here,' he thrust a newspaper bundle into my hands, 'you can take this home!'

I hadn't meant to go back so soon, but I took the hint along with the bundle—which turned out to be watercress fresh from the stream. A heat-haze drained the day of colour, and I felt cheated of my walk and a bathe. On the way home I prayed that they hadn't discovered the pool, which I now thought of as my private property. Though no faun-like figure rose up from the bracken to join me in my sport, I treasured those expeditions as closely as a lover's secret.

The bright day, also in June, when I first came upon the pool had an unexpected ending. But it began in a shimmer of heat with the entire insect world alive and a-spin. Bees throbbed in foxgloves; flies and beetles drilled the air; and gnats in ecstatic swarms zig-zagged above the stream. When suddenly I saw the kingfisher—a luminous flash between ferns. I had only seen him once before; and I knew that this was to be an unforgettable day. Hadn't Mrs Mooney told me that the kingfisher was an omen, a portent? Otherwise all was still; the wind's blue flags were folded away, and not a twig stirred. As I walked I breathed in the honeyed smell of thyme and bedstraw. The birds were silent—only a lark, inde-fatigable, mounted up and up like a singing rocket to dissolve into nothing. It seemed as though I and the lark were the only creatures awake; even the moor itself, tawny-maned and shouldered, drowsed in the heat.

On such a day the lead mines would be arid and dusty, so I made for the neighbouring valley where the Green Withins divides to run through a glade of oaks, birches, and rowans. Pushing my way among the rising bracken, I came upon a sheep-track bordered with late bluebells. A cuckoo's broken call mingled with the sound of running water. Presently the path twisted and steepened down-hill so that I slid the last few yards to land unexpectedly beside a pool. And *what* a pool—deep and dark as nettle-beer. Dappled with lights and shadows, the water threw reflections upwards on to the enclosing rock wall so that the rock itself seemed to be moving, running with ribbons of watered silk. Two rowan trees were interlaced above the inlet where the rapid stream frothed and sprayed in a considerable fall to the pool. Bubbles, constantly forming, spun upon the water and burst in the sun. All was fleck and foam and rippling light till the stones seemed to be as mobile as the water itself. I guessed this to be a haunt of otters, undiscovered territory, cool and quiet as moss. For a few moments I sat there lost in contemplation of dazzling water and dripping ferns—hart's tongue and stag's-head sprouting green feathers from narrow ledges.

Soon it occurred to me to take off my sandals and dip my feet in the water: it was too deep to paddle. I longed to swim but feared I might be spied upon because the pool was sunk at the base of a sun-shaft in a valley bordering farmland. On either side steep banks rose above the rock walls, and looking up I could see the wooden fence of a hayfield. That was the only obstacle. Meanwhile the sun beat down and I was alone with temptation growing stronger every minute. Suddenly, throwing caution to the winds, I stripped and plunged. The cold shock was exhilarating; I felt like a naiad among ferns and freckled shadows. Finding I could swim four strokes back and forth across the pool I grew bold and hoisted myself up on to the ledge under the rowans. With difficulty I crawled against the stream up the slippery rock-basin until the power of the water forced me back. I gave up and sat on the ledge in the middle of the fall, idly flicking the pool below with my big toe. Hours melted away. Shadows began to creep out from rocks and trees while the slow sun, like a ripe fruit, reddened and sank among the branches.

I had hardly buttoned up my dress and was shaking my wet hair when a movement in the trees startled me. I flashed round, and to my amazement and dismay the dark, ungainly figure of Mr Mooney precipitated itself down the bank to my feet. Slowly he uncrumpled and stood up ruefully dusting his jacket and sleeves. This operation filled a gap for which there were no words. 'Lovely evening,' he remarked presently, adjusting the field-glasses slung around his person, 'and a lovely place you've found here.'

'Lovely,' I agreed, 'I only discovered it today. I didn't know *you* knew about it.'

'Oh, I didn't—by no means. The fact is, I've been following a kestrel—she's nested somewhere up this valley. Please don't let me disturb you.' His glance wandered anxiously to my wet hair.

'You don't mean to say you've been bathing?' I laughed at his consternation.

'I must admit to total immersion this time—the most effective form of baptism.'

'But isn't it very cold?'

'Colder than Jordan, perhaps, but far more invigorating.'

'But this stream feeds the reservoirs. Surely bathing here is forbidden?'

'Strictly speaking, yes, this is forbidden water, and just as delicious as forbidden fruit, but without the consequences, I hope. And I hope, too,' I added hastily, 'that I haven't shocked you?' There was a considerable pause while the vicar, much bewildered, arranged his thoughts. 'Oh no, it's not for me to . . . but there *are* other considerations . . . people and so on. Someone might have seen you,' He nodded towards the railings above.

'It was a risk, but well worth it. In that pool I felt as happy— and as innocent—as Eve before the Fall. And I wasn't found out!' 'Not this time,' he agreed doubtfully. And then, consulting his watch: 'I must be getting back. It's quite late, and supper will be waiting.'

Rather than linger behind to give him an obvious start, I clambered up the bank after him. Relaxed from the bathe and a day in the sun. I enjoyed that walk home which revealed an unexpectedly good companion. The vicar's oblique humour sharpened my wits after sun-drenched hours of pure being. While we were walking through the fields above Yarrow reservoir he told me that he'd come to believe that most people, in the end, did what they wanted to do. Eagerly I agreed: 'And if you do the right thing while wanting something quite different, then you do no good?'

' "Sooner murder an infant in its cradle than nurse unacted desires." A dangerous doctrine for a clergyman,' he smiled gravely. 'The important thing is to try to want to do what is right: the real virtue lies in the enjoyment.'

Thus philosophizing, we found ourselves all too soon at the wicket-gate and crossing the green. We passed Mrs Birdwhistle still sitting on her steps chatting to Mrs Seed. 'Been a beautiful day!' she sang out. Mrs Plodder's view of us through the muslin curtains was followed next morning by light-as-feather questions over the garden wall. I played shuttlecock and battledore with her till she gave up. One couldn't even walk out with the vicar without raising dust. Living in a village means that you can keep no secret —even the vests and pants on your washing-line are counted.

After this adventure I took good care, when escaping to the pool, to set out through the bracken behind the house rather than cross the green. If these bathing expeditions were discovered I would be in serious trouble with the Corporation: water-pollution affected Mr Bull as a red rag, and my recent victory of the trees would go against me. The fact that cattle waded in the stream depositing there whatever they felt inclined, was accepted as an accident of nature. A woman bathing was another matter. Nor did I fancy being spotted from the boundary by a farmer; and because mundane objects such as towels and bathing-suits would have been out of harmony, the five minutes' process of getting dried and dressed were sharp with apprehension—which heightened the pleasure. I was lucky; during a fortnight's heatwave I bathed nearly every day until that enchanted world seemed to be entirely my own.

On the hottest day of all—before the weather broke—I tempted providence by a last visit to the pool. The dwindled waterfall murmured a lullaby as I floated face to the sun. Now and again I crawled out to dry on the warm rocks. The leaves above hardly flickered in the heat, and I was almost asleep each time before slipping back, easy as a seal, into the water.

Morning melted into afternoon; shadows began to finger and dapple the pool. At last I gathered sufficient will-power to drag myself out and up the grassy bank where I had flung my clothes. They were not there. Yet they could not have been moved because no one had come near the pool all day. Hunting hopelessly under the trees, I felt a movement nearby, and looked up to see a very young man sitting on a log. He had fair curly hair, and was brown-skinned, naked to the waist. In his candid blue eyes was an innocent gaze of pure admiration. I leapt behind a tree, and he smiled disarmingly. 'Don't hide yerself,' he pleaded in a soft rural accent. 'It's just like a picture—better'n fillums.'

'How dare you take my clothes? Give me them at once, and go away!' I was too taken aback to be angry. ''Ere they are,' he stood up and picked a crumpled bundle from the bracken. 'But please, miss, give us summat ter go 'ome with . . .' he fumbled for words, and went on hesitantly, '. . . it's such a temptin' day, warm an' sweet. An' watching you in t'water I felt I wanted it bad. Just this once miss, please, before I git back ter milkin'.'

'Well!' I exclaimed in bewilderment, 'you *are* in a bad way. I'm very sorry for you. But I really can't oblige. Haven't you got a girl or anything?' He shook his head. 'No girls I fancy round 'ere. An' I never felt like this before. Honest.' Slowly, sadly he came over to where I sheltered behind the trunk of an oak, and handed me my clothes. 'It would be t'first time,' his eyes pleaded as I said 'No.' He sighed. 'I s'pose I'll 'ave to make do wi'out.' Saying which the beautiful, blond, gentle creature turned into the trees, and was gone.

During the almost-as-hot summer of Mrs Plodder's suspicions, I was descending the bank one afternoon in the usual state of exhilaration to stop short in dismay. Voices and laughter. Taking cover under a line of bushes, I crept down to one side, and saw two bundles of clothes and two striped towels, a few feet apart, staring offensively at me. Cautiously I clambered further down to get a view of the pool which remained screened, and there, to my consternation, were Byrony and Michael unashamedly splashing in the sun. Trespassers. Intruders. Anger and disappointment overcame me, and for the first time I felt plain jealousy—not at their enjoyment, but at their discovery of my private paradise. Even though I had been warned, I had a childish impulse to seize one of their belongings and hurl it into the pool. Then I noticed a red sandal flung apart from its fellow and lying temptingly within a few feet of my grasp.

Wriggling through the bracken, I held my breath manoeuvring to reach that sandal. Even as I stretched towards it Byrony, now treading water, turned her face in my direction. I froze instantly like a petrified rabbit, staring back at her through green fronds, seeing yet unseen. Suddenly Michael caught her unawares and ducked her under. To the accompaniment of spluttered protests I closed my fingers round the sandal and retreated inch by inch up the bank. As I clutched it with rage and elation, an overpowering curiosity compelled me to look back—like Orpheus ascending from the Underworld. I saw Byrony pulling herself naked out of the water to sit on the mossy ledge, and, exactly as I had done, flick her big toe in the pool. She mocked at Michael, a mere mortal floundering beneath her. And then, shaking the drops from her hair, she stood up, stretched to her full height, and flung out her arms towards the sun.

Standing there, tall and narrow-waisted, water drops glistening on ivory flesh, she might have been Aphrodite. In two strokes Michael was clutching the ledge, seizing hold of her knees and pulling her back into the water, drawing her into himself. 'Oh, you beast!' she cried, thrashing up a spray as he towed her to the opposite bank. He grasped her by the waist and kissed her neck before pushing her gently back upon the grass. For a few moments he stood quite still, poised expectant above her. The two of them, naked among leaves, freckled by shadow and sunlight, seemed unreal as figures in a Greek legend, and though I found myself playing the rôle of spy, I couldn't turn away. As though from another world I gazed on unbelieving while Michael lowered himself beside her, running a light finger down the length of her body and up again to circle those small round breasts. She flexed her toes, and the instant he rolled towards her sprang up and disappeared into the bracken.

When I got home I dropped my trophy into the hall chest among masks, brushes, and other relics of the chase. At least I had one secret unshared by the village.

18

Making Hay

Rivington shut one eye and slept in the sun. Its kitchens were deserted because on our side of the green those housewives' altars face east and are most dismal at three o'clock in the afternoon. Mrs Seed and Mrs Birdwhistle sat on their steps knitting, their needles and tongues occasionally falling silent in the drowsy heat. Even Chink, legs stretched out behind him, lay panting on the grass. While the others had withdrawn to the shade of their gardens, Mrs Dapple, her front door wide open, stayed inside and watched the cats dozing upon burning flagstones. For once Mr Dapple's saw was at rest in the warm woodshed, and on the Taylors' roof seven white fantails were clustered like a spray of blossom.

The three o'clock bus, scarlet and shining-hot, slid alongside the green 'as silent as a painted ship upon a painted ocean'. No one alighted, nor was there anyone sitting in wait for it on the wall. On such a day, 'blessed is he who stays where he is', I thought as the empty bus departed to Horwich. From there its custom was to turn round and return immediately to collect the children bunched in waiting around the school gate. As already implied, the return journey of the bus was a 'sleepers awake' signal for the village. Of those children who were not carried away over the water, the younger ones interminably climbed up and jumped down the post-office steps, then Mrs Birdwhistle's and finally, greatly daring, the School House flight forbidden by Mrs Plodder. Meanwhile the elder ones flashed around on bicycles: dizzy wheels powdering the grass with dust.

Eventually Mr Plodder and Mrs Mooney appeared round the vicarage corner. Nodding a mutual 'good-bye', she went through her gate while he mounted the steps to the green. At that moment Miss Whittle, revived at the sight of this daily ritual, came hurrying towards the post-office. With a bare acknowledgement in her direction Mr Plodder disappeared into his house. She resented the fact that he never took off his hat to her; and today he had seemed more off-hand than usual. "E's a dark 'orse, 'e is,' she remarked to Mrs Seed who, because of her deafness, shook her head and asked if she wanted stamps. 'Not fer me,' replied Miss Whittle tartly, 'I've more ter do 'n write mi time away. Too many folks around 'ere lives on paper,' (she gave me a look) 'wot wi Miss Morel an' suchlike making waste-paper o' their lives. An' wot does it end in? smoke!' She puffed contempt.

Mrs Seed looked reproachful at this half-heard pronouncement while Miss Whittle came to the point of her visit. 'I've clean run out o' tea. Can yer lend me a pinch?' Mrs Seed, resigned to this sort of thing, retired to the kitchen and returned with a quarter-full packet which she handed over the counter. A village post-mistress becomes a butt of borrowers. A packet of tea, a drop of paraffin, half a loaf here and there—not all repaid by any means. Miss Whittle had even borrowed the mowing-machine and step-ladders—this last liberty earning Mrs Birdwhistle's indignation: 'Wot's wrong wi an upturned bucket? Post-office ain't a bloom-ing public convenience!'

Meanwhile, as I stood in wait for a postal-order, Byrony came in. This was the first time I'd seen her since the pool episode, and I couldn't help staring, almost undressing her with fascinated curiosity. As once before, she seemed totally unconcerned. Indeed, her wide-apart love-in-a-mist eyes answered my gaze with unnerv-ing confidence. Miss Whittle gave her a sour sideways look and went out. Bryony, noting nothing, breathed fulfilment. I knew then for certain that she was in love, in the delicious stage of anti-cipation.

After a brief interval she told me she was on her way up to Sheephouse Farm to help with the hay. 'We were at it all yesterday afternoon. Why not come and join us? You'd love driving the hay-rake machine.' I wondered whether after this performance she cooled herself off in the pool. Anyway, she had no call to patron-ize—while she had made her own variety during the war, I had been concerned with the genuine thing, and was expert with the hay-raker.

In those days I used to get up at six in the morning to find that Ben had been out since half-past four. The actual start of haytime varied from June in a good year, with plenty of sun following sufficient rain, to August in a cold and patchy summer. However thin the crop might be, Ben only once delayed till August, by which time the grass had seeded, all its goodness blown to the winds, and the mouse-coloured hay fit for nothing but bedding. That year he had to buy fodder. Another farmer, intimidated by a run of bad summers left his hay out till September. There it lay, rotting under water, fit for nothing but burning—if it could be coaxed into flame. Though this man's field might have looked romantic in June—with yellow-rattle, a parasite that feeds on grass, and butter-cups freshly varnished amid frothy fool's parsley, it was poison to cattle. None of your twitches and dog's tail for Ben. His good meadow was laced with sheep's fescue, cock's-foot, clover, and rye-grass.

After the early morning cutting Ben went in for breakfast, and told me to return in an hour or two when the dew had dried. Then it was raking-up time—a job hard on the hands, good for the hips. Occasionally I was promoted to the spinner which, with its deli-cate spokes, resembled a catherine-wheel flying around flinging up wisps of hay. 'Now for the hair-drier!' Ben would exclaim glancing down the long rows of moist, freshly-cut grass. All three machines—cutter, spinner, and raker—were horse-drawn. Though this lengthened the working hours, it added, for me, to the romance of the labour. My view was coloured by the bright bay mare, Ruby, whose shining buttocks swinging before me as I drove gradually creamed into a surfy sweat.

This particular year, when I put the suggestion of hay-making to Aubrey, he agreed at once, delighted to help Ben who always welcomed hounds over his land. An hour later when we arrived at the farm we found half the village lending a willing, if inexperi-enced, hand. There were Johnny Thatcher, Mrs Dapple, Bob Taylor and the twins, and Ronnie Seed with Jimmy, now a tall, awkward lad of fifteen. As he raked the fresh-cut grass into waver-ing lines, his eye strayed to the curves of the girl beside him. Sally Haythornwaite last year had been leggy as a filly. But much had happened since her fourteenth birthday with the blossom setting, rounded and tipped with pink. Though naturally dark, her face and arms were not yet over-tanned—she was in the schoolroom during the heat of the day. All blushes, dimples, and shy smiles, she was at the stage of becoming, unknown to herself. But Jimmy, ignorant of a young girl's dreams, took the credit for these signals to himself. He was set on winning her back from David Mooney, now become a miserable bookworm who would never volunteer for hay-making.

Another in a romantic mood was Byrony driving Ben's dapple-grey in the raker while Michael, a new arrival, looked on admiringly. 'Fancies herself as Boadicea,' I whispered to Aubrey, who, preferring action to criticism, was selecting two wooden rakes, one of which he handed to me. Silently we joined the others in combing up the new-cut fringes into crescents—like waves of an incoming tide. After two hours' hot work only a handful of rakers remained in action; and my palms were so blistered that I had to give up. Ben, indefatigable, was still rattling back and forth like a shuttle in his new machine glinting red and yellow in the sun, while Bryony, seeing me idle, jumped down from her chariot and offered me the reins. Thankfully I climbed up into that little iron cup of a seat. Though the machine was clumsy and slow, there was deep satisfaction in bumping along behind the grey's ample hind-quarters and switching tail. And, at regular intervals, in pulling a lever to release a loose bundle of whispering grass. Elation at this exercise combined with the reassuring rhythm smoothed away any resentment towards Bryony and Michael—now leaning together over a gate and looking towards the sunset.

Presently Ben clattered to a halt; and in the distance I saw the four figures of his wife and three daughters coming towards us bearing earthenware jugs. With cheerful groans the last of the rakers downed tools and straightened up. And at Ben's signal we gathered together to receive mugs of nettle-beer or cider. 'Takes yer 'ead first!' Ben laughed and threw back a pint till his face glowed red as a Worcester Pearmain. Jimmy Seed and the girls drank the home-brewed beer, more powerful than its name suggests. Sally giggled as Jimmy slid an adventurous arm around her. 'My head's full of waltzing cottonwool!' exclaimed Bryony suddenly sinking down on a pile of hay. After the second round even the men were none too steady. Ben offered the jug to Bryony, but she shook her head: 'It's taken the edge off reality already.'

That raw cider, aided by the warm honey-and-clover air, was enough to unhook the lot of us. As I thanked Mrs Haythornthwaite for her strong golden brew, which had mellowed even her sharp tongue, I wondered if it had also blurred her vision of Sally running back to the farm—ostensibly for more drinks, which no one wanted, but actually to lure Jimmy, who followed behind, into the coolness of their still-room. 'Yes, it's Sheephouse draught—a bit tangy, but does its work,' she was saying, turning away from Jimmy and Sally to watch Bryony and Michael who were drifting away hand-in-hand. I tried to divert her gaze: 'However d'you find time to make it with so many other jobs? And what about the housework?' Mrs Haythornthwaite, having followed the pair out of sight, at last gave me her attention. 'Housework?' she echoed in astonishment. 'Oh, that's only a sideline.'

Impressed by this sense of values, I realized that for all her ambition and jealous pride of her daughters, she was a good wife to Ben. After his fiery outbursts he must have found her refreshing as rain. And when he was depressed—over a poor crop or a still-born calf, she could be as comforting to him as autumn sunshine. How she managed to damp Sally's ardour for Jimmy—newly-kindled after this frolic in the hay—which continued all summer, we couldn't guess. But she'd set head and heart on the vicar's son for her daughter. And sure enough, by the autumn Sally had turned away from her faithful Jimmy of the devoted dog-brown eyes.

Our walk home through the darkening fields took us past Primrose Cottage. Bryony and Michael must have gone very slowly indeed because they had only just reached the gate in front of us, in spite of a good half-hour's start. 'No use asking you in for a drink!' Bryony laughed as we drew level. We thanked her and said good-night. Just then the Newhall barn-owl gave a long wavering call—like a clarinet—from the nearby lime trees. 'Coming in?' we heard Bryony's soft invitation as we moved on, hurrying away from Michael's reply. As the wicket-gate clicked behind us the lights flashed on in the cottage.

19

Show Ring and Hunting Field

That summer yielded a record hay crop, but the rich grass proved too much for Richard's pony, Windri. After stuffing himself full as a bolster, he developed laminitis and became very lame. Though we kept him up, almost at starvation point, he did not improve. By now the summer shows were in full swing, and Richard, longing to compete in the children's classes, begged us to buy another pony.

It was Bryony who told us about Little Nut belonging to Jim Harker, a lean, leathery man who farmed the land beyond Anderton. We tried the bright bay Welsh cob over gates, bars, and an open ditch. His performance was superb. 'Mummy!' shouted Richard leaping down from his back: 'We *must* have him—he's a stunner.'

'An' yer can 'ave 'im fer fifty pound,' said Jim hissing through the gaps either side of his one front tooth. So we brought home our third pony.

Little Nut, hog-maned and dock-tailed, shone in summer more brightly than any polished hazel-nut. Moreover, he was equally round, compact, and tough. If his nature was sweet as his namesake, his mouth was equally hard—a fact not apparent when I tried him out at Smithills Horse Show. We never suspected his owner of being over-anxious to sell.

The cob, thirteen-hands-one in his three black and one white socks, was so much the smallest competitor in the adult jumping classes that he immediately became the focus of interest. Compared with the sixteen-handers ridden by the Colonel and Humphrey, he looked like a toy. And I had to crane my neck to look up at Aubrey astride his mountainous roan. As I rode round the enclosure in such outsize company my pride evaporated to hear someone comment: 'Sithee, 'e's no bigger 'n a guinea-pig!'

Indeed, after taking him to view the five-barred gate, I decided to withdraw. But his owner persisted: 'Go on, be a sport. I swear 'e'll not let yer down!' Wavering, I was lost, and endured frighten-

ing butterflies while Humphrey on a clumsy lolloper made twelve
faults—forelegs knocking down two bars, and bricks off the wall.
Next, the Colonel's chestnut refused the stile and retired. After a
few goodish performances came Aubrey riding Samson, expert at
the game, who took his time, reserved his strength, and achieved
a clear round. A storm of clapping made me feel even more inadequate, while Little Nut snatched at his bit, thudding impatient
forefeet into the turf.

When my name was called I felt disassociated from the whole
proceedings. As in a dream I saw my kind brother-in-law lower
the gate a fraction and give me a wink as I rode into the ring. Amid
loud cheers Little Nut flew it like a tom-tit, and was over the fence
and stile before I came to myself. The cheering was tumultuous.
Before us loomed the wall, and for once the cob, unable to see over
it, was daunted. He refused. The crowd yelled at me to turn him
round, ride back, and try again. Gamer and more resourceful than
I, he crashed into it knocking it down, and clambered over on to
the other side. I looked at the judge, but he nodded at me to proceed. Proceed we did—one foot in the water, one bar off the in-
and-out, and then . . . knotting and spreading himself like a
kangaroo he sailed gloriously unbelievably clear of the triple-bar.
The crowd rocked and roared and threw up its caps. With sixteen
faults Little Nut had won the day. We couldn't understand why
his one-toothed owner had let him go for fifty pounds.

We found out soon enough. Within a week we condemned
Little Nut as utterly unsuitable for any child—or any adult, for
that matter. To begin with he had only half a mouth—the left side
must have been numbed by brutal handling—and therefore could
only be circled to the right. Richard discovered this when he first
tried him out in Ben's twenty-acre field. All went well to begin with
as he did figures of eight on the right rein. But when Aubrey
shouted at him to change legs and lead with the near fore something happened. The cob spun round like a top uncoiling and shot
away to the left. Fortunately a six-foot stone wall prevented him
from disappearing into the next field; he swerved and bounced,
unseating Richard who hung for a sickening moment, left foot
trapped in the stirrup. Then, heedless, crazy, he pounded along
the length of the wall bumping Richard, head on the ground,
alongside. Those thumping hooves attracted another horror:
from a gap in the wall two huge hairy cart-horses thundered on

to the scene, manes and tails a-fling, nostrils a-flare, as they rocked and snorted galumphing within inches of Richard's body. Helplessly looking on, we both seized up. And then by a miracle the stirrup was released leaving Richard motionless in the grass behind those devilish hooves. By a miracle, too, the inflamed cart-horses charged ahead after Little Nut and his backwash of flying earth.

Not surprisingly 'Nuts-and-Bolts', as we sometimes called him, proved to be unsaleable: useless for children, he was too small for adults. But he was up to my eight stone, and there was plenty of fun to be had on him—if I dared—in the hunting field as well as the show ring. We decided to keep him for a time, and put him out to grass till October.

Meanwhile, golden day by golden day the year ripened with the corn, and bowed like a sheaf towards the autumn. Of all seasons autumn is the most harmonious with the twittering swallows balanced like crotchets on the telephone wires, and plumed seeds of rosebay floating soft as snow in the sunlight. When the bracken turns a warm fox-red village feuds seem to resolve themselves in the sudden realization that nothing lasts for ever. For myself, I have always preferred autumn to spring, especially in the north. Up here spring is captious and wayward, fooling us early in March with a spell warm enough to prise open the kingcups. Then a week later we may wake up to see crocuses thrusting purple fingers through a bed of snow. Plantings, sowings, and settings forth, though green-edged with promise, are sharp with uncertainty. And the word 'poignant', according to the *Oxford Dictionary,* means 'painfully sharp to the feelings'. That sums up spring for me.

Whereas autumn, all golden lights and leaves, is a season of gatherings: promise fulfilled; the apple in the hand. A rounded season completing the circle of labour in seed and egg, so that all things growing under moon and sun are curved in accord to the curves of space.

When Ben bought a machine which disgorged square bales of hay I believed it was the beginning of the end. 'Why,' he laughed, 'In America they're not even selling eggs in the round! Tak' up too much space in packing. They're breaking 'em into squares, freezing 'em, an' setting 'em into blocks—ready fer t'pan.' When it comes to squaring the egg I'm nothing but a round peg in a square world.

Autumn, for our household anyway, meant the start of hunting again. Richard was able to ride Windri, now sufficiently recovered for the bye-meets before the season proper, and I decided to take a chance on Little Nut, choosing a day when hounds met at the Cavendish Arms, Brindle—scene of my débâcle at the brook. This is a country of wide fields, fences and ditches. On that sparkling autumn morning the Colonel was mounted on the four-year-old chestnut thoroughbred, gleaming like a new-minted penny, which for months he had schooled for the hunting field. And for months, likewise, we had been schooled regarding the pedigree, starred with two Gold Cup winners, stretching behind this paragon of horseflesh now being shown hounds for the first time.

As usual when riding Nuts I was nervous—never more than a passenger on this twopenny-worth of muscle and hot Welsh blood. Though not speedy, Nuts of the iron mouth and will was totally unstoppable. With the one-track mind of a bulldozer, he simply went over everything that happened to be in his path. What was Brindle Brook to him? Or a fence with a six-foot drop? At this unpleasant obstacle he jumped so high under an overhanging bough that my bowler was swept off and I swept down (as in a lift) and onwards—hatless, helpless, yet marvelling to be still alive behind those indomitable black-pointed ears. From the height of a lofty hireling Aubrey occasionally encouraged me. 'Left 'em all standing at that post-and-rails!' he shouted as he thudded past giving me mud in the eye and hope in the heart. A few minutes later he was back: 'They're stuck at an awkward gate. Come an' give 'em a lead.'

Obediently I plodded along to where a bunch of refusers, including the Colonel, were digging in at a gate whose top bar was overlaid with a formidable tree trunk. Aubrey, piloting me, cleared the field and drew aside. My dock-tailed, nerveless Little Nut, now the centre of attention, arched his neck, snorted, and made three cat-bounds, prelude to a tremendous spring and bounce clean over without touching a twig. Three fields sped by before my Welsh marvel ground to a halt, so that I didn't see who followed in our wake. But for the rest of the day the Colonel refused to look at me.

It turned out, however, that even hurt pride came before a fall. During a slack interval later that same day I found myself on the heels of the 'new-penny' thoroughbred. I needn't have feared getting too close to those burnished hindquarters, so earning a kick or a vivid oath. Suddenly hounds were in full cry—music enough to go to anyone's head, let alone that of a green four-year-old. Like a flash, horse and rider were off downhill and out of sight. Minutes later I thudded round the corner of the wood where they had disappeared from view to come upon a group of riders dismounted. One of them was holding the Colonel's horse, and alongside in the grass lay the Colonel himself. Crumpled against a hedge his face, for once, was the colour of putty. Seldom had I seen anything alive lying so still—I hoped he was alive. Presently the one doctor in the Hunt galloped up, leapt off his horse and, nodding to us to move on, attended to the injured man.

Apparently the chestnut had stumbled in a rabbit-hole and come down. 'Folded up like a jack-knife,' someone said. 'Never saw anything so quick. Ambulance on its way—Sheila raced off to telephone.'

All at once the glory was gone from the day, and hounds were called off. For a week the Colonel lay unconscious in hospital; and our anxiety grew with each succeeding day. Humphrey, who sat by his bedside every evening, was nearly out of his mind. Then, on the ninth day came the good news that all was well; the Colonel would be back in the saddle within a month. We could have ill-afforded to lose so colourful a figure.

20

On Death and Birth

Whether or not the riding had aided Richard's recovery, he was now well enough to go away to school—and very unwillingly he went. But when Mr Plodder assured us that he spent most of his schooldays here cracking nuts under the desk, we felt that the time had come for a change.

Wrongly influenced by its position in the Lakes, we sent him to a spit-and-polish prep. school. Under the iron-rod discipline he was miserably unhappy. 'They won't even let you pick up snow here,' he wrote, and 'I have been put in silence for a week.' But it was the end-of-term report in the summer that finished the school for us: 'This boy not only knows nothing, but is unteachable.' And since health and happiness go hand in hand, Richard began to wilt. The ear-abscesses started again, and we were obliged to bring him home. A few days later he was in a nursing-home undergoing a fifth operation—a radical mastoid after the three mastoid operations of the war years.

It happened on a Good Friday, an unforgettable day with the cherry coming into bloom as we drove him in. Then, after being told that the operation was not quite straightforward, followed two unforgettable hours in the waiting-room. I tried not to watch the clock, but every minute the black finger clacked forward, signing away the afternoon. Outside a thrush sang in a flurry of blossom: 'Hurry! Hurry! Hurry!' The door opened, and Sister came in: 'He's all right,' she said. 'Come and see him tonight.'

For the next few days his life held like a fine thread. But on the fourth afternoon he seemed more than usually limp. On his bedside chest a thermometer stuck out from its cushion of pink gauze. Surreptitiously I took his temperature. It was a hundred and four. After seven weeks we were allowed to bring him home, and, as before, he made a slow recovery. Then came the day for his first ride on Windri—too distended with summer grass to move at speed.

One morning brought a letter from Irene telling of her mother's death. Could she come and stay with us? We were overjoyed to have her back, and though there were no lessons this time, Richard's exploits must have taxed her weak heart. As, for instance, when he called us up to his bedroom to see his home-made electric fire. There on the floor it stood, gleaming with challenge. 'Go on Irene,' he said, 'you be the switcher-on.' Rather dubiously she knelt down and pressed the switch to dart back in alarm as a blue explosion forked the room. Undaunted, he wired the hen-cabin, and made a wireless set—untrue to its name, crackling with complicated wires. Then there was the house in the tree outside the kitchen window. In this nailed-together nest of planks he would swing alarmingly to-and-fro daring Irene to come up and have tea with him. And neither of us will forget the wild afternoon of east wind with Mr Dapple knocking on the back door: 'Yon Richard's walking on t'roof—'e's got up by t'work-men's ladders.' He grinned in sympathy as we dashed outside into the gale to stand gazing up helplessly from the lawn.

The tent, a birthday present, provided difficulties throughout the summer. No matter how it rained he slept in it under the labur-num tree. Once during a thunderstorm Aubrey ran outside in dressing gown and slippers to try to persuade him in. But Richard shouted through the thrashing rain: 'It's lovely, lovely. Go back to bed, Daddy!' He ought to have lived outside.

Following this idyllic summer came a year with a vicar in Malvern who tutored him, treated him as a son, and led him to the standard required for public school entrance. But we chose instead a 'progressive' school, co-educational and vegetarian. (His last abscess cleared up completely during the first term, and he never had another.) But he didn't take to boarding-school.

A week before the start of his first term we were together in Ben's twenty-acre field catching Windri when he suddenly set down the bucket of oats he was carrying. 'Mummy,' he said, 'I don't want to go away to school any more. Please send me to the grammar school, and I'll promise to work very hard.' That same week he asked, during a game of 'Questions and Answers': 'Who's going to die first in our family?' And later that evening when Aubrey was saying good-night, he called after him: 'Daddy, when I'm dead will I be able to walk through walls?'

Telling myself that all was for the best, I saw him off to school from Piccadilly station, Manchester. He was still waving good-bye as the train rounded the curve out of sight. Suddenly I felt apprehensive, though he went off happily enough with a friend and my promise to take him out at half-term. This happened to fall during the fortnight we had already arranged for our longed-for holiday on the Isle of Iona, where, in the year 512, St. Columba landed from Ireland with his message of Christianity. We tried to alter the date, but every place on the island was booked for the season. After much discussion we decided to keep to our plans, and to take Richard out for the autumn half-term instead.

The first Sunday away began with a service in old St. Mary's and a glimpse of the reconstruction of the ancient Abbey. As we walked home I saw a new threepenny bit shining in the white sand. 'What luck!' I exclaimed, picking it up. The bright day ended with a sunset walk along the Machair where, looking out to sea, we shared our joy in Richard's restored life. After lingering awhile in the failing light we turned reluctantly towards our lodging place, Sithean (Hill of the Angels), a farmstead sheltered from the sea. In the distance I saw a man coming towards us—it was the shepherd who was our host. I wondered what brought him out at this late hour. Avoiding me, he went up to Aubrey and spoke to him in a low voice. I could only hear odd words, but instinctively I knew—Richard. Richard had been drowned.

When we returned home his last letter lay open as I'd left it on the piano before going away: 'Do please come and take me out. You haven't been to a half-term at this school yet. . . . I've worked out the trains for you. . . .'

All that had been built, brick by brick, was fallen in. I blamed no one but myself. We should have cancelled our holiday. The pitiless inquisition went on; and there was no answer. No merciful God bent down out of the sky to comfort and explain. It was then I discovered the only God I could know—in the kindness of other people. They helped in more ways than writing letters and sending flowers and coming to the funeral. But when that small coffin was lowered into the ground I could only echo the words of Oscar Wilde:

> All my life's buried here:
> Heap earth upon it.

And there under the grass he lies by the boundary wall of the peaceful churchyard—a few paces from John Fisher and family who lived in this house. No wonder the rooms echo with footsteps and memories conspiring against our resolution to leave. I felt more than ever like a cutting grafted into the bricks of its history.

In the weeks and months that followed I realized how little I had really known our neighbours. When I went into the post-office Mrs Seed's unspoken sympathy was my undoing. Sometimes I called on Mrs Dapple and though we talked about her cats and how Rosie Thatcher wasn't giving Johnny proper meals, a vital communication flowed at a deeper level between us. As for the Mooneys they were more than merely kind; they filled me with hope—of purpose in suffering, and relationships completed in 'another world than this'. Mr Mooney recalled the epistle for the Sunday of Richard's departure: 'I tell you, the sufferings of this present time are not worthy to be compared with the joy that shall be revealed in us.'

He didn't think of death as a tragedy, and had once confessed that he preferred burying people to marrying them: 'The day a man dies is the day he goes home. When he marries, why, you never know where he's going!' Mrs Mooney, instead of looking slighted, had heartily agreed. At least they saw life not as a succession of accidents, but as a meaningful journey. 'And those who die young,' Mr Mooney had continued, 'are especially privileged—their task here finished before they've had time for wrong-doing.'

When the vicar was talking about the 'fuller life', as he called it, his face lit up and his eyes shone so that you felt his vision to be far more than merely personal. All his parishioners were agreed on this, especially the Haythornthwaites. After their eldest daughter died of leukaemia, the vicar walked many an afternoon up to the farm; spent many an hour talking in their kitchen. 'An' every time 'e left us,' Ben confided, 'we felt proper lifted up.' He sighed deeply and shook his head. 'Ah well, I daresay as it 'ad ter be.'

On the whole country people, farmers and gardeners and those who live close to the earth, accept the fundamentals of birth and death, love, grief, and disappointment, with a grace that comes less easily to intellectuals. Aubrey, a born countryman, never tortured himself with asking unanswerable questions. He lived in a straight line and from day to day.

Before long Mrs Mooney had persuaded me to give talks to the

Mothers' Union, which probably did me more good than the Mothers. Likewise Mrs Plodder, still president of the Women's Institute, encouraged me to join, so that willy-nilly I was dug into the community, and was now on 'borrowing' terms, sure sign of integration. A packet of tea was to be had from the post-office, or half a loaf from Mrs Dapple. In return such things as hammers and hose-pipes went out on loan from us. And a system of barter allowed a loaf to be repaid by, say, a lettuce. These unwritten laws were violated only by Miss Whittle, who refused to buy anything that might be borrowed, and Bryony who took to borrowing strange objects from us. One day a clothes-line, then a hot-water-bottle, a dust pan—all spirited away never to be returned. I made up my mind to put an end to this embarrasing situation.

Months went by and she never came near. Then one afternoon, looking a little sheepish, she appeared at the front door. 'I've come to ask if I might borrow something rather surprising. . . .' Before she could finish I cut her short by burrowing into the oak chest beside the door. 'And that reminds me,' I straightened up, 'this time I've got something to return to you.' Triumphantly I handed her the red sandal, long-treasured and long-forgotten through the upheaval of Richard's illness and death.

Puzzled, she turned it over and over. 'Mine?' she asked uncertainly. Anyway, whether or not she remembered the occasion of losing it, she departed with hasty thanks, forgetting what she'd come for.

As I stood at the window watching the chequer of light and shadow upon the water and through the trees across the road, came news that a stranger was to arrive in our midst. Bryony was expecting a baby. Astonished, speechless, I came down from the clouds to hear Aubrey saying: 'Now you *have* put your foot in it!'

Eyebrows rose questioningly; unspoken questions hung in the air when her name was mentioned. But in view of Humphrey's grateful acceptance of a threefold cord there was nothing to say. And when Johnny Thatcher announced that Mr Marchbanks and Mr Laycock had been playing bowls together at the club and celebrating afterwards over several pints of beer, Mrs Seed shook her head: 'There's naught so queer as gentry!'

We wondered which of the two would be 'favoured' by the baby. Already bets were being laid in the club; and we looked forward expectantly to April.

F

April came and it was a boy. Would his blue eyes turn dark like Humphrey's, or his silver thatch brown like Michael's, we asked each other. But to Bryony, incongruously wheeling a pram instead of riding a pony, we could only exclaim: 'Isn't he lovely?'

She had us all foxed. Blue eyes and fair hair remained, and Julian John, as she called him, grew into the image of his mother. Bryony took to washing nappies as effectively as a hen-reared duck to water. I startled her one morning with her mouth full of clothes-pegs she was filling the line between the apple trees with those gratifying white squares. 'I love to see them shrilling in the wind!' she exclaimed standing back to view them with pride. She might have been putting out white flags in surrender to domesticity. The next moment I was following her tip toe to the pram in a corner of the orchard. Lovingly she lowered the hood a fraction, turned it ten degrees south to catch the sun on Julian's sleeping body while shielding his face. Then, finger to lips she drew me away. From the look on her face, we might have been visiting a wayside shrine.

The next thing was the christening. I'd expected Bryony to bap-tize her child in the stream. But no. After deliberating for a month she decided that Julian, with his two saints' names, should be re-ceived into the Church and given, as she put it: 'The chance now and the choice later.'

Everyone in the village was invited to the service and to tea after-wards at Primrose Cottage. I had agreed with some misgivings to be godmother, and thrusting away the past helped to decorate the font with lilies of the valley from our garden, instead of the white hawthorn she would have chosen in defiance of superstition. And thus we buried the sandal.

When the moment arrived Mr Mooney in his enthusiasm splashed Julian John so thoroughly that he yelled through the service beyond my power to quieten him. Later, at Primrose Cottage, Mrs Twigg was sipping champagne and prophesying the gift of self-expression for this child born under the sign of Aries, the Ram: 'Perhaps he, too, will be an artist.' At this moment he was demonstrating hunger with angry fists and screams. Mellowed by champagne and sunlight, nobody minded; and the vicar ex-plained that the infant was overcoming the devil by shouting him down. Mrs Mooney and Mrs Plodder, in concord discussing the next Rose Queen, took turns in rocking the pram so that their new-found agreement might not also be shouted down.

Meanwhile, Michael was making himself agreeable to everybody in turn. 'Though wot *'is* part is in all this, 'oo can tell?' Mrs Seed whispered in my ear. I reminded her that strange things happened in Rivington, and were even recorded on the gravestones. Immediately she pricked up her not-so-deaf ear, and I told her that according to an inscription screened by the holly tree the youngest of the Reverend Fisher's grandchildren, Alice, was born in 1834, seventeen years after her father's death. 'My, that wer a long pregnancy,' she exclaimed in delight. 'And believe it or not,' I went on, 'she was born in her mother's sixty-second year.'

'Go on,' Mrs Seed was laughing. 'A bit of a Sarah, wasn't she?' We agreed that if the stone told a true story, then the holly tree had seeded itself with good reason.

We remarked on the contrast between this day and the last occasion of such a village gathering—the Professor's funeral more than nine years ago. That had been a sombre affair: death in snow, black hats and port, with the Colonel being pompous and Mrs Plodder pouring her drink into a plant-pot. Just now the schoolmaster's wife seemed almost feather-headed as she floated up to the Colonel (one of the godfathers) of whom she usually stood in awe. From his splendidly moustached height he looked down on her as he might have looked at a partridge boldly advancing from the nest. 'About time we had some new life in Rivington,' she beamed, congratulating him on his godson. Then, as Humphrey came alongside, the rays of her well-being were switched like headlights upon him. 'A beautiful child, *so* like his mother . . .' she began, hardly protesting at her glass being filled for the third time.

Humphrey's lavishness with the champagne effectively blurred any sharp issues that might have arisen that afternoon. From now on Julian John was accepted as an asset to the village. Did he not provide Mr Plodder with a potential new pupil? While Mr Mooney was glowing at the reception of one lamb and one almost lost sheep into the fold. The two men stood together clinking glasses as they drank to an expanding future.

And so, with a death and a birth, the wheel once more turned full circle. May was giving way to June; the cuckoo's call faltered; and meadows foaming with chervil were threaded with vetch and red-beaded sorrel. Where the last patch of bluebells had withered away brand-new buttercups opened in the sun. Already a year had gone by since Richard's death, and I was cutting yellow flag-irises for his grave—the same yellow flags that grew so thick in the valleys of Iona this time last year.

'This time last year'—a phrase that drags you into pits of nostalgia. Yet in looking over your left shoulder you may discover how sorrow—after many years—can slowly be transformed, with anguish ripened into a state of creativity. All experience enriches, and suffering digs deeper than joy. Life has two hands—one to take away and one to give.

21

Fisherman Poet

Three summers before this, in 1946, a new and colourful figure had crossed my path—the angler-poet, Herbert Palmer. Old enough to be my father, he became my literary critic, mentor, and source of encouragement. And true to the two-handed nature of life he also became an active source of irritation—the necessary smarting sand in the oyster.

At our first meeting he seized joyously on the fact that I lived in Rivington—'An angler's paradise; I knew it as a boy!' he shouted, virtually inviting himself to stay the following May.

In Rivington, land of many waters, the coming of May means the rise of the may-fly and the appearance of fishermen. Because water is considered more important than people, the compensation of a little trout-fishing is welcome. And though many anglers look with contempt upon reservoirs, these are not to be despised. If the trout are small and few, they are happily uneducated—thus attracting both fly- and worm-fishermen. During the season these most patient of all human-beings are to be seen standing intent and still, hour after hour, on stony shores. Casting, reeling in changing flies; and content to toil all day and take nothing.

Once I applied for a fishing licence—merely for the pleasure of being allowed to climb the high walls that barricade ordinary mortals from a hidden world of reeds and willows, a lyric world inhabited by grebes and divers and splashing water-hens crying alarm from the rushes. Anglers enter a paradise all their own. To walk along the shores of Anglezarke is to feel a touch of Lake Country magic only slightly subdued by the grey film of industry. Here is a path through a wood whose branches hide the glittering water and give shelter to wood-pigeons and wood-peckers, while underfoot beech-mast and pine-needles allow one to travel softly as a cat.

The morning after Herbert Palmer's first arrival here was wetter than wet with the rain tilting slantwise in grey hill-weather fury. We needn't have worried that he'd be around the house all day;

on the contrary, blessing the weather he set forth arrayed in oil-skins and waders, and carrying a net and basket. It was after seven in the evening when his glowing face and grey moustache dripping raindrops appeared round the drawing-room door. Gleefully as a schoolboy he set down his basket on the sofa, opened it and displayed seven shining, speckled trout—that was the moment we nicknamed him Tarka.

But it was Herbert Palmer the poet I had first met the previous year when he read his verse to a gathering of the Poetry Society in London. At first sight he was wild-looking, almost repellent, with his glinting hazel-brown eyes, yellowing teeth, and voice rasping as a thistle. But when he began to read that farouche exterior was transformed. Grey-haired, dynamic, he stood and declaimed—a Blakean figure in whom 'Energy is Eternal Delight'.

After his first visit he often came to us for holidays in which fishing and poetry were happily intertwined. He loved the place, loved the house, and begged us never to leave. 'This is your destiny!' he shouted across the breakfast table. Certain that the house was haunted, he vowed he heard children's footsteps on the landing at night, and felt presences emanating from the walls. In company with Blake and AE he found nothing odd in the manifestations of spirits. As for the reading of portents, a rainbow or a pair of magpies might lead to a trail of speculations. When I mocked him he insisted that superstition is rooted in racial myths, and reveals the dark side of the religious image. At any rate, he was fascinated by this dark side with its daemons and devils; and we challenged his preoccupation with the idea of hell. 'Perhaps, like all true poets, I'm of the devil's party—but I know it. Milton didn't!' Roaring with mirth at his joke, he stamped out of the house to catch more fish.

If racing is the sport of kings, angling, he assured me, is the sport of philosophers. 'When I'm fishing,' he explained, 'my poems go on underground—or underwater.' He loved expounding, thrived on disciples, and was in his element when I invited people to meet him. One evening I asked Frank Singleton (my erstwhile employer on the newspaper) and his wife Rachel, my dearest friend, to dinner. Frank, a poet himself, has more respect for poetry than any other kind of writing. And though a brilliant raconteur, he was content on this occasion to sit at Tarka's feet. Indeed, Tarka's egotism was so outrageous, so superb, that there was little choice. Tonight he rode us full tilt. Unable to get a word in, we gave him our ears until, on impulse, I quoted some obscure, much-praised modern verse. I might have lighted a firework under his chair. He shot up spitting fury: 'Pretentious rubbish—written out of the top half of the brain. No spiritual light in it!' Having had his roar he sat down like a lamb and then, with supreme confidence, 'A major poet is never afraid of being downright and simple. Simplicity is a mark of genius.'

'Yes, Tarka,' I agreed, 'but why do you use such old-fashioned, even archaic language in your own verse?' Not in the least rebuffed, he rather rebuffed me: 'I never did wish to write in the peculiar ephemeral diction of my time. Nor did Shakespeare, Milton, and Wordsworth. Like them I have always sought a timeless language.'

We sat back, effectively silenced. Tarka set about re-filling his pipe—a ritual which began with knocking out mounds of black ash in the hearth. Then from a shabby pouch he dug for a fingerful of loose-leaved coltsfoot tobacco which he proceeded to roll and squeeze and stuff, all fraying ends, into the bowl of his pipe. Many matches went to that lighting, much sucking ensued to draw out the pervading clouds of smoke in which we were all enveloped. 'Never be afraid of being yourself,' he went on as though there'd been no break. He manipulated the matchbox to encourage a freer draw until his pipe hissed fiercely and sparks shot on to the carpet. 'Take no notice of fashion. When I read this modern stuff I can't remember a single line of it. Whereas,' he paused for another vigorous pull, 'genuine poetry clings to the brain.' He waved his pipe in the air as if writing this declaration in smoke.

All good humour, Frank put in a plea: 'I go with you most of the way, Tarka, but surely there are *some* contemporary poets who will be remembered? What about Eliot, for instance?'

'Eliot!' he thundered, rising to his feet 'I obliterated Eliot in my lecture at St Albans. I crushed, annihilated and utterly and finally disposed of him.' All at once he broke off and sat down. Then added with a rueful grin. 'And they only gave me three guineas for doing it.'

On the subject of fishing there was no controversy because we knew nothing about it. I used to watch him making flies, twiddling fragments of feather and silk into strange, exotic creatures the like of which I never saw beside an English stream. With a mother's pride he would survey his gaily-coloured offspring: Dark Snipe and Purple, Partridge and Orange, March Dun, Red Spinner and Soldier Palmer, all of which belonged to the world of poetry. The Red Palmer provided him with the best stories though he vowed that his namesake brought him ill-luck.

We were walking together along the stream one day when he suddenly bent down and demonstrated how, as a boy, one blazing afternoon, he had fished with the Red Palmer over a similar stretch of water. 'It was clear as gin,' he recalled, 'only a lunatic or a beginner would have dared his luck on such a day. But the fly dropped beautifully; and in less than ten minutes a mature trout slid past; had second thoughts; returned and bolted it.' He stopped, entranced by the memory before going on: 'He raced downstream, so I reeled him in and soon had him standing in the water below me. We had a fearful tussle, but I couldn't land him. To begin with I tried lifting him out, but he struggled above water like a whippet, and I nearly broke my rod. In the end I had to drop him back, and after several more attempts he got away. I nearly wept. The triumph would have been so complete.'

He walked on head down in front of me, haloed in golden recollections. Just short of the far wicket-gate we came upon two boys fishing a forbidden trout pool. 'Catch anything, gov'ner?' asked the elder holding out a jam-jar throbbing with minnows. The 'No Fishing and Paddling' notice was generally ignored by boys, always by cows who literally splashed contempt into our drinking water.

On the evening I'd asked the Mooneys and Bryony to dinner I set out to meet him—in case he forgot the time. It was a mild and early spring evening with the willows alongside Anglezarke breaking into the first yellow-green. All too soon I came upon him standing knee-deep in reeds at the water's edge—silent, watchful as a heron over his rod and line. The sound of his reel harmonized with the leaf-and-water music where silken ripples plucked at the roots of alder and willow. A mist of midges zig-zagged above his head. But Tarka, patient and gifted as his namesake, was longsuffering, even angelic when he fished. I called out to him. Without looking round he shouted back: 'I've been bitten something awful! I've had enough bites—from the midges—for a week.'

When we arrived home he took five trout from his grass-lined basket and laid them lovingly on a giant dish. He insisted that I cook them for dinner, but I pointed out that there was one short, and suggested splitting the largest fellow, a full twelve-incher. Tarka looked hurt, as though, like Solomon, I'd suggested splitting the baby in half.

After some persuasion he agreed, consoling himself that his biggest prize must have been a cannibal: 'Because I got him in the stream, and the acid in the peat-water here keeps them very small.'

Punctually our guests arrived, and Aubrey handed round glasses of sherry. Tarka drained his at a gulp and gratefully accepted another which disappeared in the same way. 'I drink wine like beer!' he exclaimed later at dinner as he tossed off a third glass of hock. A being of fire and air, he could never be quenched by thimblefulls, nor enclosed in the atmosphere of a drawing-room.

That evening we sat on late in a haze of tobacco smoke while our guest, mellow with wine and moorland air, dwelt on his favourits subjects : poetry and religion. Both had the power to soothe and to stimulate. We baited him, holding out first the red rag of modern verse and then the blue ribbon of border ballad. By turns he stood up and sat down; raved and rejoiced. The Mooneys led him on, and soon he was riding the wind, tilting at stars : poetry welled up in him and he carried us enchanted into the heart of the wild :

For the red grouse is a wilding bird that's mightier than the lark;
He's lightning to the weary heels, and drumfire in the dark.
I dread no more the tarry wheels that grind the pinewood track
For the voice of God calls out of him: 'Go back! Go back! Go back!'[1]

He could be thrilling and tender by turns, and caught up in a world of song his harsh voice became lilting and mellow. Believing himself to be a reincarnation of Ishmael, he read his own poem with the superb confidence of an Old Testament prophet:

And Ishmael crouched beside a crackling briar
Blinded with sand, and maddened by his thirst,
A derelict, though he knew not why accursed.
And lo! One saw, and strung the dissonant lyre,
Made firm his bow unto the arrow's spire,
And gave him dates and wine.[2]

[1] From *Summit and Chasm* (1934).
[2] *Collected Poems* (Benn, 1933). (Re-printed in Quiller-Couch, ed: *Oxford Book of English Verse*.)

During a rare silence I slipped on a record—the *Tannhäuser* overture. The effect was electric. Leaping to his feet he waved his arms in time to the music, and with flashing eyes proclaimed: 'My poetry is akin to Wagner's music!' But the great crashing harmonies overwhelmed him and he sat down. When the music died away he seemed unusually subdued for a while, and then quietly picked up the thread he had been silently following: 'I am a super-melodious poet and have also been compared with Beethoven. . . .'

'Oh no,' Bryony interrupted, 'You're pure Wagner—tempestuous and barbaric.'

'All great art is barbaric!' he cried triumphantly, standing up once again to hold the floor. 'A major artist works from the roots upwards. Think of Shakespeare, Rembrandt, and, of course, Wagner.'

'What about Mozart and Jane Austen?'

'Too "drawing-room" and mannered. I think the only composer I almost dislike is Mozart.'

For once he was drowned in dissent, and after a controversial interval Aubrey steered us into the quieter waters of fishing. Bryony disapproved of this sport as only one degree less barbarous than hunting: 'Whatever you may say, fishing with hooks is cruel.'

'No, no, you've got it wrong!' Tarka ran eloquent fingers through his unruly grey hair as he strode up and down the room. 'There's something akin to godliness in fishing. It's a delicate skill that makes men good-tempered and patient. A day's fishing will solve problems and dissolve anxiety. A bad man was never a good angler. What say you, vicar?'

'By some Divine co-incidence,' Mr Mooney acquiesced, 'the initial letters of the name and title of Jesus spell the Greek word *'Ichtheus'*, a fish.'

'Exactly. No wonder so many of the disciples were fishermen! Fishing is reflective, contemplative sport; it brings a man to himself.'

Overwhelmed by this torrent of persuasion, we let him have the last word; and satisfied at last he sat down almost purring in his armchair by the fire. After a pause he turned graciously to Bryony: 'You should read my *Roving Angler*[1]—much smaller, but I believe

---

[1] *The Roving Angler* (Dent 1933. Reprinted 1947).

even better than *The Compleat Angler*. This was no idle boast of
a book praised in *The Observer* as a leaf from Izaak Walton's note-
book 'with sunlight or green shadow on every page.' After all,
Tarka had for many years been fishing correspondent for the
Manchester Guardian.

Next morning it was raining hard enough to drown the daisies,
but he set off jubilant in the usual welter of oil-skins, gum-boots,
basket and tackle. 'It'll be a good day,' he announced, incurably
optimistic as he stuffed sandwiches and thermos into a haversack.
By half-past seven in the evening there was no sign of him. We
gazed through the window at cold rods of rain thrashing the
sycamores. 'I think I'd better go out and meet him,' Aubrey
decided, 'the old boy'll be wet to the skin.'

An hour later, draggled as water-rats, the two of them returned.
Tarka, rain-battered and exuberant, displayed seven smallish
trout. 'I had to throw five back. The best catch I ever had up here!'
Trickles of water from his oil-skins expanded into a pool on the
kitchen floor. He bent his head and a cascade flowed from the brim
of his hat. 'I fished the stream at the top end of Anglezarke,' he
explained ignoring my unspoken comment. 'The water was as
brown as Guinness—with a fine head on it. You'd have thought
the life-blood of the moors was pouring in. And *haven't* I had a
rough time—clambering over stones and nearly getting myself
drowned. The water was so fierce and strong.'

Tarka's frequent visits provoked comment in the village. People
wanted to know where he lived and what he did and whether he
was married. When I explained to Mrs Seed that my friend was a
writer and a poet she was unconvinced. 'But wot's 'is bread-an'-
butter?' A question prompted by his threadbare suit and well-
seasoned hat. Here everyone worked hard, and to sit down and
write was considered no job at all—as I had already discovered.
Writing might be tolerated as a 'nice hobby' for a married woman;
in a man it was seen as a sign of decadence. The village frowned
upon my eccentric visitor.

Though Rivington has attracted so many eccentrics, an off-
pattern and oft-returning guest is not so readily accepted. Mrs
Twigg, however, found his vibrations in harmony with her own.
'His aura glows,' she told me in confidence, 'a little redly, perhaps.

But then Mars was in conjunction with Saturn at the moment of his birth.'

A mixture of Wolf-Knight[1] and prophet, his vision was apocalyptic rather than immediate. He would wander round the fields wrapped in dreams, seeing nothing before him. And not only fields but also the house, which led to domestic difficulties. On one occasion after a hard day's fishing he went to bed with his boots on. Another time he used a new bedspread as a bath-towel. I reproved him, 'We might as well try to tame the north wind as teach you the social niceties.'

Everywhere he went he left a trail of spent matches and tobacco-ash. And at table, forgetting to eat, he would stare out of the window then suddenly get up to pace about the room expounding on poets and poetry. Yet something heroic shone through these disregards. He never flattered or deferred to gain recognition in the literary world. Nor ever stooped to insincerity. On the contrary, his habit of speaking the truth made him many enemies. Hating hypocrisy, he befriended every potential poet—and every potential angler too. He must have spent hours at the river side teaching all-too-impatient pupils the other art at which he excelled. It was this quality of patience so unexpectedly allied with passion that made him a craftsman—master of rod and line; maker of song.

And this quality won for him the ultimate admiration and respect of Mrs Seed. Her son Jimmy had suffered much over his rejection by that 'hoity-toity piece of goods', Sally Haythornthwaite. Lately he had taken to drooping around the house like a good-for-nothing—until the day he came upon Tarka fishing, and, watching fascinated, followed him home. Tarka, revelling in the thought of a new disciple, set about teaching the boy to fish. More than that, he inspired him with love for the sport till his melancholy brown eyes shone with enthusiasm. For Jimmy life began anew with thrilling days spent beside the stream or knee-deep in rushes at a reservoir's edge. He learned how to cast a fly, and soon hooked his first trout and brought it home for tea. Morbid longings for Sally's dark eyes were drowned deep in pools of light and shadow where if one fish slipped away another was sure to be found.

Tarka's triumph was completed the day Bryony and I accompanied him on a fishing expedition, along with the Taylor twins. It was a green-and-white May morning with the blackbirds singing

[1] 'The Wolf-Knight' from *The Two Minstrels* (1922).

themselves silly in the hedgerows, and racing clouds inciting us to follow, follow our leader over the hills. We waited in turn to climb the stile from Dean Wood into the field above Yarrow reservoir, but had only gone a few yards when we came upon Ben's prize Friesian bull grazing among the cows. This was an untrustworthy and belligerent creature, nearly always locked in a loosebox, though occasionally, trying to sweeten its temper, Ben would tether it in the small enclosure on our right. Obviously the animal had broken loose. As we approached it lifted its head in our direction, and snuffing in warlike manner lumbered towards the path to stand foursquare and menacing in front of us. Bryony cried out in alarm; the children shrieking with excitement clustered behind us. 'Keep calm!' Tarka ordered. 'Don't run away, and I'll master him!' So saying, he levelled his fishing rod at the animal's nose, and as it advanced snuffing steam and thunder he, too, moved forward one step at a time, fixing the beast with his eyes. The antagonists drew closer together; we drew back. The bull was tossing its head, whisking a muscular tail, and snorting big business. Trying to make ourselves small, we shrank behind our protector who, with deliberate slowness, continued his course until the tip of his rod was within an inch of the bull's flesh-pink nose and flaring nostrils.

The moment was suspended. Then, miraculously, the creature suddenly halted and swayed its lowered head from side to side like a metronome which Tarka's unfaltering glance brought to a stop. They stood there, locked eye to eye in motionless combat. The wind itself seemed to shrink around them; we spectators were unable to move a muscle. After a timeless interval the bull drew itself up, and with a powerful scuffle and bellow skidded round and made off to join the cows. So complete was our faith in Tarka that we continued behind him through the fields and past the whole herd.

Before nightfall this exploit was bruited around the village. From then on his battered presence was welcomed in the post-office. Even Mrs Taylor greeting him on the green addressed him as 'sir'. Quite suddenly he found himself in demand—if only as a fishing instructor.

Although we admired and appreciated his uniqueness, Tarka never settled down into being an easy visitor. A true poet, his spirit was untamable; and when roused to ire or exuberance he would shout so that he could be heard all over the house. His physical untidiness kept us for ever in search of papers, pens, pipe, and spectacles. If one worn carpet-slipper was downstairs, the other was sure to be up. Yet his scholarly mind remained logical and orderly to the end.

22

Race Days and Riding

After Richard's death it was Tarka who made me see that all experience, however painful, must be not only accepted but actually welcome. He encouraged me to write articles and give talks. Like a mother he nursed my first collection of poems through publication. He tutored, inspired, understood, and provoked me by turns. Above all, he kept me alive. 'And some day,' he urged, 'you must write a book about horses and hunting and life in Rivington. In another fifty years there'll be no villages like this—perhaps there'll be no more fishing. Thank God, I'll be dead.'

Next spring he arrived from his home in St Albans to find us frozen-up—water-pipes, stream, and reservoirs alike were silent and unresponsive. Up here spring often hides behind shivering fells until May when like a forward child it will rush forth in a burst of leaves and blossom, with the bracken uncurling green crooks above a mist of bluebells. And then, as soon as cotton dresses are put on, in goes the sun, and we're six weeks back in the middle of March. This year it meant long discussions indoors. After poetry, angling, and religion, his favourite subject was astrology. One afternoon over the tea-cups he and Mrs Twigg became absorbed in star-talk, so I left them in the clouds and went out to chop wood. Half an hour later they were discussing their previous incarnations—Ishmael and Bernadette—and the certainty of future meetings.

'Remarkable woman!' hissed Tarka after she had gone. 'She really does have contact with the spirit world. But her one foot on this earth is a very practical one.' A true mystic is Martha and Mary in one. 'Yes,' he growled on to himself, 'I feel myself to be on her wave-length.'

'Do you honestly believe in life after this?' I asked throwing a log on the fire. 'Don't we just burn away to ash?' He stood up and looked me straight in the eyes: 'No. Whatever I may doubt, I am certain of that. We have to go on whether we want to or not.'

Tarka's beliefs never led him to question the cruelty of blood-sports. On the contrary, his attitude to hunting was the same as to fishing; he was always encouraging me to encourage Aubrey to keep it up. But that season if fishing was off, hunting across the iron-buckled land was impossible.

Mid-March, in fact, sees the end of hunting and the beginning of training for the point-to-point races. With most horses being roughed off before going out to grass, likely candidates are worked up for the races. At this time of the year the Colonel and Humphrey settled seriously into their saddles. Every morning soon after six o'clock the village was awoken to clattering hooves as the two greys stepped briskly alongside the green. No trotting, mind you, nothing but a measured two hours' stiff walking. No matter how the frosty air nipped the rule was unvaried, except for a pipe-opener twice a week. This meant a glorious gallop on the moors in which Aubrey and I often joined, though by now I was reduced to riding Nuts, who was left far behind, like a truck uncoupled from an express train. Once again bets were laid in the village club—on the Colonel's Searchlight, who was local favourite, and Humphrey's six-year-old mare, Regatta, game and speedy, but green to racing.

At Moorside and the Yew Tree, hunt meetings gave place to even more frequent steeplechase meetings which lasted long into the night. And every Sunday morning the men went off to the racecourse to build the jumps, so that we saw less of our husbands than ever. Even so, since Julian's arrival Humphrey had spent more time at home and had once been seen pushing the pram down Rivington Lane. 'If it's not 'is, 'e's going ter show us as it *is* 'is!' Miss Whittle remarked to Mrs Birdwhistle. It seemed that Bryony had received the bath-water back with the baby, though at the cost of other interests. 'I've had to give up painting,' she told me, 'there just isn't time enough between jobs to get down to it.' This when Julian was several months old and a relentless tax on devotion. 'Of course, you can't talk to babies,' she went on, adjusting his pull-ups, 'and yet people say I'll never be lonely again. But I'm very lonely tied at home all day—I can't even go out on Pegasus!' For the first time Bryony was discovering herself as a woman in a man's world.

Meanwhile, fit men and horses became fitter; and arrangements for marquees, enclosures, and race-cards were completed well before the first Saturday in April, hallowed on huntsmen's calendars as Race Day. There was no soft treading for April's entry this year. The ground was still unyielding as rock; and every night Aubrey went outside and stamped on the lawn as though to stamp away the frost. Every day long anxious telephone calls were exchanged, and then, as if in answer to intense longing, the most sporting Deity ordained a thaw. The hard surface began to ooze, and flurries of snow whirled in the wind for three days. After much consultation these barely sporting conditions (apparently the Lord had only lent one ear) were gratefully accepted as just passable for the races.

On the great day an excursion coach was run through the village—the Taylors, Johnny Thatcher and Mrs Birdwhistle were devotees; and even Bryony was taking a day off this time. Many locals and most of the farmers attended the 'Millworkers' National' as the Holcombe Hunt Steeplechases are popularly called. A stranger to this meeting must be impressed by the vigorous northern mixture of millstone-grit, bright colours, and rich dialect. In a moorland setting, ringed by mill-chimneys and smoke-grey towns, a huge crowd is gathered. White tents belly in the wind; scarlet flags and white flutter beside fences; and jockey colours flash across moorland-brown and pasture-green. For sheer vitality no poet or painter could do better than capture the surging, seething spirit of the crowd and the quicksilver movement of horses weaving across the fabric of the scene.

Will the starters never get in line for the first race? A long, fidgeting pause and they're off—pounding along the straight, up the first hill out of sight, and back into view along the skyline. Oh God be with them in that thundering gallop from the top fence down to the perilous open ditch at the bottom of the hill!

'And on a bend too, by Jove!' a carried-away visitor cried out admiringly as his field-glasses followed the riders in this year's Ladies' Race. One and all they galloped fearlessly towards this bristling obstacle. 'Yes, it takes real courage to ride all out at that jump,' replied the Colonel whose own glasses were glued to the image of his niece, Sheila ('the Plaited One' of the hunting-field) as she streaked downhill, slim body parallel with her horse's neck. 'Steady girl, she'll never rise to it at that speed. . . .' But the nimble-footed chestnut mare gathered herself on the instant and with a

G

tremendous spring cleared the water by yards, a length and a half ahead of the field. The crowd roared.

She was still leading from a close bunch, rapid hooves drumming over the straight which was lightly powdered with snow. Now murmuring approval, now falling silent, the crowd watched them attack the hill on the second time round—degrees steeper than the one on the first circuit. For all but the most stalwart it was a hill of punishment. A third of the way up Sheila was overtaken by a great iron-grey Vulcan of a horse, who himself might have been forged on a blacksmith's anvil. The strongest animal in the race, he pulled slowly ahead into the lead, stayed, and won. But the cheering for the game chestnut only two lengths behind was even more tumultuous than for the winner.

Meanwhile Aubrey, enclosed in the secretary's tent, saw little of the racing. I never understood what mysteries were performed in that dim interior of money-changing, beer, and inquiries, hub and motive force of the entire meeting. The Colonel and Humphrey were similarly immersed for long periods, but just now they were both in the changing-tent, donning chequered colours for their epic ride in the Holcombe Hunt Maiden Race. This was the moment for which the two greys had for so long been polished and prepared. Bookmakers in full cry were tick-tacking and waving their arms with verve and passion—they might have been conductors of a vast massed band. 'Six to four on, Redskin! Two to one bar one, Comet!' In the excitement no one seemed to notice that the wind had dropped leaving an ominous calm. Bryony and I pushed our way through the crowd to the paddock where the silken darlings were being paraded in thick rugs emblazoned with coloured initials. The odds on our two had shortened from tens to eights. The Colonel was out first, his moustache more twirled than usual under a maroon cap as he mounted Searchlight, Number Four, in the ring. Humphrey's mare, Regatta, rather smaller, arched and bridled under a navy rug until the last moment when her owner appeared, lean, tall and dark in emerald and white quarters and emerald cap. The rest of the field was already cantering towards the start when he mounted. Regatta, who bore the number three, tossed her head, pirouetted and gave a graceful sideways buck—which he only just survived—and plunged ahead. We heard: 'They're off!' and had to wait while they disappeared round the shoulder of the hill. A few goosefeather flakes of snow floated in the still air.

At last they were breasting the skyline, over the fence, and charging downhill. Two casualties at the water-jump still left eight runners. 'Evens Comet; six to one Searchlight!' cried the bookies to our joyful surprise. A huge silence fell with the thickening snow padding tent tops and racecourse alike, and felting the hooves scudding along the straight. And now the hill on the second circuit. Redskin and Comet, bay and chestnut, were still leading from two others with 'our' two greys going well fifth and sixth. The first four clustered together at the turn; with the snow whirling faster every moment it was impossible to distinguish the colours. All we knew was débâcle at the water-jump and the two favourites out of the race. The following four separated, jumped clear and were lost to us in the crowd. We watched the two stragglers approach the water; one refused and the other fell. The going was becoming treacherous. Suddenly a voice ahead cried out loud and clear, 'It's Number Four: Searchlight! Searchlight first over the last fence!' And now we could make out the snow-speckled maroon cap travelling above the heads of the crowd, followed by two others—a blue and an emerald running neck-and-neck. 'Humphrey!' Bryony was actually shouting as these three came into the straight. Crazy with excitement we scrambled on to the roof of a van and watched them battling it out like toy figures in a snowstorm. The soft thudding hooves were thrilling to hear as the beat of muffled drums; and the crowd rocked and cheered when one of the neck-and-neckers challenged the leader into a neck-and-neck finish. All three wore white caps now. The crowd was bewildered; applause suspended until the judge roared through his megaphone the magic word: 'Regatta!' A torrent of cheering was loosed from the crowd who love a surprise victory above all else. For a green six-year-old to win a race under such gruelling conditions was almost unheard of. 'Be in t' National next!' grinned an admiring farmer.

Everyone in our neighbourhood had backed one, and some both of the greys, so a cheer went up from the green when the triumphant horse-box returned. With the vicar's sporting permission Humphrey and the Colonel arranged to give a party in the Sunday school. And it happened that the least sporting people, the Mooneys and Morels, were the first to arrive. No sooner had they got inside the door than Michael went up to Humphrey and shook him warmly by the hand. Humphrey seemed to have won on all counts. At supper he and the Colonel toasted each other because no winner could have chosen a better runner-up, and vice-versa. Mrs Darley, the Colonel's timid wife, remained at home. Unlike Bryony, she disliked racing, with its implication of gambling, even more than hunting. 'Vice in men, my dear,' she had once whispered in her ear, 'is more to be deprecated than cruelty to animals. Hunting *does* keep them clean—*don't* discourage your husband.'

23

Eccentricities

If spring brought the snow, the races, and the first swallow, it also brought the sheep. This, because the grazing in Rivington is unfenced, and at lambing time the ewes seek out greener grass and tenderer shoots than are to be found on the moorland. Towards the end of April we watched apprehensively our late-unfurled daffodils and newly-bedded plants. Sure as the first cuckoo came the morning when all were found nibbled away. The common vegetable-plots were similarly raided as the spring advanced bright with promise, sharp with vexation. As if marauding rabbits, moles, and slugs were not enough, Dapple cabbages and Plodder potatoes were all in time to be plundered by sheep. Even Mrs Seed's carefully fostered clematis was neatly nipped in the bud. Cloven hoofmarks printed our newly-sown annual bed; and not even the vicarage garden was sacrosanct. 'Those great lonks have bitten off all my pansies!' was the first complaint I ever heard from Mrs Mooney.

We soon discovered that sheep can jump anything—walls, netting, barbed-wire—to reach their bleating lambs always, for some reason, on the wrong side of the fence. Distance does indeed lend enchantment. For what more haunting sound than the sheep-lamb duet quavering from far, far away—redolent of shepherds among blue mountains? Not so the harsh vibrato of *Baaa* under your window at four a.m., endlessly repeated, endlessly answered till you are driven out of bed to make a cup of tea.

But the sheep, like the Great Snow, brought some compensation by uniting us as a village. We conspired to build better fences with the flimsiest material—poles, branches, netting, and sacking. Grimly we hammered wooden stakes into the ground. And after school one day when the sheep had come down as wolves on the vegetable-plots, we banded ourselves together to drive them out. Mrs Plodder plump and breathless, waving a broom, Mr P., a little behind, waving his arms, and in their wake the Mooneys, ourselves and the children in a cordon. The idea was to collect sheep and lambs into a bleating, baaing bunch before driving them out with shouts and rustic weapons.

Perhaps the Almighty disapproved of the vicar driving away sheep from green pastures, because one frigid April, after a funeral oration in the snow, the good man was stricken with pneumonia. No penicillin in those days, and as the crisis approached, Mrs Mooney got down on her knees and prayed as never before. Next morning all was well, and she went out into the yard for coal. There, lying stiff in her path, was a dead sheep. 'It died instead of him,' she insisted. After this the sheep were welcome to as many pansies as they chose.

At that time Mrs Mooney had other preoccupations: David for one. Now nineteen, he was travelling daily to a theological college, which meant rising early and working late, a programme he ran parallel to his love life. Yes, Sally with her black eyes and bright glances had prevailed, and kept him up even later than his books. 'It's a case of opposites,' Mrs Mooney declared. 'She never reads a book. I don't know how deep it goes with her, but she's got him hooked.'

Eileen, on the contrary, made a vow to keep her heart to herself till she had finished training as a teacher. 'My career is going to be fixed before my partner,' she decided. 'Partnerships dissolve but diplomas remain.' Nearly two years younger than David, Martin seemed indifferent to all local girls. Now a student at the Oxford School of Architecture, he was going through the 'critical' stage— not only of girls, but of parents and home. At this time we possessed neither Hoover nor fridge—acres of stone floors and slabs spared us the need for such things. And we were still shovelling coal into a voracious kitchen-range. 'You don't realize this is 1949!' Martin reproached us. 'Look at this horrible brown-and-cream paint— don't you know that brown and cream went out years ago? Stung by the criticism of a seventeen-year-old, we buckled to with white distemper and paint of pastel shades. And then, greatly daring, we bought a Hoover and ordered an electric cooker. For some reason the vibrations of the house refused to co-operate. No fewer than four teams of men with four up-to-date cookers struggled through the back quarters, but in spite of a new electric cable, each one of them refused to work. After the fourth failure the foreman scratched his head. 'I'm beat,' he said; 'nothing like this 'as 'appened in *my* lifetime—every cooker worked perfect in t'shop.'

His eye fell disapprovingly on the cracked sink, rose deprecatingly to the rusty ceiling hooks, and finally came to rest above the door where a row of battered bells bore witness to the days of servants. Under his disapproving scrutiny the grandfather clock growled and struck the hour. 'The only thing that goes in this 'ouse is Time, seemingly,' he mused picking up his cap. Before departing he suggested we try out an old-fashioned type of cooker which they happened to have in stock. We took his advice, and to our relief the back-dated, second-hand model immediately lit up and grew hot.

After this I did some surveying in the attic, hoping that we might convert the top storey into a modern flat. Crossing one of the dusty floors I happened to tread on a rotten board, and, to the accompaniment of a horrid rending sound, discovered myself up to the thigh in the room below. Startled and bleeding, I managed to rescue myself, and while being stitched up reflected that Fisher House had even taught me what it feels like to go through the floor. This one was removed by the Corporation, but our troubles were not over. A few years later we were dismayed to feel the floor in the drawing-room swaying so alarmingly during a party that once again we called for help. And they came and took that one away too.

During this period, with Richard gone, Martin away, and Aubrey involved in still more committees, I was glad of Tarka's tempestuous visits—his praising and damning of poetry in general, his interest in my work, as keen as that in his own, his denunciations and exuberance. Above all, his zest for life made life seem exciting and unpredictable. It was during one of his stays that I had a miscarriage. In my disappointment I blamed him—for being so stormy and provoking. 'Now I call that downright uncharitable,' he reproached me. 'You know I wanted you to have the baby—how could you blame me?' He was pretty well undauntable, and even when I had to retire to bed he departed with extreme reluctance.

No sooner was I fit again than he was back on the door-step complete with fishing-tackle, arguments, and enthusiasm. When next I discovered I was having a baby I kept him at bay for three months. And then, late in the summer he arrived, gentle as a lamb.

'If you only knew,' he grinned, showing his yellow teeth, 'I'm nothing but a sheep in wolf's clothing!' Always an optimist, he insisted that having a baby at this stage would do me nothing but good. 'Teach you patience,' he said, 'and you'll write fewer but better poems. In fact, I think you ought to have two more children—though this goes against myself. You'd have so little time for me.'

Though it was hardly primroses, primroses all the way, I did once again begin to feel stirrings of spring. That was the year we had our front-door painted yellow, and I insisted on a modern stove in the kitchen. Not daring to experiment with a new one we got this, too, second-hand. Though it didn't heat the water and cooked nothing more solid than meringues, it kept the place warm. And that was a triumph.

With the coming of the stove I was able to face the winter and look forward to the baby's arrival in February. Already we spoke of 'him' and his name was Nicholas.

The young days of 1950 were brisk with expectancy: something to look forward to is the best cure for looking back, and my present state of mind intensified everything. So that one frosty-bright afternoon returning home across the moors it seemed that the Green Withins beck wriggled like an eel beneath a skin of ice; and against a turquoise sky three stone-pines bristled black as flue brushes. Two top-heavy magpies tumbling among the branches recalled Ben's comment: 'Naught but a bag 'o feathers when it cums ter shooting!' At that moment came a new sound, fluty and faraway like sea-shells, and there, above me, was a skein of swans flying towards the west. Then, planing downwards in formation—perfect as ballet-dancers—they landed in a flurry of foam on Anglezarke reservoir: white wings thrashing through white spray.

Nearer home the big stars pricked out one by one, and ahead stood the vicarage poplar, tall and dark and slim as a broomstick beneath a sliver of moon. Now I was through the wicket-gate and crossing the green where the cottage lights shafted through the frosty air on to the grass. How I loved the place.

Candlemas Day came in with sleet; and after another afternoon walk—this time round Yarrow—I took a short cut home by jumping off a wall. Next morning, six days early, the baby arrived —a red-faced, auburn-haired girl—and immediately I realized that of course I wanted a girl. So Nicholas became Catherine. In this new-found happiness we asked one question—how would

Martin accept his seventeen years younger sister? Always reserved, he was more guarded than ever. Then one day I saw him, through the drawing-room window, examining the baby's fingers and toes, lightly touching her cheeks. The expression on his face dissolved all doubt. Not to be jealous—of my grief for Richard and joy in Catherine—was quite something.

Coping with another baby at this late hour seemed rather like being sent down to the first form to learn many lessons. And to unlearn even more. Washing nappies felt like washing out old mistakes. 'Quite a Lady Macbeth!' I laughed one day when Bryony caught me at it. All the same I found myself restricted, and became dependent on Mrs Dapple who came in to baby-sit. A true mother takes the process in her stride, whereas I worried over every rash and pimple. Vaccination, colds, and injections were torture, but in spite of all, Catherine thrived and was soon crawling so expertly that we blocked up every gap in the garden. Then one day she escaped. While I was combing the bracken at the back a loud knocking on the front door made me start up with fright. With thumping heart I raced to open it, and there stood Mrs Seed with Catherine in her arms. 'I wer coming round t'vicarage corner,' she explained, 'an' there she wer, crawling neat as a daisy round t'white line.'

One morning Bryony and I sat in the orchard exchanging views on the problems of belated motherhood. She complained that her painting was constantly interrupted. 'But it must be easy for you,' she added, 'to toss off an article in odd moments.' I pointed out that 'writing oneself in' requires just as much time and quiet and concentration as painting: 'You can't just seize a pen and sit down and write *words!*' At this moment Julian fell and cut his knee. He screamed without pause until Bryony picked him up and carried him to the kitchen tap. During this performance I noticed a red-checked cloth on the table set ready for breakfast, while in a corner stood a trolly arranged with the tea things. It was eleven o'clock, and Bryony followed my glance: 'Part of my attempt to make time. And if you look through the hatch you'll see lunch laid ready from yesterday. I've given up putting things away. A waste of time.'

I was pondering this Alice-in-Wonderland method of saving time by living tomorrow instead of today when Mrs Twigg came in with two red apples—one each for mother and son—to keep the doctor away. Julian, naturally, was a vegetarian baby for whom Mrs Twigg had foretold a mild and peaceable childhood. 'Children born under the Ram are *so* sunny and uninhibited!' At that moment Julian was in the sitting-room, alone and ominously quiet. 'Better see what he's up to,' Bryony frowned. We followed her in and there, black-faced and fisted, he sat by the hearth, a nut of coal in either hand, licking each in turn. Once more Bryony rushed him to the tap. 'Let him eat coal,' smiled Mrs Twigg. 'He's taking in, unconsciously, all the carbon he needs from our buried forests. A true vegetarian baby, bless him.'

Both she and Bryony shook their heads over the barbarous diet of liver and herring-roe spooned into my red-blooded infant, though they couldn't deny that she was far the more contented child of the two, sleeping long hours, waking with a smile, and cutting teeth without tears. Whereas Julian was rampageous and destructive. 'He'd grow up to be a murderer if I fed him on meat!' Bryony laughed, and Mrs Twigg, convinced that red blood inflamed the animal passions, agreed that this would be tempting providence because Arians can also be wilful and ruthless. She suggested that Catherine's vibrations might be raised and quickened by a more enlightened diet: 'Rarefied food makes a rarefied being.' But I remained obstinate, partly to avoid schism in the home—I could never convert the men to lettuces and nuts—and partly to avoid becoming a social nuisance.

A new baby means numerous visitors—never before had so many people come to tea—curious to see how I was 'making out' after this long gap in motherhood. On the hot summer Sunday of our church 'Sermons' day I had invited the preacher, the Dean of Manchester, his wife, and two friends for tea in the garden. Martin, home for the week-end, was entertaining three of his friends on another part of the lawn. That made ten. Before half past four eleven others just turned up.

When, therefore, one Saturday afternoon, at the ungodly hour of half past two, there came a vigorous knocking on the front door I groaned and went reluctantly (in my old clothes) to answer it. Two strangers, a tall man and a girl, stood outside. 'My name's Harry Pilkington, and this is my daughter,' the man introduced himself. 'I wonder if I might ask you some questions?' Mystified, I invited them in. He wanted the name of my father's mother. 'Didn't you know,' he went on, 'that we share the same great-grandmother, Eleanor Pilkington? And she is directly descended from the Richard who built your church?' This was the first I knew of it. Nor had I realized that this Eleanor was also Aubrey's great-grandmother—for we are second cousins. We were equally surprised to learn of our cousinship with Sir Harry (now Lord) Pilkington, the glass millionaire and so modest and gentle a man. Perhaps, after all, destiny had guided us to Rivington where the Pilkingtons had been lords of the manor since the Conquest. Sir Harry went on to tell us how in 1605 Richard's grandson left the Hall to the last Pilkington to have a share in it. Her name, like the first of the Rivington branch, was Catherine.

All this while Sir Harry's daughter had sat silent and dark, listening to the talk. We heard nothing more of her until some years later when we read in the *Guardian* of her tragic death by drowning. Her name, too, was Catherine.

After this visit I got hold of the family tree and discovered that the eldest son of the last Rivington Pilkington was Richard, who died young, while Catherine was his years-younger sister. How strange that knowing nothing of this we should have chosen the names Richard and Catherine for our own children—both, as I thought, by chance and at the last moment. Stranger still was the unfolding pattern of life which had brought our Richard to rest near the only remaining wall of the church built by Richard, his ancestor. And now here was Catherine growing up in the same place.

24

Ringing the Changes

By now a new batch of children were shouting around the green; and once more our garden became the focal point. The back door grew hot with the knocking of another generation. The new estate agent, Mr Patchett, successor to Bob Taylor, had four children under ten; and the Dapples' neighbours were shaping towards half a dozen. Across the road things were quieter. With David and Eileen away, the vicar was enjoying the peace of a childless household while he pored over his book on folklore and fairies. 'He's living in a new Celtic Twilight,' Mrs Mooney confided. 'It's a good thing *my* head is well screwed down on my shoulders!'

Not only at church council meetings, but even in church the vicar became abstracted, lost in visions and dreams. After the early morning Communion service, for instance, he seemed to float away from us forgetting the final 'May the peace of God. . . .' The third time this happened Mrs Mooney stood up in her pew. 'Please dear,' she said as he gathered up the chalice, 'May we have the Blessing?'

Apart from new neighbours we also had a new Waterworks Engineer, which made me realize that we were being slowly engulfed by another tide of trees, and that I should be driven to seek his help in having some of them cut down. More than twenty years had gone by since we came to Rivington, and Johnny Thatcher was now over seventy. The Plodders were streaked with grey, and Mr P. had to be careful of his heart.

But at Primrose Cottage the threefold cord still held—to prove that in some marriages three are better than two. Except at weekends Rivington was not changed. As Johnny had truly observed: 'Only t'trees an' people cum an' go.'

Nor did we wish our village any different: living here on unassailable land makes conservatives of us all. 'I hate all changes—even changes for the better!' declared the Colonel at a parish council meeting discussing the future of Top Barn where big changes were already on the way. This barn belongs to Rivington Hall, seat of the Pilkingtons until the early seventeenth century when it passed into the hands of the Breres. By which time the original hall of wood and plaster was largely pulled down. It was pulled down still further in 1774 by Robert Andrews who built the Georgian mansion of wallflower-coloured brick which stands to-day. After the Andrews came the Cromptons, one of whom lived at Fisher House after marrying the niece of its owner, Aunt Dorcas. They were the last family to drive carriages and pairs up and down the avenue of chestnuts.

The Colonel stood out against tarmacing this sandy drive. 'We'll only be inviting racing cyclists and sports cars,' he pleaded. But so it came about. Soon after this Rivington's finest beeches were felled. Not even the Corporation of Liverpool could deny that their roots were undermining the Hall's foundations. 'Let 'em be undermined,' groaned the Colonel,' and we'll be spared a deal of noise and trouble.' True blue words to be ground down by the wheels of progress. Top Barn, thirty-five yards long, had been stocked during the war with sacks of flour and sugar—those immediate necessities were hardening like rock while we were pulling sledges to Horwich for food. Outside, concrete blocks, Nissen huts, and barbed-wire made the park look like a concentration camp. Through the dead years these remained to be overwhelmed by spring tides of scrub and willow herb. Gone for ever was the sylvan paradise left by Lord Leverhulme to the people of Bolton.

Soon after the war the Barn was stripped of cobwebs and mouldy stock to make way for a very different traffic under its massive timbers. It became a vast restaurant and dance hall which radically changed the character of Rivington, Village of the Mountain Ash. Yet it brought pleasure to thousands who drove out at weekends parking their cars around both Top and Lower Barns, and on every available verge. Thus our sleepy summer Sundays were shaken up so that windows rattled, and you hardly dared to cross Sheephouse Lane after midday. During the height of the season we sat indoors, windows shut, while motor-bikes roared back and forth across the water, uphill and down.

In vain the Colonel protested against indiscriminate parking, transistors, and litter. The rising tide of democracy surged over us; at week-ends we rivalled an inland Blackpool. 'The sheep's in the meadow; the cow's in the corn!' sang Ben Haythornthwaite at the sight of picnickers spread out in his hayfield, and family cricket-matches enlivening the best pasture. The Colonel, anxious for the safety of his animals, erected forbidding notices on the drive gate: Beware Horses! Beware Dogs! under which some wit from the town inscribed in large letters: Beware Tenants!

New neighbours meant new dogs. And now Miss Whittle, to compensate for the loss of Chink, kept two Alsatians penned up in her yard. Every visitor and van resulted in a storm of barking enough to drive us crazy. When Mrs Birdwhistle demurred she was told to be grateful for the protection of two guard-dogs. 'Guard dogs, my foot!' she retorted. 'Why, if Jesus Christ hisself came by they'd tear 'im ter shreds.'

Soon after this, at a Women's Institute meeting we were asked to submit resolutions which, if accepted, might eventually reach Parliament. We listened to Miss Whittle's uncomfortable sugges-tions—a tax on cats and bicycles, and the banning of fireworks. An idea came to me. I stood up and proposed a tax of one pound on dogs, and heavy fines for those penned up. Mrs Mooney, Mrs Seed, and Mrs Birdwhistle chimed out: 'Hear! Hear!' which provoked a torrent of dissent.

In England, where the Dog is the sacred animal, such a subject cannot be rationally discussed. This particular evening we were divided at many levels. Mrs Haythornthwaite declared that dogs are meant to work, and accused me of keeping a sheep-dog with-out any sheep. True. But Bobbin was so well-exercised by long walks and longer rides that he reserved his noise for the postman, milkman, and butcher. Furthermore, he was obedient, unpam-pered, in fact a real dog—often seen but seldom heard. Protesting that I was not anti-dog, but anti-barking, I nearly lost Mrs Plodder's goodwill for ever; and caused another cat-and-dog fight between her and Mrs Mooney, still smarting from the demise of Mimi. Mrs Birdwhistle intervened: 'Dogs are noisy, smelly, and destructive. Dogs are scavengers; they mess pavements, cause acci-dents and give children worms!' Which provoked a chorus of: 'Dogs are man's best friend ... More faithful than people ... A world without dogs would be dead!' The battle raged on till nearly ten o'clock—bus time; and the evening's dignity was barely res-tored by Miss Jackson sitting at the piano and thumping out 'Good-night, ladies!' with the loud pedal pressed down.

Relations in the village were strained for some time after this. We endured the Alsatians in silence. Then a few weeks later came news of disaster: fourteen of the Haythornthwaites' sheep had been worried by dogs. 'The field wer like a slaughterhouse!' Ben almost exploded with rage and dismay on our doorstep. The Alsatians, Rinto and Tinto, it seemed, had escaped the previous night and by moonlight started running the sheep. 'It wer Sal wakened first wi' t'noise,' Ben went on. 'She cum running into our room shouting an' blocking 'er ears. I git up an' ran outside, an' th'air wer thick wi' groans an' gurgles from t'sheep. An' them two damn dogs ravening wi' blood—round an' round in circles. I'll never git o'er it.' At the time he had scrambled into his clothes, reached for his gun and, exercising sufficient control to keep himself hidden behind a wall, waited until the dogs were in range, and shot them both. Fourteen of Ben's best ewes was a high price to pay for peace and quiet.

But calm, bright days, like beads, are strung on a tenuous thread. Later that same year, one wild September night a thunderstorm struck the gable-end of Sweetloves, and left one bedroom roofless except where the bristled top of a stone-pine writhed above crumbling walls. Next day the Corporation engineer walked up to assess the damage. In a landlord's eyes Sweetloves was an even greater liability than Fisher House. Not only did everything leak, there was not even a road for a car—let alone lorries for vital repairs. After much consultation it was decided to pull the place down and install the sisters in a modern bungalow on the Rivington boundary. How many more houses, we asked, were to go the way of the wind?

If the Morels were provided with a bungalow, Michael was left, literally, with no roof over his head. Then one afternoon at the post-office Mrs Seed told me that he had found shelter at Primrose Cottage—where she had directed him when he first came to Rivington. When next I went to see Bryony I found her light-footed, light-hearted, springing from house to garden, and hanging out sheets with the verve of the newly-wed. 'It's only a temporary arrangement,' she explained, her mouth full of pegs. But shrewd Mrs Birdwhistle took a longer view: 'Well, now she's got a permanent baby sitter.'

25

Wedding Ring

One thing that had not changed was David's affection for Sally. Now a tall, pale curate of twenty-three he remained faithful to his first love. And she with her wild gipsy beauty, skin the colour of wheat, and long lashes curving like black daisy petals, had set her eyes on no one else since she set them on him. In spite of Mrs Seed's refusal to believe that 'bold Sally', as she called her, had scored a bull's eye with the vicar's son, the wedding was fixed for next month. Mrs Mooney took a more charitable view. Rose-Queen rivalry long forgotten, she welcomed her future daughter-in-law who was intelligent as well as beautiful. Though Eileen, now a teacher, had skirmished on the edge and refused to be drawn in, she had been won over in the end. Sally had protested that she'd call the wedding off unless Eileen consented to be chief bridesmaid.

And that was a wedding to remember—a real country wedding heralded by the red moon of harvest coming up over the Pike, and the blackberries gathered for wine. Because no farmer can give his heart to such revels with the ripe corn standing, Ben, this year, had cut his oats a week early. It was a full crop, rustling-dry; and Ben who reaped the only cornfield in Rivington drove his machine with the pride of a charioteer. After a long day's work his rounded hilltop, smooth as a shaven head, glistened with stubble; and the drop-eared sheaves bowed over one another with the weight of their offering.

The wedding took place the day after the stacking of the corn. One barn, kept empty for the party, was decorated by Sally's mother and elder sister with oat strands, flowers and fruit like a proper harvest home. 'Now is the ripe time, the right time for a wedding!' laughed one to the other; and Ben, pinching his wife, the plumper of the two, praised the longer nights and the bedding of the straw above the starkness of spring. 'Too cold up 'ere in April—an' too much ter do in t'day time!'

As for the church, Mrs Mooney and her 'Mothers' excelled themselves in preparation for the Harvest Festival happily arranged for the Sunday after the wedding. Corn-sheaves, cauliflowers, melons and marrows abounded. Tomatoes, shining red like billiard balls, adorned every window-ledge; and pyramids of apples and pears basked in the stained-glass sunshine. From the hooked beak of the lectern-eagle was suspended a bunch of grapes large enough to diminish its dignity and authority. But when we demurred at this the Mothers refused to defy tradition. 'Feed grapes ter th'eagle,' reasoned Mrs Birdwhistle in a surprising burst of poetry, 'an' t'lessons 'ull bear good fruit.'

Font, reredos, and pulpit, aglow with marigolds and ruby-red dahlias, were transformed into flower-show exhibits. Two baskets of eggs and twin giant cornsheaves, were offered with plaited loaves beside the prayer-desk. Even the central candelabra was wreathed in roses. So that when Sally, curved seductively into white satin, dusky under floating veil, glided up the aisle on Ben's left arm ('I mun 'ave mi right free ter defend 'er.') she struck the single virginal note among all this rounded fertility. Jimmy Seed, now heart-whole, had pulled the solitary bell at racing speed while Ronnie galloped on his heels with the friskiest bridal march ever heard in church. Already bride and groom were standing side by side, kneeling and making their vows. During their brief absence in the vestry the petalled hats of the congregation fluttered to a murmuring crescendo, were hushed to audible silence as the wedded pair reappeared and stepped confidently down the aisle. Eileen, red hair shining, was followed by a cluster of small bridesmaids bunched fluffy as chickens into yellow tulle.

Up at Sheephouse trestle-tables spread with white linen and ivy trailers, offered every imaginable sort of home-grown food from hams and poultry down through the scale to sandwiches and cakes, fruit, nuts, and sweets. Corks exploded from bottles of elderberry, blackberry, and, best of all, parsnip wine. I found myself in the appreciative company of Mrs Twigg and Bryony, both glowing over wineglass rims and enthusiastically offering each other nuts in nibbling agreement. 'When the Church and the earth are united, all is harmony,' announced Mrs Twigg raising a glass to the young couple now hidden behind the giant wedding-cake. She strained on tiptoe for a better view. True enough, young David was full of the spiritual ardour of the newly-ordained, while his bride, rounded with the ripeness of growing things, represented the good earth. 'And did you notice the dominant colours in church?' Mrs Twigg went on. 'Red and yellow: passion and inspiration intertwined? Saturn in conjunction with Venus. . . .' She dwelt on the thought and sighed deeply, perhaps pondering on the deficiencies of Mr Twigg.

At that moment Anna came up. Since she had left Sweetloves and taken another teaching job, we saw little of her. Bryony greeted her with the graciousness a woman with two men can afford for one with none. But something had happened to Anna—a bloom on her skin seemed to come from within; and there was new light and depth in her hazel eyes. Always beautiful, she had before carried with her an air of sadness. Now she rippled with life, supple as a spring willow in every movement. Just now she was smiling at Bryony's confidence, holding up her wine-glass, turning it delicately as if it were a flower. No looking over the left shoulder, only spontaneous pleasure in the moment which had nothing to do with the strong country wine.

Today, even Mrs Plodder was expanding under the influence of fermented parsnip. As she held out her glass for a refill she explained that beverages made from fruits were permissible, even to teetotallers. 'I never touch anything bought and labelled,' she blushed. And then, fortified by another sip, 'We can't forget the turning of the water into wine.' She lifted her glass to the light: 'Pure vegetable juice and sun!'

'Go on,' teased her husband, 'down it—we're here to enjoy, not to justify.'

A rapping on the table announced that the bride was about to cut the cake. At Ben's request the first slice was hacked out with a harvest knife while he murmured something about the throwing of the corn. Humphrey, always on warm terms with Ben, proposed the health of the bride in his usual clipped and courteous fashion.

'*Such* a gentleman,' sighed Mrs Plodder, 'and *so* much to put up with—'

There were rumours that the Marchbanks were soon to leave the district, and in Michael's absence (he hadn't been invited) Bryony drifted towards Anna. Together the three of us watched Sally, dewy as a moss rose, blushing at Humphrey's compliments while looking up with frank adoration at David. He, paler than usual, seemed overwhelmed by the sudden silence, and unable to speak.

Then, hesitantly, he thanked us for coming and for our presents, thanked the parents for their 'considerable' part in the production of Sally, but when he looked at Sally herself he could find no more words.

'Well!' exclaimed Bryony after the speechifying, 'He *has* got it badly! First love. But it doesn't last.'

'You're a cynic,' replied Anna. 'Sometimes it matures, like wine, into something far better. Tested by time.'

'Wait till your turn comes. . . .' Suddenly Bryony viewed Anna with suspicion: 'You look very happy today—what's the matter with you?'

'Matter?' she laughed.' I suppose *you* would call it trouble—and the trouble is I'm going to be married myself.' Bryony's gasp of surprise was interrupted by someone urging us to look at the presents laid out in the farm parlour. Just now the table-lamps, arrays of silver and glass were obscured for us by overriding curiosity at the enigmatic smile on Anna's face.

After an aimless interval with the bride off the scene, we found ourselves clustered in field and farmyard for a view of the send-off. The Seed boys were deluging the bride with a mixture of confetti and crushed oats—enough to keep a horse for a month. 'Put yer on yer mettle!' sang Jimmy as she struggled into the black hired car while clutching a petalled velvet hat of forget-me-not blue.

And so the harvest moon rose on a wedding that signified both the end and the beginning of an era with the older folk's children grown up and marrying, and a new generation shouting around the doorsteps; with vicar and schoolmaster turning grey, and new families moving in. Next day when Bryony came to collect Julian, half-buried beside Catherine in a pile of leaves, we congratulated each other on the grubby, demanding infants who prevented us from growing old in peace.

26

Full Circle

The years flew by and once again I was taking a child to school and cooking twelve o'clock dinner. Ideas of writing were submerged in the immediate business of bringing up this daughter who was already visiting Mrs Dapple and asking school-friends home to tea. I found myself making friends with the young mothers of Catherine's friends and once more involved in children's parties. Involved also in household troubles. When the pantry fell in and the roof was declared unsound, we girded ourselves up, and for the second time went in search of a new house.

The bungalow we looked at boasted everything that Fisher House lacked—from labour-saving kitchen to underfloor heating. The rooms were square, sensible, airy. And the sun beat unimpeded through wide one-pane windows from which we observed the tiny, orderly, treeless garden. 'No more dark days here,' Aubrey echoed my thought. And no view either—except of identical bungalows and garden patches. We looked at each other across the raw characterless sitting-room and once again fled back to Fisher House.

Apart from structural difficulties, our 'help' problem had increased with the years. Even 'dailies' prefer town to country; a modern house to one like ours. Then one day an Irish widow, hardworking, well-mannered, and one of the 'old school', applied. For nine blissful months we saw her as a flawless treasure. Then suddenly my rose-coloured spectacles broke to the fact that cups, plates and other trifles were vanishing overnight. Aubrey missed one of his carefully-fostered cyclamen plants; the hens withheld their eggs, so that I made up my mind to call on Mrs Reilly who lived in Wigan. She was out, but her daughter-in-law invited me to sit down while she made a cup of tea. With some embarrassment I observed the table spread with our (admittedly faded) willow-pattern cloth. On a shelf a long-lost coffee cup and saucer sat beside a familiar china foal minus a hoof. Other half-forgotten friends confronted me at every turn—that hunting-scene tray (a wedding present), a never-used gong, and a tea-caddy. Determined to see no more, I turned my gaze to the window and, blow me down, there was the pink cyclamen peeping roguishly between the curtains. Tea arrived and was poured out from our neglected pewter teapot, now winking new. 'Sugar?' enquired daughter-in-law helping herself from the companion basin. 'No thank you,' I replied getting to my feet and making for the door. 'Just tell Mrs Reilly I called.'

Miss Roberts, on the other hand, touched nothing but drink. One day I filled a whisky bottle with cold tea and quinine, lightly powdered the neck and went to the hairdresser's. On returning I discovered the expected finger-marks grasping the bottle, after which I withdrew my net from town, and relied on the good countrywomen nearby.

As we grew older the need for an easier-to-run, more comfortable house was opposed by our deepening roots. We looked over many houses, but not one had the character, situation, and charm of our own. Where in England today, within reach of friends and cities, can you step out of your own front-door and walk for miles across unspoiled moorland? But time was bending our neighbours, if not ourselves, to its will. One brisk March day of lamb-fleeced clouds Mr Plodder had a stroke. He died the same evening; and the village mourned as it had never mourned before. We couldn't believe that this familiar figure would be no more seen rounding the vicarage corner at five to nine every morning. Mrs Plodder and Mrs Mooney wept on each others' shoulders : they were now firm friends, and Mrs Mooney lamented the inevitable departure of Mrs Plodder—from School House—as much as that of her husband. But Mr Mooney himself was growing frail; soon after the Plodders had left he retired to Ireland. And that meant good-bye to two good friends. A few months later Mrs Seed rocked herself to sleep and out of this world. All this meant a new vicar, schoolmaster, and postmistress, so that I dare not write a word about them except to say that the postmistress has set up a little shop, and nevermore need we run out of tea.

Though Rivington still remains an oasis for refugees from the world of industry, we who live here have been deeply affected by the grievous changes around us. Depression in textiles reached out an arm to our green valley as mill after mill was closed down or taken over. Colonel Darley, retired by his firm and too old for another job, retired properly with his wife to a bungalow on the south coast. Perhaps not a change for the better, 'But at least,' he consoled himself, 'we'll be free of midges, sycamores, and puddled clay!' Soon after this Humphrey was made redundant and found work elsewhere, so it was good-bye to him and to Bryony who had brought such colour into our lives. They gave a farewell tea-party with Michael surprisingly calm. 'At any rate,' he confided, 'this has solved a problem which was becoming confoundedly knotty.' At last the threefold cord was loosened, and Michael got a post in a school far away from here.

Hardest hit of all sections of the cotton industry was the fine-spinning to which Aubrey belonged. The family firm, T. M. Hesketh and Sons, with its six mills limped along till 1954 when it was taken over by another company. But the prospect became no brighter. One by one all but one of Heskeths' mills were closed; work-people—many of them Aubrey's comrades of forty years—had to be sacked; and management, including a brother and cousin, drastically pruned. He watched the demolition of the mill in which he had spent most of his working life, saw the great chimney sway and fall and crash into smoking rubble. Something of himself died with it. Decrease in demand for high quality fine-counts—the finest in the world—led to complaints from grudging buyers and bitter struggles against competitors. And still the profits diminished. All this, added to the inhuman strain of the war years, led gradually to his breakdown. Unable to pull his weight in a sinking ship he, too, at the age of fifty-eight, had to go overboard.

And now we were faced with the ultimate reason for leaving Fisher House—running costs. Ironically, a month before Aubrey's retirement on a meagre pension, our £50-a-year rent was trebled. Catherine's boarding-school fees alone were higher than his net income. Knowing there was no answer but to take her away from school, we did nothing. Then one morning, like a green leaf over the Flood, came a letter from a friend indeed. Inside good wishes and a text on the need for faith was a tiny screwed-up scrap of paper. It was a cheque for £1,000. (Some of the nicest things have been said on cheques). So we stayed put and re-learned how to 'cut our coat'—as we'd been obliged to do when we married in 1931 on £500 a year. In those days what riches. And now we were thirty-four years older with Aubrey unable to work. But

we loved the place, belonged to it, and determined to manage somehow.

Soon enough we found that a lower standard of living can
mean a higher standard of health; and the practice of economy in
this house provided the three of us with an obligatory 'keep fit'
campaign. Using the car as little as possible, we cycled or walked
miles a day. Then cutting down fuel bills meant cutting down trees
—however that may be forbidden, saplings are permitted—and
this stimulates the circulation. Aubrey sawed and chopped wood
without end. In no time he had reduced the hen cabin to fire-
lighters though I argued that eggs would have been more benefi-
cial. Ministering to fires and stoves allows little time for settling
beside them and thereby cultivating chilblains. We shared the long
labours of carrying coal, coke, logs, and drums of paraffin across
flagged floors and windy yards. No hot water till bedtime was the
new rule which still keeps us kettlewise; and no warm room till
afternoon keeps us on the move. When the winter winds blow we
have always had to sleep in headscarves—as well as bedsocks. But
the winters, these days, seem colder than before. How we welcome
the hesitant summer when, armed with spade and hoe, we rush out
into the sun.

Having dispensed with our one-day-a-week gardener, more
energy is required of us outside than in. Energy replaced in the
form of spinach, cabbages, lettuces, beans and herbs, which enable
us to follow (almost) Mrs Twigg's requirements. In fact, our meat
bill was soon stripped down to five and nine-pence a week. The
answer to unbelievers is: half a pound of liver, one rasher of
bacon, three neck-end chops. Proteins were made up by herrings,
mackerel, eggs, plenty of cheese, and still more eggs. Occasionally
we did see red—in the form of minced beef for spaghetti bolognese.

We still maintain some healthful economies, and others which
consist of margarine mixed with butter, condensed milk rather
than cream, no biscuits, cakes and other 'farinaceous rubbish'
scorned by Bryony. Fruit and nuts are heavy on expenses, but to
compensate for this we have given up smoking, thus knocking out
threats of coronary thrombosis and a speedy end to enjoyment.
Because, in spite of all, we enjoy many things—that evening aperi-
tif, for example: Cyprus sherry diluted with Ribena is enough to
blur the rough edges after a hard day's washing. Nevermore the
laundry (it goes without saying). But doing the washing keeps

one supple: the bending, stretching, and doubling. Then the skill required in flinging the line—especially since Aubrey has sawn off the one stout laburnum branch which used to support it. Rain on wash day and indoor drying is almost welcome. And rain, if nothing else, is still plentiful.

The friendly rain—it still drips through the trees and through the roof into the attic, thus making us run upstairs and down with jugs, bowls, tarpaulins to prevent yet another stain on a bedroom ceiling. This because our present condition implies home-decorating. As in our 'early married' days we are again become expert at climbing ladders and walking the scaffolding (if not the plank) bucket in one hand, brush in the other. And there is no Miss Whittle to interrupt and criticize.

Further savings include hairdressing: Catherine and I set each other's hair; I cut Aubrey's, though not to his satisfaction. And we seldom buy clothes: compassionate friends send us bulky parcels of intriguing cast-offs. Nor do we go to the theatre or eat out—thus blueing a week's housekeeping in a single night. We go to bed early and save both energy and fuel. Cynics maintain that losing your money means losing your friends. On the contrary, such a so-called calamity reveals your friends; and in this respect we have never been richer. Fairy godmothers lend us summer cottages and give us a great deal more. Frank and Rachel (my oldest, dearest friend already mentioned) have helped in ways beyond describing here: we are rooted in their friendship as the gorse bushes are rooted in the moors. Days of ill-fortune have taught us more of the nature of kindness than days of plenty.

27

Everything Changes

'Everything changes, yet everything remains the same.'

One stormy winter of rain and snow we became seriously alarmed at the state of our roof. Rain dripped not only into one attic room but into three; and we discovered the rafters and floor-boards to be full of woodworm. 'Perhaps, after all, we shall be eaten out,' I sighed putting through yet another call for help to the Corporation. But they were weary of tenants and the endless demands on their mouldering property. Though fungus grew on the woodwork and paper peeled from the walls, nothing but patching was done. Then one day Martin, architect's interest aroused, made a thorough survey. 'If you don't leave here soon,' he said, 'the roof will fall in.' Then, after a pause, 'Why not buy the place?'

'Buy it!' I echoed in astonishment, 'You must be crazy. Besides, Liverpool would never sell.'

'I bet they would—they're not going to re-roof for you, but they've got to keep you weatherproof. I believe they'd be glad to be rid of the house—that is, if you're determined to stay. And as sitting tenants of thirty-eight years, you could get it well below market price.'

'But what's the point when the rent is so low?'

'Some wealthy Manchester commuter would give his eyes to live here in peace and quiet, *and* in a house of historic interest protected by the Ministry of Housing. Here's your only chance of raising enough money to live anywhere else.'

We were torn in pieces, intrigued yet dismayed, by this idea. Could we raise the money? Would we be driven out by urgent and costly repairs? If it became too much for us, or one of us died we'd be forced to go anyhow. And then the worry of eternal repairs warred against the pleasure of possession—a very small pleasure to me since my desire is to be rid of property and things. Waking at four o'clock in the mornings, I was tormented by questions made more insoluble by the advent of estate agents, Borough and Corporation surveyors arguing about the price, and by the advice of accountants and friends. Why had the question ever been raised? We didn't want to improve and repair our home, or to convert it into flats, but only to live on undisturbed. Then I thought of those uninvited visitors—the wind and the rain; fungus and woodworm. Anyhow, why did we stay on when everyone else seemed to be leaving?

Before long Primrose Cottage was pulled down to leave only a foundation of loose stones tenanted by gorse and thistles—prickly reminders of the Marchbanks household. Of the ruin of Sweetloves the last remaining gable-end had bowed to the storm; two new families have lived in Moorside since the Darleys, after moving south, followed each other in quick succession out of this world. Even Mrs Twigg, the indestructible, was with us one day and gone the next, melted from our midst as though she had never been. And after Mrs Birdwhistle took flight, the last two to leave were the Dapples—Mrs Dapple, growing frailer with the fading days, floated light as a feather from our midst the day after Christmas. And he, not fancying life without her, took no pleasure in the spring plantings and spent less and less time digging the garden until, with his prize potatoes ready for lifting, he took to his bed. And that meant three burials in the chapel yard because Johnny Thatcher is also gone with the wind, and his blue-plumed bonfires are lighted by another man.

While people go and come, events have overtaken us—for one, the Ministry of Transport's over-our-heads proposal to drive a motorway—the M61 link with M6—through Anderton's woods and fields within five hundred yards of Upper Rivington reservoir. Although we defeated their plan for a service station over the finest acres, the motorway battle was lost before the start of a public inquiry. We live in an age when the bulldozers always win. There must be a motorway even though, at this rate, there may not always be an England. Everywhere the green is giving place to the grey so that more people may have the chance to run their cars over longer and longer stretches of motorway into an ever-diminishing countryside.

Every year our narrow lanes are widened, but so far the summer traffic seething around the green is not controlled by lights. Which reminds me that the once-dreaming Rivington Lane has recently been drilled, hammered, and excavated. And for what? For the laying of a water-pipe to bring us a reservoir supply from Horwich. Farewell, spring water, cool and sparkling as a spring morning. Farewell, unparalleled cups of tea. Strange that we who live among reservoirs should be beset with water problems because, lucky though we have been, some of our neighbours have complained of gravel and peat-fibres in the bath, and of objects more animated. While we continued to thrive on living water, one or two town-dwellers, after taking refreshment at Top Barn, complained of tummy trouble. Whereupon the water was analysed and found unfit for stomachs conditioned to a treated supply.

The first we heard that we too must also put up with treated water was the appearance of a journalist on our doorstep. And then electric drills bored home the unpalatable truth. 'Well,' we consoled ourselves, 'there's always the rain-tub—they can't take *that* away! And the spring up Sheephouse Lane. Whatever improvements threaten we'll still have tea brewed with vital water. No fluoride or chlorine for us.' Then we considered the work involved in carrying those daily buckets through all weathers—far worse than trimming oil-lamps under cover. So much for progress and the future of mankind. A future of people unresistant to the mildest germ, subjected to chemicals in food and water, and ultimately, perhaps, unable to reproduce themselves.

On the brink of that non-future we now stand, but 'Sufficient unto the day' crows the church weathercock swinging from north to west. English weathercocks are notoriously changeable; we must live in the present only to find it slipping forever from beneath our feet. Another change ringing in our ears is the telephone; now that we are on the automatic system our memorable two-digit number is changed to a jumble of five. No friendly voice greets us from exchange commiserating about the weather. And they've boxed in those open twin-bells so often stuffed with cottonwool to secure an uninterrupted half-hour. Were not telephones made for man and not man for telephones?

Not only telephones, but candles are in the air. The most surprising, though least technological, change stems from the church —now we have candles on the altar. Some foreseeing old lady must have smiled as she made her will leaving a sum of money for candlesticks in Rivington church. But alongside this comes another reminder of the two-handed nature of God. One Sunday morning

revealed ominous slabs of concrete lying along the grass verges of
the church path. Soon the path was tarred black with heavy concrete edges. No moss or loose stone must remain to trip us; no
particle of gravel be deposited on holy carpets. Perhaps before
long the entire churchyard will be tarmaced, and ourselves incin-
erated to the winds with only the weathercock to tell which way we
went.

Another surprise was to greet me from the toft and quillit. I
gazed down in amazement at two vast silage towers sprung overnight from a farm across the water. Though painted green, and
unlike twin towers of Babel in that they are sometimes silent, they
nevertheless dominate an attractive valley. By equating them with
oast-houses and Celtic round towers we have come to accept them
as part of the landscape and poetry of our age, like telegraph-
poles and pylons. And so, improvement by improvement, we are
being tamed, tarmaced, civilized, and speeded up. The unique
individual who held out longest against the ravages of progress—
sans electricity, sans water, sans sanitation, sans everything but
rags and an oil-lamp to light her to bed was Rosie Thatcher, the
last survivor at the manse. Untroubled by the turning wheels she
sat on alone beside a smoky green-stick fire. Mrs Dapple's efforts
towards washing curtains and clothing went unrewarded. Rosie
clung to an old coat shining with grease. Nothing would induce
her to wear the garments offered by solicitous neighbours; these
were stuffed into a cupboard and consumed by moths.

Her outings became fewer: after Johnny's death she schooled
herself to collect her pension from the post-office, and on Sundays
went to chapel. Very occasionally she appeared at chapel tea-
parties, still in her shiny coat, and stained dress hiding unwashed
undergarments, and with a faded felt hat over unwashed hair.
This caused much embarrassment because, for obvious reasons,
no one would sit beside her. Then one Saturday the foreseeing
Mrs Dapple gave Rosie her second-best hat and coat. These, being
a delicate shade of powder-blue, provoked surprised comments on
Rosie's improvement. But the following Monday morning when
Mrs Dapple called at the manse, Rosie was a long time shuffling
to the door, and eventually appeared, crumpled and dirty and still
wearing the blue coat and hat.

For some locked-away reason Rosie always cooked her dinner
a day in advance, so that a chop fried on Saturday was hidden

on a shelf ready for Sunday. The idea of enjoying a meal fresh from the pan—with nothing laid away for tomorrow—was too daring. Apart from this nothing troubled her; living alone she was neither nervous nor lonely, and shutting her ears to civilization and the traffic roaring down Sheephouse Lane, she 'retired' at half-seven winter and summer alike. Even on the night Johnny died she had gone to sleep beside him until dawn when she crept outside as usual to gather sticks, leaving him to 'sleep it out' in his rigid rocking-chair. She had not even troubled to move him away from the larger-than-usual fire (it was a bitter February), so that next morning when the police arrived they discovered the left leg of Johnny's trousers badly singed. After being reproached, Rosie answered with a delighted cackle: 'Aw well, I never did think *'e'd* set th'ouse on fire!'

During these proceedings the younger and more squeamish of the two policemen had been obliged to rush outside and vomit in the grass. Another illusion was to be shattered by Mr Dapple's description of Johnny when finally stripped: "E might 'a looked clean on top, but underneath 'e wer like a blackie from t'neck downward!' Alas for the apple-blossom complexion which had fooled us all. In truth, matters at the manse went from bad to worse, yet in spite of all Rosie continued to flourish. When we asked after her she invariably grinned in reply: 'Doing fine!' thereby exposing the double row of top teeth which may have contributed to her excellent digestion.

We could hardly believe the news that she had been taken behind the back of the village to an old folks' home. And just as surprising was Mrs Dapple's report after visiting her: Rosie, scoured, scrubbed, and fitted with new clothes, was brimming with delight to find herself on thick carpets, enjoying wholesome meals, and sitting for hours in front of the television.

Mention of television brings to mind the thousand-foot-high mast recently erected on Winter Hill beyond the Pike. Dwarfing the hill upon which it stands, it resembles a rocket on a launching-pad pointing to the moon, catching the sun. This marvel, studded at night with six ruby lights, frequently loses its head in the clouds as though destined for another planet. Less happily planted in the background are six smaller and wirier sister-masts which, bristling like pins from a mossy cushion, reduce the bold outline of the moors to insignificance. Well may we ask if better viewing is worth the sacrifice of such a view.

One thing we could never have believed—that we should live to see a great yellow bulldozer searing a path through the bracken at the back. Yet there it was, one warm August afternoon of 1968, a devil's creation (in my eyes) swinging and nodding, spilling mouthfuls of earth among the ferns. Warning of this devastation came in the form of a posse of men around the back door just as I was about to start the washing-machine. A golden Monday morning and the newly-painted rails on our drive must come up, they said. No access to the garage because they were going to dig a great trench up the drive and through the bracken. For eight weeks we endured a scene like Passchendaele—for the sake of sewage and water-pipes up to the manse. Yes, the shaky old grey ruin has been sold, re-built, sanitized and sandblasted at vast cost for the joy of living in Rivington.

Ten, fifteen years have gone by since I last saw the kingfisher, a gleaming jewel streaking upstream—harbinger of worlds where steel and concrete have no permanence, worlds of imagination ever new. However changed the countryside may be, no one, so far, can change the seasons. Though springs seem colder and summers wetter than when we were young, the roses continue to brave them out, and daisies push up gallantly from the sleeted lawn. Perhaps the seasons only appear to be more fleeting because it's quicker going downhill. Already another summer has rusted out, and the leaves are floating down to earth like crumpled birds driven helpless in the wind across the grass.

Autumn, time of fulfilment, is still my favourite season. Around the sundial late roses are glowing in the morning sun; and michaelmas daisies, yellow-eyed in heliotrope lashes, attract the light. I put down my pen to admire the red admirals palpitating on the purple flowers, and remember how, on such a day as this, we moved in. Unbelievably the one intended year of our stay has spun out into forty. . . .

At this point, on a sudden impulse, I ran outside to share the thought with Aubrey who set down his rubbish-filled barrow beside me. He was in no mood for philosophy. 'Too much work in this garden,' he remarked, 'and I'm getting too old for it. Next spring we really must look for another place.'

Next spring indeed. . . . Though the house still creaks and groans, and month by month the roof sags a little lower, we have done the craziest thing : we have given it a new coat of white paint and a fresh jasmin-yellow front door, and have actually bought it. Dreams of that centrally-heated bungalow are vanished in woodsmoke. But every time we come back here after a day out we return thankfully to its dignity and draughts. Now that the place is our own we find ourselves more possessed by it than ever—where else could we live? Here is home, and there is no escape.

RIVINGTON
AUTUMN 1971